Eighteenth-century furniture

STUDIES IN DESIGN AND MATERIAL CULTURE

general editor
Paul Greenhalgh

already published in the series

National style and nation–state: design in Poland from the vernacular revival to the international style
David Crowley

Victorian furniture: technology and design
Clive D. Edwards

Twentieth-century furniture: materials, manufacture and markets
Clive D. Edwards

The Edwardian house: the middle-class home in Britain 1880–1914
Helen C. Long

Manufactured pleasures: psychological responses to design
Ray Crozier

Quotations and sources on design and the decorative arts
Paul Greenhalgh

Chicago's great world's fairs
John E. Findling

The culture of fashion: a new history of fashionable dress
Christopher Breward

Henry Ford: mass production, modernism and design
Raymond Batchelor

Eighteenth-century furniture

Clive D. Edwards

MANCHESTER UNIVERSITY PRESS
Manchester and New York

distributed exclusively in the USA by St. Martin's Press

Copyright © Clive Edwards 1996

Published by Manchester University Press
Oxford Road, Manchester M13 9NR, UK
and Room 400, 175 Fifth Avenue, New York, NY 10010, USA

Distributed exclusively in the USA
by St. Martin's Press, Inc., 175 Fifth Avenue, New York, NY 10010, USA

British Library Cataloguing-in-Publication Data
A catalogue record for this book is available from the British Library

Library of Congress Cataloging-in-Publication Data
Edwards, Clive, 1947–
   Eighteenth-century furniture / Clive Edwards.
      p.   cm.
   Includes bibliographical references
   ISBN 0-7190-4524-X (hardcover). — ISBN 0-7190-4525-8 (pbk.)
   1. Furniture industry and trade—History—18th century.
I. Title.
TS880.E36   1996   95-47177
338.4′76841′009033—dc20

ISBN   0 7190 4524 X   hardback
            0 7190 4525 8   paperback

First published 1996

00 99 98 97 96   10 9 8 7 6 5 4 3 2 1

Typeset by Carnegie Publishing Ltd, Preston
Printed in Great Britain by Redwood Books, Trowbridge

Contents

Contents

Figures

Figures

Preface and acknowledgements

Writings about the history of eighteenth-century furniture have proliferated in recent years, from wide-ranging general histories to detailed analyses of workshops and individual products. As well as stylistic matters, discussions about all aspects of furniture production and use have benefited from skills derived from other disciplines. Therefore it should be said at the outset that this book is not intended to be a work of direct original research, rather it tries to address the history of one part of our material culture from a range of associated viewpoints. In sum, these have produced a way of seeing eighteenth-century furniture and its context from conception through to consumption. Therefore this book relies heavily upon the groundwork of previous furniture scholars, all of whom are acknowledged at appropriate times. It is intended to be a book which introduces background, factual detail, and some particular issues relating to eighteenth-century furniture studies by analysis of the processes involved in making, selling and using furniture. It is not intended to be a chronological account of eighteenth-century furniture styles and fashions.

This approach has enabled me to concentrate on the notion that objects are products of systems of thought and of political, economic and material circumstances. Therefore I am also indebted to the work of historians in the field of consumption, to geographers in the area of location theory, and to material culture studies generally for much of the framework of my discussions. The scholars that I have relied on are also acknowledged in the appropriate notes.

General editor's foreword

Furniture surrounds us. It fills the interior spaces of our public and private buildings and is one of the clearest indicators of the practical and aesthetic predilections of an age. This book explores the infrastructure of the furniture trade in the eighteenth century. The period has been mythologised as being the one in which many manufacturing industries underwent dramatic change. This was bound up with a steady rise in demand for consumer goods. Sir Joshua Reynolds, in his *Seven Discourses* of 1778, recognised a 'regular progress of cultivated life . . . from Necessaries to Accommodations, from Accommodations to Ornaments'. In the move from the necessary to the ornamental, makers of furniture acknowledged the increased significance of design. Design simultaneously attempted to create and to follow taste, to generate a confidence in the consumer that could in turn translate into economic stability within the industry.

The book is divided into four parts: trade and business, materials and techniques, the processes of design, and consumption. This allows the author to explore the industry in all its aspects, from the methods employed to make the furniture to the processes through which it was distributed. The size of the subject inevitably means that the author paints with a broad brush. The volume does include, however, a wealth of empirical material that gives specificity and colour to the story being told. The author moves deliberately away from the vision of furniture as being bound up with the fate of a few named designers, and gives us a vivid picture of a complex and sprawling range of activity. He is also careful to include in his discussion aspects of the trade that have been largely ignored until recently. For example, the role of women in the making and selling processes is dealt with, as is that most time honoured means of distribution: smuggling.

This volume brings to completion Clive Edwards's trilogy on the furniture industry from the eighteenth century to the present. He has now provided us with a historiography that allows us to position furniture within the world of objects over the last three hundred years. The volumes on the nineteenth and twentieth centuries explore parallel terrains and use similar methods as the present volume. As a trilogy, they are a landmark in the written history of furniture.

1   Introduction

The serious study of furniture is typically based on five distinct categories of research, although individual historians will normally give prominence to particular approaches. The first is clearly the objects themselves. Familiarity with actual specimens is the surest way of understanding design, materials, techniques and then being able to make comparative evaluations. Visual research in museums, private collections, antique shops and auction houses is the basis of this category.[1] Second, research into what has already been written about the topics so that the research of others can be absorbed. This secondary research is discussed below in the form of a brief historiography. Third, delving into primary sources such as inventories, accounts, newspapers, diaries, wills, and other legal documents will add substance to original study. The problem of survival of this sort of material may sometimes distort the evidence. For example, the muniment rooms of country estates have revealed a great deal abut the activities of well-known suppliers and their clients, but tell little of the circumstances of production or sale. Inventories, although extremely useful, are records of a moment in time and therefore cannot give a picture of the changing nature of a household. Fourth, an awareness of the international connections, both in terms of comparative furniture development as well as attitudes and styles of scholarship, will ensure a rounded approach to this study. Finally, the contextualisation of the above categories by the in-depth study of aspects of the history of the given period will help in a broader understanding of the interdependency of all historical research.

As a result, recent furniture studies both in North America and Europe have embraced a much wider range of sources; they have become more interdisciplinary; they have reconsidered the idea of a canon and as a result have re-examined the familiar and enlarged the range of objects studied.[2] These changes have been evident since the 1960s, not only in writings and catalogues, but also in the displays and exhibitions put on by museums. The combination of solid scholarship, enlightened curatorship and interpretative displays, based on direct access to objects, has done much to promote and develop furniture research. The exhibition on *John Channon and Brass-inlaid Furniture* held at the Victoria and Albert Museum, London, in 1994 and the Colonial Williamsburg, Virginia, exhibition, entitled *Working Wood in Eighteenth-century America* in the same year are but two recent examples of such progressive work.

However, furniture historians should be grateful to the early twentieth-century founders of the serious study of furniture who have laid so much ground work, especially in the study of the seventeenth and eighteenth centuries. *The Dictionary of English Furniture* (1924, revised edition 1954) by P. Mcquoid and R. Edwards is a store of facts and images which still remains useful. The works of R. W. Symonds, in particular his *Furniture-making in Seventeenth and Eighteenth Century England* (1955) remain valuable as do the researches of Ralph Edwards and Margaret Jourdain, Edward Joy, John Gloag, and Helena Hayward.

More recent scholars who have introduced some of the newer approaches to furniture history would include C. Gilbert, *The Life and Works of Thomas Chippendale* (1978); H. Hayward, and P. Kirkham, *William and John Linnell Eighteenth Century London Furniture-makers* (1980); Pat Kirkham, *The London Furniture Trade 1700–1870* (1988), and Lucy Wood, *The Lady Lever Art Gallery Catalogue of Commodes* (1994). For vernacular furniture types, W. Cotton, *The English Regional Chair* (1990) and C. Kinmonth, *Irish Vernacular Furniture 1700–1950* (1993) are exemplary. In addition, the contribution of scholars in journals such as *Furniture History*, *Winterthur Portfolio*, and *Regional Furniture*, have broadened the nature of furniture history as well as providing access to a wide range of writing and scholarship.

In the United States, where material culture studies developed,[3] many seminal publications have been produced. The influence of organisations such as the Society for Protection of New England Antiquities (SPNEA), The Winterthur Museum, and Colonial Williamsburg have encouraged a very wide range of publications and exhibitions. The important work by Charles Hummel, *With Hammer in Hand. The Dominy Craftsmen of East Hampton, New York* (1968), as well as *The Work of Many Hands, Card Tables in Federal America*

1790–1820 (1982) by Benjamin Hewitt, Patricia Kane, Gerald Ward and *American Seating Furniture 1630–1730* (1988) by Benno Forman, are fine examples of quality research and publishing. I have been glad to be able to include examples from these and other works.

In addition, many valuable studies of individual designers or makers have been published, along with much work on particular regional furniture types that have been either broad and wide ranging, or narrow and specific in their scope.[4]

Scholars of eighteenth-century interiors have also examined the use of furniture, and these analyses often help to explain the consumption of goods in a particular milieu, thus partly redressing the old tendency towards over-reliance on the biographical and the stylistic. For works in this vein, see J. Fowler and J. Cornforth, *English Decoration in the Eighteenth Century* (1974); P. Thornton, *Authentic Decor. The Domestic Interior 1620–1920* (1984); C. Saumarez-Smith, *Eighteenth-Century Decoration* (1993).

Apart from the works mentioned above, this book has been influenced by other approaches to history. The important work by N. McKendrick, J. Brewer and J. H. Plumb, *The Birth of Consumer Society* (1982), and the more recent collection of essays, *Consumption and the World of Goods* (1993), edited by J. Brewer and R. Porter, as well as Shammas's *The Pre-industrial Consumer in England and America* (1990) have focused attention on the end uses of a wide range of goods. The work of economic historians has also been influential, including texts by Crafts, 'British economic growth 1700–1831', *Economic History Review* (1983), and by Berg, *The Age of Manufactures 1700–1820* (1985). Specialist research such as Mui and Mui's *Shops and Shopping in Eighteenth-Century England* (1989), has thrown new perspectives on retailing. Yet other disciplines such as literary analysis, including P. Tristram, *Living Space in Fact and Fiction* (1989), and geography, including J. L. Oliver, *The Development and Structure of the Furniture Industry* (1966), have offered fresh insights into ways of looking at furniture and furnishing history.

From this it is plain that furniture history straddles a number of other disciplines. In part it is social and cultural history, although the surviving evidence in terms of objects often tends to relate to upper status owners, particularly prior to the nineteenth century. In part it is economic history, with its relation to production, trade, craft and division of labour as well as the distinction between designing and making. It is also closely related to the history of materials and techniques, furniture having been made from such a variety of materials and with a wide range of tools and machines.

Some of the questions which will be raised are based on the tensions between these various aspects. Although I am generally suggesting a demand-led furniture industry, there were other pressures on the various parties involved that were affected by differing circumstances. For example, was the demand for designs pushed along by draughtsmen and makers, or was it pulled by economic pressures? Did the choice of materials reflect a push by merchants or was it pulled by trade demands for distinction? To what extent did retailers influence customer choice and taste, and were consumers simply passive receivers? To begin to answer these questions the nature of demand for eighteenth-century furniture needs to be established.

Rise and nature of demand

If it is correct to suggest that all economic activity was driven by demand (and its corollary – consumption), then it is reasonable to investigate and evaluate the changes and developments in the furniture trade with this idea in mind. The activities of a particular trade or industry, from the design decisions and materials chosen, to manufacturing techniques and distribution methods, will all be influenced by the driving force of demand. Therefore an analysis of the processes will not only enlighten the nature of demand itself, but will also show the interdependence of the parts to create a consumption-driven whole.

That there was growth in the supply and demand for goods in the eighteenth century is not generally disputed. What is in question is the rate of change, the constitution of the market and the nature of consumption.[5] This is not the forum to take this discussion further, suffice it to say that there is general agreement that the English were already relatively wealthy at the beginning of the eighteenth century and aggregate real incomes rose during the century.[6] This economic progress was sufficient to support an expansion of demand, which was itself deemed natural. Sir Joshua Reynolds expressed the idea of incremental demand in terms of ownership: 'The regular progress of cultivated life is from Necessaries to Accommodations, from Accommodations to Ornaments.'[7] In other words, it was seen as characteristic of society that there was a progression from necessities to decencies to luxuries.

Growth in the consumption of goods was not simply an eighteenth-century phenomenon. Evidence shows that consumption patterns had begun to increase in the latter part of the seventeenth century.[8] There is no reason to suspect that the growth of ownership of material possessions, shown through inventories up to the 1730s, did not continue for the rest of the century, particularly as the middle and lower levels of society were at the forefront of the expansion.[9]

As has already been remarked, contemporary commentators from various disciplines had noted the changes in consumption patterns. Perhaps the most extreme comment was in 1776, when the economist Adam Smith pointed out that consumption was the goal and purpose of all production. Growth in consumption was to be sustained by advances that were both incremental and induced. The incremental advances were simply based on population rises, urbanisation, transport improvements, shops and nodal demand. The population increase of approximately 66 per cent over the century on estimates for 1701, indicate a growing workforce and market. Combined with a variety of social levels which encouraged concern with position and rank, and by extension the nature of their home and family, it seems that an increasing number would be clamouring for the status products of the furniture-makers of the time.[10] The induced demands are more difficult to assess, but would appear to have been made by encouraging emulative or competitive spending through shops and displays, pattern books, visual models and fashions. These created a culture of consumption that was fed and promoted vigorously.[11]

A well-known example of this induced demand was Wedgwood and his ceramic products.[12] His enterprise even touched furniture, as on one occasion he proposed to publish illustrations of cabinets that were inlaid with Wedgwood plaques. He thought that this would

> give sanction and notoriety to our productions to such a degree perhaps as we have at present no idea of. I would put these numbers into the common mode of sale in all the shops, and in our own warehouses everywhere.[13]

Although there are some extant examples of Wedgwood inlaid cabinets, it does not seem to have been the great sales gimmick that Wedgwood envisaged.

In previous centuries much of the production and consumption of furniture had been of a local nature, with businesses supplying the requirements of all groups. By the middle of the eighteenth century the geographical separation of production from consumption was important enough to be commented upon. It is clear that the division was not a new phenomenon in other trades, but in furniture it appears to have been. It was Daniel Defoe in 1745 who observed:

> Come next to the furniture of [a country grocer's] house; it is scarce credible to how many counties of England, and how remote, the furniture of but a mean house must send them; and how many people are every-where employed about it; nay and the meaner the furniture, the more people and places employed.[14]

However, in an earlier edition of his *Complete English Tradesman* (1727), Defoe discussed the needs of the same grocer and the example seems to confirm the pre-eminence of London as a furniture supplier:

> The Hangings, suppose them to be ordinary Linsey-Woolsey, are made at Kidderminster, dy'd in the country, and painted or watered at London. The chairs, if of cane, are made at London; the ordinary matted chairs, perhaps made in the place where they live. Tables, chest of drawers etc. made at London; as also the looking glass'.[15]

What do these two apparently conflicting statements suggest? The latter extract points to the pre-eminence of London for furniture but confirms the many sources from which textile furnishings could be obtained. In the slightly later version, the point seems to be that even the 'mean' furniture which was originally made locally, was now produced in many other places. This raises questions of the developing infrastructure relating to the physical means and costs involved in transportation of goods. The other question is, what were the implications of this geographical separation of furniture manufacture and consumption?

The first result was that with high status demand, the best London makers were quite able to supply all that was required to furnish a new home wherever it was situated. Secondly, in the middle to lower levels many items did not need to be made in a bespoke way, so that manufacture in batches to a general specification (often supplied by pattern books) meant that some economies could be made even by local makers. To maintain levels of trade and choice, the various models needed only to be altered in detail. However, in either case the existence of a design or visual language was a necessary part of the whole process.

The other major implication was that the development of a near-universal design language meant that the consumers' progress, from necessities to accommodations, and then on to ornaments, was often simply a matter of emulating the correct models with the assistance of the furniture trade.

Trade

To convert these demands into objects, an economic infrastructure developed. In the case of furniture, there were three major features that affected its nature during the eighteenth century. The range of material possibilities increased, the dispersion of technical knowledge was relatively quick, and the demand for both high-style and imitative products encouraged continual development, albeit in an uneven fashion. The boundaries between these factors were constantly moving as furniture-makers realised that their major task was to combine style, materials, and technology in a desirable product at a price the market would accept.

Undoubtedly as the century progressed, there was a need to change the structure of the furniture trade to cope with the increasing demands made upon it. However, it is equally clear that the eighteenth century saw no major upheavals in trade organisation. Rather, it was a gradual adjustment to new circumstances.[16] These developments were usually related to growing markets.

One route to productivity lay in policies which removed strategies that used more rather than less labour. In some industries, in fact fewer than often realised, the employment of machines did assist output, but the growing population also meant an increase in the labour pool. It is therefore not surprising to find that a plentiful supply of labour in England resulted in a slower adoption of machines in contrast to America, for example.[17] In many cases there was a positive denial of the need to change until it was forced by financial circumstances.

This myopic attitude to change in the face of the potential of machines is expressed in Henry Martyn's *Considerations on the East India Trade* (1701) when he asked the question:

> But has more than only one sawmill been seen in England? . . . by a
> wonderful policy the people here must not be deprived of their labour:
> rather every work must be done by more hands than necessary.[18]

Of course, innovation is not necessarily mechanisation, and the
distinction between various attitudes to change is more easily seen in
relation to whether the trade is capital or labour-intensive. The classic
industrial revolution allows comparison between capital-intensive
industries and labour-intensive, craft-based trades. In the first case,
changes were welcomed that improved efficiency and reduced unit
costs, particularly when the objects produced were often of a primary
nature, needing further manipulation by other trades before they were
to be consumed.[19] In the latter case the development (or continuation)
of hand and intermediate techniques (e.g. upholstery), combined
with the wider use of division of labour, often meant a satisfactory
conjunction of old and new processes. If machines were encouraged,
they were often only for primary conversion and later, simple multiple
operations.

Whatever changes were introduced in individual workshops, or
more widely within a trade, it was clear that profitability was the
ultimate aim. For furniture-makers, as well as many other craft-based
trades, business decisions were about thresholds of profitability. So
for example, when comparative costs of old and new technologies
showed little savings, there was often no obvious need for change. On
the other hand, many of the tradesmen were keenly aware of the
vagaries of taste and were well able to keep up their profitability by
energetic marketing of a continual stream of new designs and objects
to satisfy the market.

Taste and Design

At the root of much of the preoccupation with objects during the
eighteenth century was the notion of good taste. The understanding
was that there existed a generally agreed level or standard that constituted 'good taste'. This has been referred to as the 'ruling taste'.[20]
Although this is rather simplistic, the concept of hegemony, or the
dominance of one taste over others, is understood. Objects will then
represent the degree (or otherwise) of their correctness judged against
this notional ruling taste. How this preference was arrived at is another

question, but it was clearly influenced by the same social, economic and political factors that affected demand. Designs, especially in the form of pattern books, were the manifestation of these tastes, ready processed for use by the other members of the chain. However, despite the attempts of Reynolds and Hogarth[21] to lay solid foundations for taste, the idea still remained that even those who were at liberty to make personal interpretations of style continued to follow the dictates of the ruling taste.

However, the concept of a constant good taste was elusive, not least because of the regular changes required by status holders to maintain their differences from the lower levels that were busily copying the style initiatives developed by the status holders. Nevertheless, matters of taste were important. As Saumarez-Smith (1993) has written: 'Taste motivated desire; desire propelled the acquisition of goods; the need for different types of consumer goods stimulated changes in the ways that they were made'.[22] Clearly this process had a continuing impact on the range of styles, materials and techniques for all the trades involved. In the case of furniture it was these demand-led changes that meant that makers had to often adapt to new circumstances through necessity rather than choice.

Eighteenth-century society

Finally in this introduction, a little needs to be said about eighteenth-century society in general so that some perspective is given to the reader. It could be argued that at one level the developments in eighteenth-century politics were aimed towards creating and maintaining consensus. This was achieved in part by avoiding the rise of a despotic monarchy, combined with an absent aristocracy; by importing foreign kings who were dependent on the politicians who assisted them, and by the process of politics, in which similar vested interests allowed a degree of consensus to be achieved.

Underneath this surface there were clearly many injustices, but for significant sectors of the population there was a growing degree of economic stability and social harmony. This encouraged public mobility and personal development for individuals, while it also encouraged growing economic activity and prosperity, sometimes with political assistance for the country. This help might take the form of restrictions on imports that would harm the home trade, the encouragement of exports, and the control of the production of the colonies to benefit the home trade.

If consensus was the ideal of the politicians, improvement was the goal of economic activity. The pace of economic change that was spurred by both domestic and overseas trade, resulted in expanding but fluctuating economic growth.[23] The economic advance was combined with a population rise, so, as well as increases in disposable income, there was also an expansion of the market base itself. The impact of these changes on furniture meant an increase in demand at various levels. As society was organised so that the idea of self-improvement was important, it was perhaps inevitable that there would be a hierarchy of goods to reflect this. This progression, simply described as a scale of necessaries, desirables, and luxuries, was continually altering for individuals as they moved up or down the social scale.

In terms of consumption or demand, once a level of prosperity is spread widely enough through society, then the functional nature of the actual goods is often considered less important than a symbolic representation. This new type of demand makes emulation of high-style models a necessity. It then follows that less expensive models are not necessarily inferior, they are less labour-intensive and are simplified objects in the same general style, frequently offering a diluted symbolic representation. The designers are then called upon to plan these various models, so that a range of makers may use a choice of materials and techniques to sell the furniture in the number of ways explored here. These models either follow the ruling taste or begin to establish avant-garde styles which are likely to be assimilated into a new taste.

The relative domestic stability that consensus appears to have created encouraged gradual changes in social organisation. Domesticity and privacy grew in importance, and with this came the gradual develop-ment of an idea of family life that was to be fully developed in the nineteenth century. Although these changes are very difficult to quan-tify, just as hard evidence of social change is also elusive, they more or less indicate a state of mind, which was reflected in the ruling taste. These ideas were reinforced by the fact that England did not have a society that centred on court life. The aristocracy's country homes were supplements to the city houses they often also owned, which meant that the influences of their design choices could be seen in the provinces as well as in the cities. Not only were the city merchants and tradesmen able to follow the taste set, but so too could the farmer and the country squire. The house and its furnishings became a focus for society.

In addition, the sedentary nature of English people in the eighteenth century meant that much time was spent at home.[24] It could be argued that a demand for comfort was a natural result of this – comfort here meaning not only physical relaxation, but also the more intangible results such as convenience and even self-satisfaction.[25]

To complement and accommodate these changes there were ranges of special furniture devised for the various pursuits, such as gaming, reading and writing, social dining, and tea drinking. All these 'homely' pastimes encouraged the elaboration of furniture types which reflected the rituals of a developing polite society.

It could be argued that the changing status and power of the home and its furnishings tended to reflect the shifting patterns of political power from the great house at the beginning of the century, to the middle class home at the end. It was clearly economic success at a variety of social levels, rather than hereditary status, that was responsible for the growing range of furniture styles and objects.

It is also apparent that urbanisation was an important influence on eighteenth-century furniture businesses and their products. The popularity of urban living and its growth in the eighteenth century is shown by figures for the percentage of the population living in towns of 2,500 or more inhabitants; in 1700 the figure stood at 18.7 per cent, by 1801 it was 30.6 per cent. This urban renaissance was built on the surplus wealth and the expansion of the middle or merchant classes, these in turn being developed from the boom in trade and finance.

There were two types of urban centres, those that attracted wealth, such as spa towns and resorts, but especially London; and those that created it, especially the ports and manufacturing towns, including London. It was clearly the wealth-attracting centres that led the fashions that were then copied elsewhere.

The growth of polite society and the urban culture it sustained was based on two complementary elements – leisure and luxury. Leisure facilities included town assemblies, either in special-purpose rooms or in town buildings, and the development of walks and parks, all of which were designed for personal public display. The town was seen as an open society, an arena for style battles and for personal exhibition as well as a marriage market and a base for buying into society. These forums clearly assisted the establishment of codes of taste, applicable at any particular time. In terms of dress, the idea of a surface show, even if there is little of consequence underneath, is easily understood. What is less simple to analyse is the desire for statements of taste in the home. The home represented substance as well as show, so the signs required were different. Clearly, convenience and comfort were becoming more desirable for themselves, but the demands made upon a private home which often acted as a public stage, must have meant that furniture often had to play a dual role of both function and sign. The most important sign was, of course, status within the hierarchy. There also developed a particular urban aesthetic which relied on buildings that began to resemble one another externally, as the development of planned squares and streets grew.[26] This development might well have provided another reason for a demand for differentiated interiors and furnishings.

The urbanisation process was encouraged by the gradual development of public amenities within cities which meant less fire risk, safer and wider streets, and better water supplies, thus increasing the attraction of urban living. In addition, such important improvements as paved sidewalks and lighting encouraged shopping as a pastime in city centres so that shops and shopping gradually became part of the respectable urban scene and part of the round of society.

The concept of 'polite society' was based upon a general increase in income, and was fired by a prevailing optimism and confidence which resulted from the consensus mentioned above. However polite eighteenth-century society was, there is little doubt that consuming and the attendant notions of fashion, emulation and imitation, were paramount. The various notions of consumption have been argued in other forums[27] and will be looked at further in chapter 5.

What is interesting is that in the eighteenth century the nature of the consumers and their self-image was already being noted. This understanding of human nature has been of some consequence to trades and businesses ever since. It was Forster in 1767 who thus identified the main strands of society that precipitated a variety of demands based on vertical movements:

> In England the several ranks of men slide into each other almost imperceptibly, and a spirit of equality runs through every part of their constitution. Hence arises a strong emulation in all the several stations

and conditions to vie with each other; and the perpetual restless ambition in each of the inferior ranks to raise themselves to the level of those immediately above them.[28]

The social mobility and relative ease of movement, combined with the desire to purchase goods to symbolise that change, appears to have been one of the driving forces behind the continuing growth of fashion in all its forms.

These ambitions and the way people spent their money, especially on luxuries, were sometimes seen by contemporaries as undermining social mores, a change in the moral constraints which governed social behaviour. However, these complaints seem to have had little influence in changing attitudes to possession and display.

Because the furniture trade's development was demand led, its component parts had to go through periods of readjustment if its position was to be maintained. The development of a range of new operations, and the introduction of improved materials and techniques were necessary responses invoked to keep up with the demands, whilst design and designing became essential elements of the business of making and selling furniture. The final consumption of the products of the trade was the result of the stimulated demand, which for much of the eighteenth century encouraged this socio-economic cycle.

Notes

1 The number of museums and collections which have examples of eighteenth-century furniture are too numerous to list, but comprehensive museum guides for Europe and North America will indicate the potential.

2 The texts that have been very useful in developing these new approaches are mentioned at various points below, but G. Ward (ed.), *Perspectives on American Furniture* (New York, 1988) has a number of very useful contributions, especially E. S. Cooke, *The study of American furniture from the perspective of the maker.*

3 For an introduction to this topic see T. J. Schlereth, *Material Culture Studies in America* (Nashville, AASLH, 1982)

4 For further examples see the bibliography.

5 For an introduction to these discussions see J. Brewer and R. Porter, *Consumption and the World of Goods* (London, Routledge, 1993).

6 J. Styles, 'Manufacturing, consumption and design', in Brewer and Porter, *Consumption*, p. 537.

7 Sir Joshua Reynolds, The Dedication to *Seven Discourses* (1778).

8 L. Weatherill, *Consumer Behaviour and Material Culture in Britain 1660–1760* (London, Routledge, 1988).

9 Although inventory analysis after the 1730s is difficult due to the relaxation of the inventory requirement upon death, sporadic inventory examples, and other evidence can be used. See C. Shammas, *The Pre-industrial Consumer in England and America* (Oxford, Oxford University Press, 1990).

10 See B. Ford (ed.), *Eighteenth-Century Britain* (Cambridge, Cambridge University Press, 1991), for an overview of many aspects of British cultural life in the period.

11 E. L. Jones, 'The fashion manipulators: consumer tastes and British industries 1660–1800', in L. Cain and P. Uselding (eds), *Business Enterprise and Economic Change: Essays in Honour of H. F. Williamson* (Kent State, Kent State University Press, 1973).

12 See exhibition catalogue, *The Genius of Wedgwood*, London, Victoria and Albert Museum, 1995.

13 Wedgwood Manuscripts (E. 18518–25), 20 February 1774, quoted in N. McKendrick, J. Brewer and J. H. Plumb, *The Birth of a Consumer Society* (Bloomington, Indiana University Press, 1982), p. 124.

14 D. Defoe, *The Complete English Tradesman* (1745), vol. 1, pp. 263, 266.

15 D. Defoe, *The Complete English Tradesman* (1727), vol. 1, p. 333.

16 See E. Joy, *Some Aspects of the London Furniture Industry*, unpublished MA Thesis, London University, 1955. Also P. Kirkham, *The London Furniture Trade*, Furniture History Society (1988).

17 Although referring to nineteenth-century furniture, see M. J. Ettema, 'Technological innovation and design economics in furniture manufacture', *Winterthur Portfolio*, XVI (1981). Also R. Samuel, 'Workshop of the world. Steam power and hand technology in mid-Victorian Britain', *History Workshop*, III (1977).

18 H. Martyn, *Considerations on the East India Trade*, 1701, p. 615, quoted in M. Berg, *The Age of Manufactures 1700–1820* (London, Fontana, 1985).

19 'Primary' means the production of cloth, iron, and the preparatory processes of other material carried out in bulk, in readiness for further conversion.

20 S. Giedion, *Mechanisation Takes Command* (New York, Oxford University Press, 1948, reprinted 1969).

21 Reynolds, *Discourses*; W. Hogarth, *The Analysis of Beauty* (1753).

22 C. Saumarez-Smith, *Eighteenth-Century Decoration* (London, Weidenfeld and Nicolson, 1993), p. 311.

23 For a clear analysis of the various arguments both pessimistic and

optimistic that help to explain the eighteenth-century economy see Saumarez-Smith, *Eighteenth-Century Decoration*, pp. 140–2.

24 Having said that, the importance of visiting other peoples' homes must not be ignored. See, for example, A. Tinniswood, *A History of Country House Visiting: Five Centuries of Tourism and Taste* (Oxford, Oxford University Press, 1989).

25 Chapter 5 below deals with this idea in detail.

26 See J. Summerson, *Georgian London* (Harmondsworth, Penguin, 1962).

27 See the various essays in Brewer and Porter, *Consumption*.

28 N. Forster, *An Enquiry into the Present High Price of Provisions*, 1767, p. 41, quoted in Neil McKendrick, 'The consumer revolution of eighteenth-century England' in McKendrick *et al.*, *Birth of a Consumer Society*.

2   Trade and business

As in other aspects of the eighteenth century, transformations in the nature of the business of furniture-making and selling were both radical and conservative. The radical changes were based around the development of an entrepreneurial class, the growth of both local and long-distance trade, a developing but erratic division of labour and its associated specialised skills, and a growth of standardisation. In addition, the involvement of the individual with his craft changed as the idea of elite craftsmen who introduced rational business organisation methods and advanced selling techniques, as well as producing reliable technical performance, was becoming a feature of the trade. The conservative aspects of the period, in furniture terms, were related to the slow acceptance of any mechanisation or machinery, only a creeping change in other technical developments, and attempts at generally trying to maintain a status quo.

Due to the developments of major metropolitan centres, new forms of business organisation developed.[1] These were often based on the amalgamation of trades, for example, a cabinet-making business might grow to include chair-making and glass-dealing, a carver might include gilding in his repertoire, and chair-makers might become upholsterers. Partnerships of cabinet-makers and upholsterers often developed into highly successful businesses. The example of Ince and Mayhew, whose business lasted forty-five years testifies to this.[2] Over all these (and other) possible changes, the major development was the rise of the upholsterer to become the controlling force in the supply of furnishings and decorations.[3]

It was clearly most profitable, as well as being practical for the customer, for one firm to provide all the needs of a client's furnishings, even if they were not all made by the same supplier. Indeed the co-ordinator could take a profit on any sub-contracted work, therefore the more comprehensive the range of trades that were under one controlling management, the more successful the entrepreneur was likely to be. Many of the more famous names in the eighteenth-century furniture world were to organise their businesses in this way; the businesses of Thomas Chippendale, Vile and Cobb, George Seddon and William Linnell are amongst those to be discussed below.

It is important to remember that there were many thousands of other makers who made a living from furniture supply. The relatively large number of small-scale operators, although gradually augmented by bigger enterprises, remained the case for another one hundred and fifty years, which perhaps accounts for the generally tardy attitudes of the furniture trade well into the twentieth century.

Economic organisation

The economic structure of the furniture trade was such that it could handle not only a thriving domestic trade, but also a growing export-led economy. To do this the various sectors of the trade were organised on a number of levels. For simplicity, the business organisation can be generally divided between four groups: (a) working masters or journeymen making furniture in their own workshops for the whole-saler or retailer; (b) the integrated manufacturing firms operating from extensive premises combining a variety of skilled workmen; (c) craftsmen-shopkeepers working from their own premises making and selling; and (d) furniture retailers with showrooms. The latter sometimes operated appraising, auctioneering, and second-hand departments as well.

The working masters were described in 1747 as 'those masters who keep no shops nor stocks but principally follow making and dispose of their goods as fast as they are finished'.[4] The same description continues with reference to cabinet-makers and says that 'if a person is only a working master, £100 besides his tools will do tolerably, but if he keeps stock for sale it may increase accordingly to two or three thousand'. If this were the case, he would have fallen into the category of a craftsman shopkeeper.

Mui and Mui (1989) have analysed the profitability of a cross-section of independent businesses in York by investigating the income and expenditure of businesses upon which taxes were assessed. Although the furniture examples are limited, one instance in 1797 shows that the average of cabinet-makers' incomes was £163 (within a range of £100–£200), whilst expenditure averaged £120 (within a range of

1 Christopher Gibbon's trade card. Although the showroom has furniture and fabric samples, as well as funeral hatchments on display, there is still evidence of employees working in the shop.

£80–£200). The average results clearly show a healthy annual surplus of income over expenditure.[5]

Another way to develop was to expand into the second category, an integrated manufacturing firm,[6] which was able to deal with any furnishing requirement from a window blind to a complete house furnishing scheme. Well-known examples are Gillows, Vile and Cobb, Linnell, Chippendale and Seddon. These firms' surviving documents have been analysed and published in a variety of forms, but a first-hand account of this sort of business can be found in the journal of Sophie von La Roche (1786). She described her visit to Seddon's premises and noted that 400 apprentices were employed on 'any work connected with the making of household furniture – joiners, carvers, gilders, mirror workers, upholsterers, girdlers – who mould the bronze into graceful patterns – and locksmiths'.[7] This workforce was

> housed in a building with six wings. In the basement mirrors are cast and cut. Some other departments contain nothing but chairs, sofas and stools of every description, some quite simple others exquisitely carved and made of all varieties of wood and one large room is full up with all the finished articles in this line.[8]

The comprehensiveness of the firm is indicated by Sophie's all-embracing description: 'The entire story of the wood as used for both inexpensive and costly furniture and the method of treating it, can be traced in this establishment'. The firm's growth is also evidenced in their fire insurance cover. In 1756, Seddons were covered for £500; by 1770 the amount was £7,700, and by 1787 it had risen to £17,500.[9]

The third group, the craftsmen-shopkeepers were distinguished by Collyer as:

> Those who work only for shops, and keep no goods by them, take ten pounds with an apprentice who when out of his time may commence such another master with only a chest of tools of value eight to ten guineas and a little wood; but they who keep shops and vend their own goods to the consumer, or for exportation, have more with a lad, who will require a few hundreds if he sets up in the same manner.[10]

Mortimer's *The Universal Director* (1763) carefully pointed out the distinction between working masters and retailers. This publication only listed the cabinet-makers who

> only such as either work themselves or employ workmen under their direction; and that not one of those numerous warehouses which sell ready-made furniture bought of the real artist is to be met with in this work, the plan of which is to direct the private gentleman to the fountain-head in every department.[11]

There was clearly a status distinction between the two; the reliable bespoke operation as opposed to the upstart ready-made stores.

Although there was some tendency to separate the making from the vending in certain instances, there was a close connection between the various elements of a business. There was also a trend towards the combining of the distribution function under an upholsterer or cabinet-maker. The entrepreneurs who developed these comprehensive firms were mainly based in their own workshops, but employed other craftsmen to supplement their own skills. This enabled them to work at their own specialisms whilst acting as co-ordinators of others' products.[12]

Workshops

Clearly the nature of the manufacturing premises would vary according to the type of business carried on. For example, as a specialist in tapestry furniture, Paul Saunders' (1760) workshops not surprisingly included special workrooms for tapestry, cabinet, feather, upholstery, and carpet preparation. In addition to these he had a gilding shop, a silvering room, and a shed for pearching (seasoning)

2 The interior of a small-scale cabinet-maker's workshop, which represents a form of furniture-making that was to remain typical for much of the nineteenth century.

timber.[13] This range of workshops would indicate that not only did Saunders upholster his own products, but he also employed frame-makers, gilders, and possibly specialist silverers as well. This method no doubt ensured a high degree of quality control, as befitted a supplier to the Crown.

Descriptions of the Linnell business in 1763 are also exceptionally revealing of a major complete furnishing company. In this case the premises included a cabinet shop, a glass room, a chair room, an upholsterer's shop, a carver's shop, a gilder's shop, store rooms, count-ing house, the joiner's shop and a saw pit.[14] Again, here is an example of virtually complete control over all the processes of furniture-making, from primary timber conversion to finishing processes, no doubt planned to maintain company control.

Little had appeared to have changed in the quality trade by 1803, when Chippendale the Younger's premises included an upholsterer's shop, a cabinet-maker's shop on three floors, a glass room, a feather room, a chair room, and a veneering room, as well as timber-drying space.[15]

Changes had been occurring though, and by the turn of the century the powered workshop was not a one-off, even in country districts. The deposition (1815) of country chair-maker, Mark Chippindale, gives a clear overview of the nature of a chair-maker's workshop in Lancashire. It is revealing to find that the fittings and stock were considerably more valuable than the cost of completely rebuilding the workshop itself. The machinery (which was powered by water wheel) included one drum and pit-wheel, one press, one circular saw and fixture, two boreing [sic] lathes and fixtures, three turning benches and fixture, one press drill and drawer. In addition to these machines, there were other drums and shafts, belts and straps.[16] This is a clear example of specialisation assisted by some mechanisation.

It has already been seen that craftsmen had to become entrepreneurs as their businesses expanded. Therefore in a business dealing in any volume of trade, in addition to the workshops, there would be various furnishings which were necessary to the running of the office. These would have included desk(s), stool(s), nests of pigeon holes for filing, and a 'case for Compting House books with partitions'.[17] Clearly a reasonably sophisticated financial management apparatus was required for firms that were involved in vertically integrated businesses with a large clientele.

Employees and management

It is clear then that parts of the duties of being a furniture-maker or dealer went some way beyond the actual crafts and business practices involved. The employment of journeymen, the training of apprentices, membership of trade companies, and the duties and responsibilities that went with all these aspects required continual attention. In particular, the changing relationship between employers and employees meant that industrial relations began to be a feature of the eighteenth-century trade.

The role of the livery companies or guilds gradually declined during the century. From their original purpose of protecting the craft, maintaining standards, and offering welfare, they faded into fraternal associations which eventually had little to do with the crafts they once supported.[18] It is significant that famous names such as Chippendale, Cobb, and Hallet, were never members of a livery company, although it must be said that many other well-known furniture-makers were.[19]

On the other hand, the employees who organised themselves into trade societies developed useful organisations that were to ultimately

3 A well-lit and equipped French workshop employing a number of workers, and illustrating a variety of operations and equipment. The sawing of timber in the vice and the marquetry donkey at the rear are noteworthy.

evolve into trades unions. In an economic system that was essentially *laissez-faire*, it is not surprising to find that many of the workers' benefits that were once taken for granted were gradually eroded. Apprentices, for example, were provided with nominal protection by the Statute of Artificers (1563), but the decline of the apprenticeship system during the eighteenth century meant that by 1814 the Statute was repealed.[20]

Although these sorts of structural changes altered the nature of the trade in the long term, in the short term, more immediate matters led to strife. The earliest recorded furniture trade dispute occurred in 1731, and is the first example of cabinet and chair-makers organising themselves; in this case to demand a twelve-hour day.[21] The masters refused the journeymen's demands, who responded by offering the public the opportunity to buy furniture direct. The procedure was to contact the journeymen at either the Black Boy or the Apple Tree public houses in St Martin's Lane. This method of disrupting the normal channels of trade to the disadvantage of the masters was repeated later in the century. Sebastian Pryke (1989) has recorded a similar feature in trade disputes occurring in Edinburgh during 1778. Despite attempts to gain an improvement in wage rates, the Edinburgh journeymen were unsuccessful, so the General Society of Journeymen Cabinet-makers, Joiners, and Carvers established 'a Manufactory of all manner of CABINET and CHAIR WORK where the variety of the neatest and newest patterns of every article may be had.'[22] This shows a great degree of sophisticated organisation, and possibly some assistance from supportive masters, who saw a financial benefit in assisting the project.

As American furniture-makers were influenced by English methods and tastes to a considerable degree, it is not surprising that Philadelphia cabinet-makers also took the same option, having had their wage demands rejected. They opened 'a Ware-Room in Market Street' so that they could sell the furniture they made on their own account.[23] The response of the Philadelphia masters was to advertise for journeymen who would work for them, and fill the demand for labour left by the unlawfully combined conspirators. This advertising for replacement labour also occurred in Newcastle in 1784 when the journeymen struck for a twelve hour day. The masters advertised for two to three hundred men so the scale of the dispute was clearly considerable.[24]

The establishment of the Cabinet-makers' Society in about 1760 was the first enduring furniture trade employee's organisation in London. Whether it was formed to conduct a strike or otherwise, a strike in 1761 ensued, in which the members demanded shorter hours and better piecework rates.[25] The employers' response was predictable. In November 1761 an Order of Council was published in the *London Gazette*, which urged magistrates to prosecute the masters of public houses where the meetings of journeymen were taking place. This was soon followed by an advertisement placed by a group of master cabinet and chair-makers, who offered to re-employ any journeyman on the usual terms of trade.[26]

However, despite disputes, it would seem that relationships between apprentices, journeymen, and masters were close. The physical proximity of workshops within particular areas of cities must have meant that journeymen remained in contact when they moved from a particular workshop. The network that this produced must have been important, and would have constituted something of an internal labour market.

At another level, other networks affected the nature of businesses and their control. Marriages between members of families from different businesses often provided the stimulus for amalgamation; other family ties provided capital for expansion, so the establishment of dynasties was not uncommon.

Sub-contracting and division of labour

The various trade divisions that were established early in the eighteenth century meant that the sub-contracting of parts of the production process were possible, as was the full development of complete specialisms such as chair-makers. An indication of the nature of sub-contracting is found in the description of the role of the cabinet-maker by Collyer:

> all sorts of furniture made of mahogany, walnut tree, plain and carved, veneered or inlaid, go through his hands. The carvers, chair-makers and dealers in brass ornaments are employed by him, and he has a profit out of their labours.[27]

This description not only shows some of the other trades that were employed by the cabinet-maker, but also confirms the cost of 'added value' in the make-up of the final price of furniture.

Although it would appear that the supply of marquetry products lent itself to specialisation, the evidence for this is scant. An example of this sort of division of labour might be the London-based group of Swedish cabinet-makers, Linning, Martin and Fuhrlohg, who have all been associated with marquetry of the finest quality. There is little evidence that they just supplied ready-made marquetry images, although some panels of marquetry were shown at the annual exhibition of 1773–4 of the Free Society of Artists of Great Britain, from which it could be presumed that they were for onward sale.[28] It is rather more likely that they produced fine cabinet furniture fitted out with their specialism – marquetry. Firm evidence of earning a living solely as an inlayer is difficult to find until the end of the century.[29] However, the inter-relationships between trades and sub-contractors in furniture-making should not be surprising as the trade was multifarious in its demand for components for a wide variety of productions.[30]

It is more likely that specialists were developed within a business, especially as the all-round training of apprentices began to give way to the particular training associated with one part of the making process.

This development of the division of labour indicated that the supply of standardised parts, produced either by outside specialists or by makers designated to the task within a business, became increasingly important. Even in the highest standards of production, cabinet-makers would use recurrent patterns of inlay, bronze hardware, and jigs and templates for cabinet and framework.[31] Indeed these clues are often used to identify an object and supply an attribution. The example of the Dominy family workshop in New York demonstrates this point clearly.[32] They had prepared patterns (templates) for armrests, bracket feet, cresting rails, table legs and chair splats.

Interchangeable parts were no doubt used for frames for side chairs, drawer fronts, legs, etc., and in a quality firm like the Linnell's cabinet workshop, there were many examples of pre-prepared parts. In one example there were listed 79 pairs of mahogany arms for chairs, 222 Marlborough feet for tables and chairs, 112 bannisters for chair backs, 60 mahogany splats for chairs, and 35 table legs with turned toes, amongst other multiple items.[33] It is not known whether these items were made by particular craftsmen who specialised in repeat work, but as they are for simple parts they may have been made by rote. For a busy firm like Linnell these figures do not represent any real form of production for stock, rather perhaps an early form of the production system that ensured that parts are ready 'just in time' to complete orders.

In fact, the economies of scale were to be more beneficial in high turnover businesses than they would be in smaller concerns. Even if the trade was relatively unsophisticated in its understanding of economics, analysis of the costs of raw materials, production planning, and labour charges were clearly important in determining the final prices.

Costing, pricing and price books

For any business, the setting of a correct selling price was essential to survival. Whatever the size of enterprise, capital expenditure, material costs, overheads and labour charges, all had to be covered. There was no resale price maintenance in the eighteenth century, and it was common practice for buyers to both haggle about the final price and to delay payment as a matter of course. This often meant that enormous mark-ups were put onto base costs to compensate for these problems that were endemic in the eighteenth century.

Roubo, the great French author of *L'Art de Menuisier* (1772), recommended a costing system based on sound financial principles.[34] He suggested that the price of the finished article should be established by adding capital invested to labour costs, plus a 20 per cent profit margin, and an amount of 10 per cent–15 per cent to cover overheads.

Even if this equitable practice of setting selling prices was practised, other methods of ensuring profitability were clearly used. Cost benefit analysis in the use of particular materials could help to control expenditure. A minor example of this is demonstrated by Roentgen, the illustrious maker, who practised veneering *en quatre faces* so as to use small sheets of veneer in a pattern, which he found to be much cheaper and more satisfactory than the full length veneers.[35] Other examples of cost cutting include the use of stains, imitative and replica products, and so on, all of which are manifestations of economic choice.

The erratic nature of payments and the demand for continual stylistic changes also put great pressure on the cash flow of businesses. Hence there are many examples of furniture-makers entering into business contracts with partners able to supply working capital. The example of Chippendale's business relationships with Rannie and Haig are documented,[36] but the potential profits from furnishing businesses must have encouraged many partnerships on this basis.[37]

Apart from a sound financial base, the satisfactory organisation and profitability of trades depended much on the ability to measure work accurately. This would include measuring raw materials, and taking measurements in customers' homes, but most importantly it was controlling wages and the time taken to complete jobs. The wage rates were usually calculated as piecework, but could also be 'by the day'. In America, this day-rate was adapted so that specific items would be timed and paid on the number of days taken to make them. For example, dining tables took eight days to build, Pembroke tables three and a half days, and dining chairs two days.[38]

The increase in the cost of living from the mid-century onward put pressure on wage rates and caused some conflict between workers and employers, as shown above. To avoid this, joint agreements had to be reached. In one (rare?) case, American employers consented to raise wages on a per cent basis in line with the cost of living, whilst the workmen agreed to reduce wages on the same basis if costs fell.[39]

One of the most satisfactory methods of agreeing rates was the provision of lists setting out agreed work processes and costings. Prior to the publication of printed price books, local agreements were produced in manuscript form. Susan Stuart (1988) provides evidence of the earliest *manuscript* price list produced to define journeymen's wages in relation to the making of particular pieces of furniture.[40] This refers to 'Prices for workmen in Lancaster', a hand-written list found in Robert Gillow's *Memorandum Account Book*, circa 1746.

Christopher Gilbert (1985) has published an early English example from York which was devised in 1764.[41] It is an unremarkable list and interesting for this. It shows standard furniture items that would appear to have been in demand on a regular basis, and often includes prices for furniture in wainscot (oak), mahogany and walnut. It is revealing that walnut was the most expensive to work; as well as being an indication that its popularity was still evident as late as 1764, it perhaps shows that a particular skill, possibly in decline, was required to work it. Another point to note is that distinctions based on timber choice were to become the basis of other costing and price books. In the *London Book of Prices*, the basic prices were for mahogany but rose on a scale: if satinwood was used, a surcharge of 12.5 per cent was added, if 'exotic' timbers such as rose, snake, yew, or maple wood were used, the surcharge rose to 20 per cent.

The *Cabinet-makers' London Book of Prices*, first produced in 1788, was considered by the journeymen as a demand, rather than any example of agreed rates. Its success must have been considerable, as by 1793 the need for a second edition was answered in the form of a new and enlarged volume. This was not accepted so readily by the masters and a dispute ensued. The workmen involved went on strike and caused considerable disruption.

In an attempt to counter these initiatives, some London masters produced their own rival publication, the *Prices of Cabinet Work with Tables and Designs*, produced in 1797. It was, however, unsuccessful in usurping the *Book of Prices*. In 1811, a related volume entitled *The London Cabinet-makers' Union Book of Prices* was published and went into various editions until 1861.

As has already been seen, London was not the only centre of price book usage. Gilbert (1982) cites a number of provincial towns whose cabinet-makers considered it necessary to agree prices for local work.[42]

[59]

A CYLINDER-FALL DESK,

£. s. d.

Three feet long, three drawers in front, cock beaded, three small drawers, three sham ditto, and six letter holes inside, the edge of the top and sweep part of the ends moulded or veneer'd crofs-way, standing board made to slide, on plinth or common brackets - - - - - - - - 2 18 0

EXTRAS.

	£	s	d
Each inch, more or lefs, in length - - - - - - - - - - -	0	1	0
Each extra long drawer - - - - - - - - - - - - - - - -	0	2	6
Each partition - - - - - - - - - - - - - - - - - - -	0	0	7
If two short drawers in place of a long one, extra - - - - -	0	2	3
Each joint in the ends, top, or drawer fronts, either solid or to veneer on, at per joint. - - - - - - - - - - - -	0	0	1
Cutting down stuff for ditto, each cut - - - - - - - - - -	0	0	0½
Veneering each long drawer front - - - - - - - - - - -	0	0	6
Ditto each short - - - - - - - - - - - - - - - - - -	0	0	5
Each butt joint in the veneer - - - - - - - - - - - - -	0	0	4
Veneering the ends, each - - - - - - - - - - - - - - -	0	1	0
Each joint in the veneer - - - - - - - - - - - - - - -	0	0	4
Fram'd back, each pannel - - - - - - - - - - - - - - -	0	0	6
Munting in a plain back - - - - - - - - - - - - - - -	0	0	4
For the price of extra work in the carcafe — *See Dreffing Cheft.*			
For the price of work not inferted here — *See Cylinder-fall Table, or Tables of ditto.*			
Oiling and polishing - - - - - - - - - - - - - - - -	0	1	2

I 2

No. I.

4 An example of a page from the 1788 *Cabinet-Makers' Book of Prices* listing the various parts of a job and their cost. It is indicative of a more careful approach to the economics of trade.

It is important to recognise that the continual change in styles and tastes in furniture meant that the price books were not intended to be design manuals. *The Edinburgh Book of Prices* explains:

> The constant change in fashion in the style of cabinet work, renders it difficult if not impracticable, in a work of this kind, to embrace particularly the price of every article; but although this book is limited in point of extent, it is hoped that it will be found to contain the general principles for ascertaining value of work, so exemplified as to render it easy to make up the price of any piece of work by it.[43]

In America, English price books spread a common knowledge of London fashions and working practices over a wide area, whilst individual towns set their own rates for various jobs. Although a retail price list, rather than an agreement between journeymen and masters, an early example of rates is from Rhode Island, dated 1756, and entitled *Rule and Price of Joyners Work*.[44] By 1772, Philadelphia carpenters had agreed to establish prices and standards for work and published printed lists with details of rates etc.[45] Interestingly, Montgomery (1966) saw a trend in American price books which published retail prices, as moving towards price control and cartel practices.[46] Whether this was the case or not, the price books indicate a coming-of-age for the furniture business.

The example of price books give a clear demonstration of the level of business that required piecework rates for objects that were regularly made on a similar pattern. Many examples exist that demonstrate the success of the patterns being made into furniture. Most importantly, they demonstrate that the business structure of furniture supply had changed from small workshops producing commissioned designs to a multi-based, well organised and financed manufacturing system, that was moving towards the production of a limited range of objects, often with many standardised parts, to be sold through retailers. This surely proved to be one of the more significant shifts that occurred during the century.

Location

The location of eighteenth-century furniture businesses seems to have been a mix of tradition, expediency and planning. Tradition, because most trades had originally had a tendency to locate themselves in a particular quarter of a town. Expediency, as it was advisable on practical grounds to establish workshops and showrooms close to the customer, and planning, which was based on careful noting of the movement of populations, the location of raw material sources, and the changing characteristics of a neighbourhood. This last factor was particularly important in influencing the beginnings of the separation of workshops from retail establishments.[47]

The prime location for a furnishing business in England had to be London. The importance of the capital as a market was commented upon by Defoe in his preface to *The Complete English Tradesman*. He noted that all the counties of England relied upon the city of London for the consumption of their products, and employment of their peoples.[48] It was not only the pre-eminent centre for furniture-making, but also the main port for raw materials importation, as well as for the export of finished goods, in addition to being its own largest market. The example of London can also help to explain the location factors mentioned.

While the trade relied on bespoke orders and remained in a handicraft stage, it was essential for the maker to be close to his customers and his fellow suppliers. The area around St Paul's Cathedral developed a close concentration of furniture-makers which no doubt originated with the ecclesiastical demand, but continued with a middling trade throughout the century. In particular, turners' premises were located in an area west of the Cathedral right up to the 1770s.[49]

After the Great Fire of 1666, the fashionable centre of London moved to Bloomsbury Square, St James Square and Red Lion Square. In the first three quarters of the eighteenth century, in the alleys and courts around Covent Garden and St Martin's Lane, the most fashionable cabinet-makers and upholsterers worked to service this trade. Examples would include Vile and Cobb, John Bradburn, Chippendale, France and Beckwith, and William Hallett. All these cabinet-makers were of top quality and it should be no surprise to find that the Controller of the Office of Works, John Vardy, also had his office in St Martin's Lane.

By the 1750s there was another wave of migration towards more fashionable parts of London. Building activity in areas such as Hanover Square, New Bond Street, Grosvenor Square and Berkeley Square, naturally encouraged cabinet businesses to move towards Soho, Bond Street and Golden Square. Samuel Norman moved to Soho Square after a fire at his Covent Garden premises, while Ince and Mayhew had premises in Broad Street, Golden Square, and Marshal Street, Carnaby Market.

In view of this trend it is not surprising to find that businesses moved quite often. Gordon and Tait, for example, was situated in King Street near Golden Square for two years, then moved to Little Argyle Street for a period of five years. In 1779 the business moved again to Swallow Street and then finally to Oxford Street.

By the fourth quarter of the century there was a further migration of population, this time northward. The area round Oxford Street and Tottenham Court Road was developed to service the new building of Portman Square and the Bedford Square area. To support this trade, there was the well-established firm of Gillow and Co. in Oxford Street, whilst Matthias Lock, Pierre Langlois and John McLean were all to be found in nearby Tottenham Court Road.

The other area of London that witnessed an influx of retail businesses was Mayfair. According to Hughes (1964), from 1730 to 1790 at least fifty house furnishers established themselves in Bond Street alone, and there were another one hundred in other parts of the area.[50]

From another point of view, the reputation of quality businesses in London gave the impression at least that operatives who had been employed there would have the latest knowledge of fashionable practice and design. An advertisement in the *Derby Mercury* of 1795 noted that a Joseph Cooper 'has now begun the upholstery trade, for which purpose he has engaged a person from London, duly qualified to execute that business in all its branches in the best and most complete manner'.[51] There are many other examples of craftsmen using their London training as a springboard into local or provincial business in Britain and North America.

In terms of location, the role of the furniture-maker was often quite different in the provinces. At its basic level, furniture-making had much to do with local wood crafts of various types (excluding coopering and wheelwrighting). An example might be that of Ambrose Hayward of Selling in Kent, a general wood-worker who also made furniture including bed-settles, chairs and dressers.[52] On the other hand, some firms were able to offer a full service comparable to large cities. The example of the firm of William Bastard of Blandford, Dorset is instructive.[53] Not only were they offering full building, joinery, and cabinet-making services, but also had facilities and materials for japanning, silvering of mirrors, the supply of glass and the finishing of furniture.

In other cases, particular regions, both in England and abroad, developed traditions and businesses that were able to meet a local, national or even international demand, depending upon which examples are investigated.

Although developments in the European furniture trade are generally beyond the scope of this book, brief mention must be made of some aspects that affected the English trade. The two main areas of interest were design exchange and the network of technical transfers occasioned by artisans moving from country to country.

The influence of France in terms of furnishing design was very important, but it was their example of 'polite society' that was to be equally influential. This concept had been established in the seventeenth century in France, with divisions being made between state and private apartments, between formal dignity and private comfort. The idea that the house could express one's taste in the same way as dress

5 A view of shared workshop accommodation. The joiner and turner working closely together, c. 1777.

was also acknowledged,[54] and the influence of these ideas will be discussed below.

More directly, the impact of the Huguenot emigrations was to enrich the repertoire of designs and techniques, whilst the exchange of technology was surely encouraged by the relationship between, for example, the English and German Moravian communities.[55]

Nature of labour and the crafts

The main crafts that were associated with furniture-making were all well-established by 1700. Their individual characteristics changed over time, but the general distinctions between carpenters and joiners were established by 1600, upholsterers and chair-makers by the 1650s, and joiners and cabinet-makers by the 1680s.

The changes did not mean the decline of one trade at the expense of another, it was rather that the products of each group were becoming tiered in terms of intricacy of workmanship and type of product made. These differences will be explained below.

Cabinet-makers

The distinguishing processes of cabinet-makers were demonstrated in the construction of case furniture often fitted with drawers. The techniques were derived from the work of the trunk and coffer makers, who had previous experience of making rigid boxes and small cabinets.[56] It was this sort of work that employed the distinctive dovetail joint which allowed solid boards to be satisfactorily jointed together, not only to provide a rigid frame, but also to deliver a reliable substrate for further decoration.

On the other hand, the methods of embellishment of cabinets, e.g. parquetry, marquetry, and veneering, were influenced by the intarsia masters whose techniques of wood ornament involved making decorative panels from small sections of coloured woods.[57]

Cabinet-makers appear to have been established in Italy, probably at the beginning of the sixteenth century, and their influence spread from there. However, it was not until the mid-seventeenth century that the true cabinet-maker rose to prominence in his own right, mainly due to a demand for more sophisticated furniture using luxury timber veneers. High standards of cabinet work had been set in the seventeenth century in Augsburg, Antwerp and Florence, the influence of which had reached Paris by the middle of the century and London by the latter part.[58]

Sturmer (1979) has described this transmission process as 'a new language of design and technology [which] developed on the level of court art common all over Europe'.[59] This language was not necessarily related so much to trade customs and practice, but rather to the availability of printed designs and the interchange of high-quality craftsmen within Europe.

Therefore it is not so surprising to find that John Evelyn could favourably compare English woodworkers with their foreign counterparts as early as 1666. He considered that

> locksmiths, joyners, cabinetmakers and the like, from very vulgar and pitiful artists are now come to produce works as curious for the fitting and admirable for their dexterity in contriving, as any we meet abroad.[60]

Skilled craftsmen were clearly sought after. A revealing and early insight on the dearth of specialised artisans is found in the order made in 1715 by the Newcastle Joiners' Company.[61] This demonstrates the shortage of skilled workers, especially outside of London, and the problems that this gave rise to:

> Whereas by 2 several orders made 20 or 30 years ago regarding the employment of foreigners, [i.e. not from the locality] and which said orders were made at a time when there was not a competent number of free brothers to supply and assist in the art of cabinet-making, inlaying and phinearing [sic], and it was agreed that if any brother did undertake that business of a cabinet-maker, such brother might have liberty to entertain, hire or sett at work such journeyman or journeymen in cabinet work only.

The problem was that some Newcastle masters were employing unskilled craftsmen who were spoiling the reputation of the company, so the agreement had to be revoked.

In this period, skilful foreign artisans working in England were likely to be successful. One example which is revealing of trends at the time is the Dutch or Flemish born Gerrit Jensen. Jensen (c. 1680–1715) is recorded as a cabinet-maker to the Crown, but was enroled as a liveryman of the Joiners' Company, no doubt because there was no separate guild, which itself demonstrates the lack of major distinctions between the trades at the time. Stylistically his work is also exemplary of the influence of Dutch and French cabinet-makers on English furniture of the late seventeenth and early eighteenth centuries.[62] Working with different materials (tortoiseshell and brass) and using the new techniques, Jensen and others from the Low Countries brought English cabinet-making to a high standard.

The influx of European craftsmen clearly had a considerable effect on the cabinet-making trade in terms of style and technique. What is equally fascinating is the reverse of this influence. Although not necessarily renowned for their skill in design, the quality of high-class English workmanship was soon recognised as second to none. Apart from a growing demand from Europe and North America, examples of continental craftsmen receiving training with an English master demonstrate this. For example, the German-born Abraham Roentgen lived and worked as a cabinet-maker in London between 1733 and

6 The trade card of the important cabinet-maker Pierre Langlois, c. 1763. The extravagant design demonstrates not only the fashionable rococo style, but also the value of a French connection to a furnishing business.

1738, before he returned to Germany to set up his own workshops.[63] By 1761, his son David had taken over the business, and even though he had never been to England, called himself an 'Englische Kabinettmacher'.[64] Another case is the great Swedish cabinet-maker Georg Haupt, who drew attention to his London training in his application to the Stockholm Carpenters' Guild, signifying the importance attached to a London apprenticeship.[65]

This appreciation was not only a continental expression. In 1763 Mortimer wrote of cabinet-making:

> This ancient, curious and useful Mechanic Art, is brought to very great perfection in England: almost every capital sale of Furniture presenting us with specimens of the ingenuity of our artists in this branch; which renders a particular description of so well-known an article entirely needless.[66]

However, not everyone held English cabinet-makers or their work in quite such high esteem. The comments of Batty Langley in his introduction to the *City and Country Builder's and Workman's Treasury of Designs* (1740) indicated how difficult it was for him to find a cabinet-maker that could make a bookcase well, 'without being obliged to the joiners to set out the work'.[67] Although this is perhaps a jaundiced view, could it demonstrate the turn around of skills whereby the cabinet-maker has lost some basic skills at the expense of more exotic processes?

Whatever the case, cabinet-making was considered a respectable trade for a bright adolescent to enter into.[68] Collyers' *Parent's and Guardian's Directory* (1761) advised that

> The youth intended for this purpose ought to be able to write a good hand, understand arithmetic, and have some notion of drawing and designing. It requires more ingenuity than strength: a nice eye and a light hand are absolutely necessary as he is by far the most curious workman in the wood way. His success as a master must depend on the delicacy of his fancy and the neatness of his work.[69]

In Campbell's *London Tradesmen*, the possible financial rewards of the cabinet-making trade are revealed. He wrote that 'a master cabinet-maker is a very profitable trade, especially if he works for and serves the quality himself, but if he must serve them through the channel of the upholder, his profits are not very considerable'.[70]

This clearly shows the distinction between those cabinet-makers who rose to the position of entrepreneurs themselves, as opposed to those who worked as sub-contractors to the upholsterers. Examples of profitable furniture-makers could include Dale, an upholsterer who purchased the estate of Viscount Bolingbroke for £50,000, and Simms, a Quaker upholsterer reputed to be also worth £50,000. Although these were both upholsterers, cabinet-makers also feature, with the example of Mr Bylis White whose obituary reported that he died 'having acquired a genteel fortune'.[71] Even if these figures are exaggerated they give an indication of the potentially profitable nature of the business.

As was intimated above, the role of the cabinet-maker was often subsidiary to the upholsterer, who often acted as the orchestrator of the complete interior. However, the cabinet-maker was an important link in the supply of furniture. Campbell considered the cabinet-maker to be the right-hand man of the upholsterer as he

> furnishes him with Mahogony and Wallnut-tree posts for his beds, settees of the same Materials, Chairs of all sorts and prices, carved, plain and inlaid, Chests of Drawers, Book-cases, Cabinets, Desks, Scrutores, Buroes, Dining, Dressing and Card Tables, Tea Boards and an innumerable variety of articles of this sort.[72]

Whoever went into business as an entrepreneur, rather than simply a craftsman, needed other skills to survive in the jungle of eighteenth-century business practices.[73] Collyer suggested that youths entering the trade should be numerate as well as able to draw and write. Although Collyer also considered ingenuity and a light hand essential for success in the trade, in some instances the master no longer had a direct connection with the making of his products. Justus Moser, writing in 1767, observed the changes that were occurring.

> The trading craftsman in England first learns his trade, then he studies commerce. The journeyman of a trading cabinet-maker must be as qualified an accountant as any merchant. The master himself no longer touches a tool. Instead he oversees the work of his forty journeymen, evaluates what they have produced, corrects their mistakes, and shows them ways and methods by which they can better their work or improve their technique. He may invent new tools and will observe what is going on in the development of fashion. He keeps in touch with people of taste and visits artists who might be of assistance to him.[74]

It is perhaps a surprise to read this. The education of a journeyman who might aspire to become a leading craftsman did not seem to prepare him for the multiple roles of accountant, businessman, manager, inventor and designer. However, the success of pattern books, tracts on economics and trading practice, as well as encyclopedias, bear witness to the demand for learning in these spheres.

In the country the situation was different. The local furniture-maker had to be diverse: both a joiner and cabinet-maker, able to turn his hand to most jobs involving wood. The economist Adam Smith noted that contrary to the division of labour found in towns, the 'country carpenter is not only a carpenter, but a joiner, a cabinet-maker and even a carver in wood'.[75] However, some provincial towns did develop flourishing furniture trades, sometimes supported by published price lists. Examples include Birmingham, Leeds, Nottingham, York, Bristol, Norwich and Lancaster.[76]

In America, opportunities for skilled cabinet-makers were considerable. As the market for furniture expanded with the growth of the country it was inevitable that European cabinet-makers would emigrate to the New World to take advantage of prospects there. Another benefit was that the trade was never controlled by guilds, although craftsmen took on apprentices who became journeymen under a civil system. Prior to the middle of the eighteenth century many American cabinet-makers also followed other crafts in their businesses, usually to develop their business more quickly. However, after the mid-century the growing population and the expanding coastal trade meant that specialisation and division of labour became more desirable.[77]

Carvers

There were a number of subsidiary crafts that were intimately associated with wooden furniture-making. Carving was one of the most important, but it suffered a variety of swings of fortune as the pendulum of taste changed through the century. In the early part of the century, the preference for highly carved chair frames made with cane seats and backs was decreasing, so the workers were divided between those that carved fully in wood for gilded or painted finishes, or those who rough carved, ready for gesso application and then finished the carving in this material.

Specialisation continued but the divisions had shifted, so that by 1747 the *London Tradesmen* could state that there was 'a class of carvers who do nothing else but carve frames for looking glasses'.[78] In addition to this group were the artisans who specialised in producing carvings for furniture from heavier timbers, such as mahogany. Campbell defined these as 'a Species of Carvers peculiar to themselves; who are employed in carving Chairs, Posts and Testers of Beds or any other furniture whereon Carving is used'. As for their education, clearly drawing was essential, but Campbell considered that 'the rest of their education may be as mean as they please'.[79] Fifteen years later, drawing skills were still considered important for a carver, even though a higher quality education would seem to have been required. According to Collyer, carving

> [has] lately been carried to great perfection, it requires much ingenuity, a lively and elegant fancy, skill in drawing with great neatness foliages, fruit, flowers, birds, heads, etc.; a good eye and a steady hand.[80]

When the climate was favourable, carvers were clearly successful, but as the *Parent's and Guardian's Directory* (1761) pointed out, they were dependent upon the public, but at that time, 'as a taste for carved work in chairs and other furniture prevails, the ingenious men among their kind of carvers are never out of business'.[81]

The fickle nature of public taste continued to have an effect on the carving trade as the century progressed. As tastes moved towards marquetry or painted decoration, the demand for carving fell away and this resulted in a decline in numbers and skills. By 1803 Sheraton recorded that carvers were further sub-divided into four specialisms. First, those who prepared architectural work, second, the workers in internal decorations for furniture (i.e. mirror frames, bed cornices, etc.), third, a group who specialised in chair work, and lastly, a section devoted to ship's carving.[82] Even Sheraton's description was qualified by saying that chair carvers worked in simple flat work or scrolls, whilst the impact of alternative compositions in frame-making must have signalled a decline in this area as well.

A close connection existed between carving and gilding which often resulted in many of the practitioners being combined into the one trade of carver-gilder. Indeed, Campbell says that 'gilders are generally carvers',[83] and this seemed relevant 'as gilding at present seems to be out of Fashion, there is employment but for a few hands who do not understand Carving'.[84] Distinctions between gilding craftsmen in terms of process or material (water gilding or oil gilding, metal, wood or plaster), as well as in the objects gilded, seem to have been relatively few. Dominique Jean (*c.* 1783–95) however, was recorded as a gilder and founder as well as an ormolu worker.[85]

Veneerers and marqueteurs

As mentioned above, the nicety of marquetry work might have suggested that specialists would have been employed at an early stage because of the expertise required in the process. However, in 1728, Chambers *Cyclopaedia* noted that it was 'the cabinet-makers, joiners and toymen among us who work in marquetry'.[86] The comment is revealing in that the distinctions between the roles of joiners and cabinet-makers still seem to be blurred, and there is no indication of any specialisation towards marquetry in this part of the trade. The reference to toymen would perhaps allude to the small fancy goods made from wood and decorated with marquetry, such as treen or Tunbridge ware.

Having said that, the practice of marquetry was often more complicated than an average cabinet-maker would be able to accomplish, or indeed would want to devote the time to. It is not surprising then to soon find evidence of some specialism, either in the furniture types produced by a business or by an enterprise devoted to the supply of prepared marquetry designs.

A prime example of the former group is the well-known French-trained cabinet-maker Pierre Langlois who advertised his commodes as 'inlaid in the politest manner', whilst a contemporary commented that 'this artist performs all sorts of curious inlaid work, particularly commodes in the foreign taste inlaid with tortoiseshell, brass, etc.'.[87] The latter, the specialist supplier, could be exemplified by Philip Hunt (1680–1720) who offered, amongst other cabinet work, 'curious inlaid figures for any worke'.[88] It seems likely that these might have been made in bulk for later application by others. At the end of the century (*c.* 1790–93) Joseph Binns advertised himself simply as a cabinet-inlayer, which clearly indicates a degree of specialisation.[89]

It therefore appears that although many workshops produced their own marquetry work, there is evidence of some cabinet-makers becoming specialists in this part of the trade.[90] In the United States, the inventory of Thomas Barrett of Baltimore, who was described as an *ébéniste*, is revealing of specialisation. His stock, as at November 1800, included 1,316 'shells for inlaying into furniture', and seventy-six yards of banding. In addition there were debts from over fifteen cabinet-makers who had been supplied from his prepared stock.[91]

Other examples exist of marquetry designs that were clearly available in bulk and were, on occasions, exported. An advertisement of 1796 from the New York *Argus* offered

> Shells for cabinet-work to cabinet-makers. A gentleman has just arrived from London with an assortment of Shells for cabinet-work which he will dispose of on reasonable terms for cash.[92]

No doubt these would have been attractive in a country where high-grade cabinet-making craft skills were at a premium.

Like other decorative processes, marquetry was subject to changes in taste and by the end of the century it had lost its prestige. In 1803, Shoraton noted that marquetry was an expensive way of decorating furniture, that it was subject to speedy decay, and this problem had accounted for its decline.[93] The trade of the turner was also affected by changes in furniture taste.

Turners

Although the high point of the turner's craft could be said to have been in the late seventeenth century, the craft skills were still important as a subsidiary to cabinet-making during the eighteenth century. Whereas it might be true to say that it was not until the last quarter of the eighteenth century that turners found work with high-style furniture-makers, it is clear that they were not redundant until this time. For example, in the case of simple wooden chairs, *The General Description of All Trades* stated that 'common turned chairs were sold at the turner's shop',[94] whilst the supply of pillars, legs, and bed frames to cabinet-makers clearly flourished. With the classical revival, the turner, often in combination with the carver, brought out many variations on themes for legs of tables, chairs, and bed-posts which were often fluted or reeded. At the other end of the scale a connection with common chair-making continued throughout the century.

7 A well-equipped turner's workshop complete with a foot-powered
treadle lathe.

Chair-makers

The nature of chair-making in the eighteenth century was quite complex. Early in the century the business was a branch of the joiner's
trade, simply because most chairs were made using mortise and tenon
or dowel joints that did not demand superior skills. In fact, it was not
long before a number of furniture-makers declared in their advertising
that they also supplied or made chairs, so any particular divisions are
difficult to determine. Nevertheless, the idea of the division of labour
and the specialist craftsmen who just made chairs or even particular
types of chairs is still valid. Sheraton confirms that by the end of the
century

> Chair-making [was] a branch generally confined to itself: as those
> who professedly work at it seldom engage to make cabinet furniture.
> In the country manufactories it is otherwise; yet even these pay
> some regard to keeping their workmen at the chair, or to the cabinet
> work.[95]

The distinctions between types of chair-making were also recognised
by the specialisations that occurred at varying times during the century.

8 A country chair made from oak complete with wooden seat. The design is derived from a high-style original but could be up to 20–30 years later.

At the beginning of the period there was a distinct group of cane chair-makers who had already established themselves in the previous quarter century.[96] The continuing demand for lightweight chairs (especially dining) made these chair types fashionable until the taste for wooden splats usurped them. When the taste for caning returned in the last part of the century, it was the trade chair-makers rather than specialists who met the demand.

During the last quarter of the century the making of fancy chairs also became a specialist trade. Fancy chairs were designed to be a lightweight but sophisticated addition to the interior. The intention was to harmonise with the decorations and hence they were often painted in a delicate manner, with a caned seat to maintain the elegant image. This fashion for painted or japanned chairs was promoted by the publications of Hepplewhite and Sheraton which helped to provide employment for specialist fancy chair-making businesses.[97]

As with other processes, specialist chair-makers had to adapt to changing fashions. The case of the cane chair-makers was noticed by an anonymous writer in 1747:

> The Cane chair-makers not only make this sort, [cane chairs] now almost out of use, but the better sort of matted, leather bottomed and wooden chairs, of which there is a great variety of goodness, workmanship and price; and some of the makers who are also shopkeepers are very considerable dealers employing from £300 to upwards of £500 in the trade.[98]

The better sort of chair-making work was considered to be a satisfactory occupation, but the making of 'the white wooden, wicker and ordinary matted sort', commonly called 'kitchen chairs' was thought to be an inferior employment prospect.[99]

In the same way that other craftsmen developed their businesses, some chair-makers became entrepreneurs:

> The Chair-makers formerly used to deal in nothing but chairs, and were frequently employed by the cabinet-maker or upholsterer, but now they keep large shops themselves, and sell almost all kinds of household goods; such as tables chests of drawers looking-glasses as well as chairs of all sorts.[100]

What must be stressed is that sub-divisions of chair-making were also related to the supply of parts, the turned members being the prerogative of the turners, the carved decoration being supplied by chair carvers, while the textile components were fitted by upholsterers.

Upholsterers

It has already been established that the upholsterer played a pivotal role in house furnishing. His specialty as an arbiter of taste was recognised by contemporary commentators and established a relationship between retailer and customers that has remained. Campbell was happy to say about the upholsterer that

> He is that man on whose judgement I rely on the choice of goods; and I suppose he has not only judgement in the materials but taste in the fashions, and skill in the workmanship.[101]

Campbell continues by describing the upholsterer, who

> was originally a species of the Taylor, but by degrees has crept over his head, and set up as a connoisseur in every article that belongs to a house. He employs journeymen in his own proper calling, cabinet-makers, glass grinders, looking-glass framers, carvers for chairs, testers and posts for beds, the woollen draper, the mercer, the linen draper, and several species of smiths and a vast army of tradesmen of the other mechanic branches.

As if this was not enough, Campbell continues: 'This tradesman's genius must be universal in every branch of Furniture; though his proper craft is to fit up beds, window curtains, hangings, and to cover chairs that have stuffed bottoms.'[102]

The co-ordinating role of the upholsterer as a full house furnisher was always important, but the specialist emphasis on material and draperies never went away. Indeed the 'proper craft' of upholstery itself demonstrated some sub-division. For example, the actual cutting out of expensive materials was seemingly left to male workers, whilst cheaper female labour was usually employed for all the sewing as they 'never served an apprenticeship to the Mystery'.[103] Other examples of division are in the evidence of chair-stuffing being a separate skill, whilst the chair-frame maker had been a distinct trade for a long time.[104]

The role of upholsterers was not only to 'fit up beds, window curtains, hangings and to cover chairs that have stuffed bottoms',[105] they were also involved in the business of undertaking and appraising (valuing). The application of black cloths throughout the house as well as the supply of coffins and other paraphernalia that were associated with the funereal rituals kept upholsterers busy.[106] The connection between death and appraisal is obvious in the preparation of inventories, but descriptions of this trade seems to indicate that they were also adjudicators in conflicts between parties. Campbell suggested that they always valued things at a low price as 'they are obliged to take the goods if it is insisted on, at their own appraisement'.[107] Upholsterers sometimes also called themselves 'Brokers of old goods', an aphorism for second-hand dealers, no doubt resulting from their work as appraisers.

Other trades

Other specialists were enlisted to complete the repertoire of furnishings. For example, the business of fret-cutting appears to have been a

9 An example of part of the process of filling and covering the upholstered parts of a chair.

sub-division, as the trade is separately described by Campbell in 1747. He pointed out that 'the fret-cutter must have a much lighter hand and a quicker eye than the cabinet-maker as he is employed in work much more minute and elegant'.[108] Did he supply ready-cut parts or was he employed to prepare parts to order? It is likely that both forms of business were enjoyed at various times by a variety of sub-contractors.

Glass-workers were also a separate craft but often acted closely with the trade. The glass grinder, who prepared the glass and then silvered it ready for the framers, was part of a chain of opera-tives.[109] This sequence continued with glass frame-makers who were joiners who specialised in preparing the frames for the carvers at the next stage. Campbell had little time for the frame-makers, describing them as 'no more than a cobbling carpenter or joiner'.[110]

Although detailed discussion of the provincial furniture trade is beyond the scope of this book, a few comments are useful. It seems clear that the supply of furniture in country districts for local consumption was not generally a separate undertaking until the mid-nineteenth century when businesses were set up in towns to supply a particular region. During the eighteenth century however, the supply of furniture was a part of the role of the local craftsman who also met demands for many other sorts of woodworking, apart from specialised trades such as wheelwrighting. Recent scholarship has provided an insight into this vanished world by using old account books.[111] The examples examined confirm that for those businesses, the supply of furniture was often only a small part of their repertoire. The product range was varied and depended on the nature of the demand, but all items seemed to have been made, including cupboards, kitchen tables, dining tables, tea tables, beds, bed-settles, dressers and chairs. At another level, the example of the firm of William Bastard of Blandford, Dorset demonstrates the range of work undertaken. They were variously known as joiners, architects or cabinet-makers, and their inventory demonstrates activity in all these fields. In the case of furniture, they seem to have been busy: at the time of inventory they listed 260 chairs in stock or in progress, 27 assorted tea-tables, 6 oval tables, 27 tops for walnut tables and 10 chests of drawers. In addition there was a large quantity of timber clearly intended for furniture use.[112]

Provincial suppliers were also capable of fulfilling exacting commissions from local and national customers and these are to be firmly distinguished from 'country work'. The well-known firm of Gillow of Lancaster is one of many such examples.[113]

Women and the trade

Although the trade was dominated by males, there are many references throughout the century to women as principals of businesses.[114] They were often wives who operated alongside their husbands; sometimes they were relatives of widowed cabinet-makers, as well as being crafts-people such as upholsterers in their own right. It is difficult to estimate how common it was for a wife to follow the trade of her deceased husband, but at least one widow sold her husband's stock by advertising that she was 'not designing to follow the trade'.[115] This could indicate

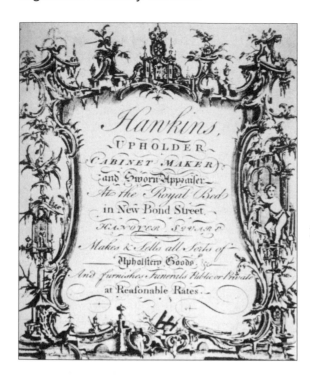

10 The trade card of Elizabeth Hankins in a fashionable Chinoiserie style. She was one of a number of women who ran furniture businesses in the eighteenth century.

that it was not unusual for wives to do so. Kirkham (1988) has pointed out that Defoe in his *Complete English Tradesman* actually recommended craftsmen to select a wife who would be able to assist in the daily running of an enterprise or be capable of continuing the business in the event of his death.[116] Interestingly, some daughters of members of the Upholders' Company were admitted by patrimony during the century, and clearly carried on their deceased father's business.[117] Even royal patronage was no bar to females as there are examples of wives taking over the royal commissions upon the death of the husband.[118] It would seem that although some eighteenth-century women had high profiles in furniture businesses, there were many others working in parts of the trade who have had no such acknowledgement.

Distribution and sales

There are few descriptions of premises, little in the way of archival material relating to retailing practices,[119] and even less visual remains to assist in interpreting the commercial activities of eighteenth-century cabinet-makers.[120] Nevertheless, this section will explore the general nature of the shops and warehouses that sold furniture in the eighteenth century, as well as touching on other methods of distribution and selling, including auctions and the second-hand market. The importance of the import and export trade (as well as smuggling) will be discussed and this will lead into a brief analysis of the methods of transport used in furniture distribution.

The structure of the distribution system was clearly affected by the major eighteenth-century developments already mentioned, such as the expanding population, the development of urban centres, the changes in standards of living, and improvements in transport infrastructures.

Without doubt, the eighteenth century saw the growth and consolidation of a retail sector that was distinct from manufacturing and making. In one calculation it has been estimated that by the 1750s, the ratio of shops to population in London was not to be exceeded until the end of the nineteenth century.[121] Clearly this was not simply a linear pattern, and the changes that occurred were piecemeal and very varied. Nevertheless, the commercial basis of trade had begun to change; no longer was it subsistence on the one hand or bespoke on the other.

It might be assumed that it was relatively easy to establish a business, but to operate profitably over a lengthy period was quite another matter. The skills associated with successful retailing had to be quickly assimilated, often alongside the production and development of the products that were being sold. The selection of an appropriate site, the choice and training of staff, the shrewd purchase of stock, the promotion of the business, the setting of levels of service, and the importance of client satisfaction were all of utmost importance in maintaining a viable business. However, before the urban markets could develop and prosper the full-scale development of the marketplace was necessary.

Urbanisation

The growth of urban centres in general, and the importance of London in particular, have therefore become major factors in any analysis of distribution and consumption patterns in the eighteenth century. This is not surprising, bearing in mind that London accounted for 10 per cent of the population; that it had more shops and therefore more opportunities to display new items; that it handled 80 per cent of the imports and had a monopoly of the Far East trade and, that as well as playing a central role in inland trade, it was a centre of manufacturing in its own right. Naturally enough other regional areas that had trading contact with London were likely to follow the patterns of urbanisation and consumption that were set there. To support this development, urban improvements such as lighting, paving, and cleaning became part of a developing system that was partly fuelled by the needs of distributors and consumers.

In addition, the public display of goods, the establishment of social codes and manners, and the development of polite society, were also crucial to urbanisation and the development of trade. The physical size of London meant that public activities where the *nouveau riche* could demonstrate their newly-acquired possessions were plentiful, but the domestic interior remained one of the most potent arenas for demonstrative gestures. As these factors clearly applied to other cities as well, the status of home was becoming universally more important at many social levels.

Changes in interiors were not just to be seen in terms of new technologies, increases in wealth, or a growing aesthetic awareness or sophistication; there were new ideas about objects and their place in the home. The importance of interiors stemmed from the way in which they could reflect social positions and it was part of the retailer's job to communicate these trends to his customers.

Retailing

The divisions of the furniture trade discussed above, make it clear that the separation of the making from the retailing functions was not complete by any means. The divisions did include shops which sold ready-made goods but it was a slow process of development from craftsmen-shopkeepers, who made goods and sold them from their own premises, to full-scale retail-only businesses. Even the simple maker-seller arrangement could be varied. The example of William Russell, a mahogany turner and cabinet-maker, is one such variant based on location. He was able to supply goods from either his shop in Bond Stables or from his house in Fetter Lane.[122]

The example of the turner's trading methods demonstrates another distinction by the mid-century. Turners were clearly divided between 'real mechanics, and a set of shopkeepers, many of them in a very large way [who] engross as to the buying and selling part, all the produce of the real turners and many trades beside'.[123] As the turners were divided between makers and sellers, so it was with the upholsterers who were the leaders amongst the furnishing businesses of the mid-eighteenth century: 'They keep large shops in which they sell beds, blankets, quilts, counterpanes and some of them deal in all kinds of furniture which they buy of the cabinet-makers, chair-makers etc.'.[124] The separation of showrooms from workshops, even if on the same premises, was likely to have become common during the century. In the case of the firm of Linnell, the main showroom was on the front ground floor whilst workshops and stores were at the rear and on other floors.[125]

The establishment of retail-only businesses may have developed through the acquisition of premises solely for selling, and often situated in fashionable parts of towns. For example, in 1759, Caldwall's carpet and bedding warehouse which was situated at Holborn, published a

11 An example of a French upholstery warehouse and showroom showing female workers, various furnishing items and a delivery service.

trade card which noted that 'persons residing at the court end of town may likewise be served at his warehouse in Piccadilly'.[126]

The eighteenth-century use of the term 'warehouse' was often synonymous with a retail display. The business of Warren and Co., who in 1763 were listed in directories as Proprietors of a 'Warehouse for all sorts of elegant furniture, pictures, china etc.' in Vine Street, Piccadilly, was clearly a retail operation. In this example, no mention is made of making or wholesaling; indeed the stock selection might indicate a business that specialised in being only a supplier of house furnishings.

By the middle part of the eighteenth century, these kind of 'warehouse shops' saw an expansion both in numbers and in the splendour in which they were fitted out. One anonymous writer described cabinet-making showrooms in the following manner:

> Many of their shops are so richly set out that they look more like palaces and their stocks are of exceeding great value. But this business seems to consist, as do many others, of two branches, the maker and the vendor; for the shopkeeper does not always make every sort of goods that he deals in, though he bears away the title.[127]

The last part of this statement is important as it not only indicates that shopkeepers sold other makers' goods but that they had instigated a form of 'own label' branding to identify the goods they sold. Therefore it is quite likely that some trade labels found on items of eighteenth-century furniture refer to the retailer rather than to the actual maker.

By 1788 retail-only outlets appeared to be seriously challenging the existing workshop selling arrangements. The *Cabinet-makers' London Book of Prices* complained that

> The goods manufactured for the use of sale shops is a grievance which it would be pointless to point out to you [the masters] – every man of the smallest consideration must see from what cause that evil arises, and wherein lies the remedy to prevent impositions on the public, and to secure to the fair trader that approbation he so justly merits.[128]

'Sale shops' certainly meant retail outlets; it is speculative to suggest that they may have been offering goods at reduced prices so as to gain trade, but this could be inferred from the *Price Book* statement. Even more frustrating were the itinerant sales which competed with established businesses. One example temptingly offered the public 'a large assortment of new furniture to be sold at the lowest prices in the large Assembly Room' in Kirkgate, Leeds in 1781.[129]

Whatever the case, many who were designated as cabinet-makers may well have been entrepreneurs buying and selling as a shopkeeper, rather than being primarily engaged in producing furniture. A further distinction between the functions of wholesaling and retailing was also often blurred. Trade cards of the period frequently state specifically that the business is wholesale or retail, or a combination of both. For example, Stephen Wood, a London cabinet-maker, stated on his trade card that 'Gentlemen, Merchants, and Country Chapmen may have the best of goods, wholesale or retail at the lowest prices'.[130] The reference to Chapmen perhaps indicates a truly wholesale function as a supplier to itinerant traders.

In contrast to these general suppliers of all sorts of furniture, there were specialist retailers who were established to meet a particular branch of demand: the concept of niche marketing was well understood in the eighteenth century. Deciding to specialise in a particular type of merchandise and becoming known as an authority was often a key to financial success. Specialists like this included dealers in japanned furniture. Two early examples of this type of trade were, coincidentally, both run by women. Mrs Savage ran an 'East India Warehouse over the New Change' (1732), and Mrs Ann Wraughton (1694) sold japanned and Indian cabinets in Covent Garden.[131] Other specialist businesses included dealers in mirrors. Examples of these enterprises might include Minshall's Looking Glass Store, Hanover Square; Luke Young's Looking Glass Manufactory; and Gumley's looking glass shop which was established in the gallery over the Royal Exchange. In the latter case it is clear that the store was more than just a mirror business as a description of the shop interior shows: 'In the midst of the walk are set in order a long row of rich tables, on many of which lie cabinets, inlaid or wholly of corals, ambers, in the like parts.'[132]

It is difficult to evaluate how goods were actually purchased. It seems evident that some purchasers at least wanted instant gratification by taking possession of their purchase(s) as soon as possible. The advertising, often on trade cards, that indicated availability from stock was surely an incentive to purchase from that particular dealer. One example will suffice:

At Hodsons Looking glass and cabinet warehouse in Frith Street Soho is *ready made* a great variety of all sorts of furniture in the neatest and most fashionable manner by choice and experienced workmen employed in his own house.[133] (my italics)

Selling from stock clearly went on, perhaps even for the majority of sales, but often customers must have required something slightly different; in the case of upholstery, for example, a cover differing from that in stock. In these cases, the bespoke special order was taken and would have been the prerogative of a different retail outlet.[134]

As has been shown, the range of sales could be from a simple ready-money cash sale to a full-scale furnishing of a home. The progress of a major commission for a house furnishing was quite complicated and therefore needed a considerable degree of managing. The first task would be to arrange a site visit to measure up and discuss requirements. This would be followed by the preparation of small sketches and estimates. On commissioning, large working drawings would be prepared along with a cutting list as well as internal estimates of materials and time. After dispatch of the finished goods, the assembly, setting up and fixing of the many aspects of the commission followed. On completion the bill could be rendered.

For the selection of bespoke items or special orders, much use must have been made of pattern books, both of textiles and of furniture designs. To further assist customer choice, the selection process could have included the inspection of samples of finished work or even models made up for the purpose.[135] The Philadelphia business of Benjamin Randolph had six sample carved chairs specially made to show the quality of the workshop's products. In France, the famous cabinet-maker Jacob is attributed with making beeswax models of furniture, whilst the practice of offering a model for a Royal commission is well-known.[136]

For the purchaser, the process of shopping itself was clearly part of the pleasure of the consumption process. In response to, or even because of this, shopkeepers spent large amounts of money on premises and their fitting out. The German diarist and blue stocking, Sophie von La Roche commented upon this phenomenon:

[she] was struck by the excellent arrangement and system which the love of gain and the national good taste have combined in producing, particularly in the elegant dressing of large shop windows, not merely

to ornament the streets and lure purchasers, but to make known thousands of inventions and ideas and spread good taste about.[137]

Sophie saw that shops were more important than simply being an economic conduit. Their role as arbiters of taste was also crucial. If some were content to visit the fashionable streets and simply indulge in window shopping, others took the business very seriously. Lady Shelborne records in her diary that she

> called my Lord with whom we first went to Zucchi's, where we saw some ornaments for the ceiling . . . from there to Mayhew and Ince where is come beautiful cabinet work, and two pretty glass cases for one of the rooms in my apartment and which though they are only deal and to be painted white, he charges £50 for. From there to Cipriani's . . . from there to Zuccarelli's . . . and from there home it being half past four.[138]

Shopping could clearly be exhausting.

In the above case it seems evident that Lady Shelborne was a decisive force in the purchasing process, but this may have been exceptional. Amanda Vickery (1993) has usefully examined aspects of the gender divisions of domestic purchases. She suggests that while women were involved in most minor purchasing decisions, in the case of capital goods, the men had an 'ultimate sanction' over the purchases. She gives two furniture examples recorded by Elizabeth Shackleton in the 1770s. Although Elizabeth ordered small items of common furniture, it was John Shackleton who went to Gillows in Lancaster to make important purchases, and it is his name that appears in their ledgers; when her newly-wed son departed to Lancaster for his furniture she noted: 'Tom [is] going from Newton to Lancaster to buy new mahogany furniture'.[139]

The whole question of the relationship between genders and the interior, as well as responsibility for purchasing, is difficult to assess, but it appears that there was a gradual change over the century. Indeed, it has been suggested that during the second half of the century, a division between the feminine and the masculine in domestic matters was becoming apparent.[140] The choosing of colour schemes and domestic furnishings was beginning to be seen as suitable for women at home, especially if they were decorating rooms that were intended for their own use. This was also connected to a gradual change in room use which meant that libraries for example, were becoming less of a male preserve and more of a family room.[141]

A sound financial underpinning for business, often based on credit, was essential when liquidity problems caused by delays in payment were often combined with chronic bad debt. It would appear that many firms suffered at one time or another. Chippendale, in correspondence relating to his firm's commission for Nostell Priory during 1770, revealingly says: 'I have been obliged to do business for ready money only, in order to support myself in the best manner I could and that but very poorly'.[142]

Whilst many cabinet-making firms suffered cash-flow problems through wealthy patrons delaying payments of their accounts, in other circumstances profit margins were squeezed by demands for discounts. The correspondence of Bristol business man, John Pinney, illustrates this. In 1791 he wrote to one cabinet-maker:

> As I am desirous of paying ready money for every article I purchase for family use, I request you will furnish me with your Account charging the lowest Cash prices, or allow me a discount, if charged at the credit price, whichever you please.[143]

This clearly shows that goods were often priced for either cash or credit transactions.

In addition to account customers, other payment systems operated. Cash or ready money sales were easily arranged, whilst extended payments or easy terms were also a useful selling point for one business at least. Robert Mulligan of Mint Street, Southwark noted that he 'buys and sells all sorts of household goods both new and second-hand, makes cabinet and upholstery work in general, *furnishes houses on easy terms* . . .'[144] (my italics).

These various examples indicate a marketplace which was supported by a variety of financial mechanisms that were widely recognised and are a further demonstration of the beginning of a mature and established trade.

Apart from retail outlets and bespoke work, auctions and public sales were alternative sources of supply. There were distinctions of course. Mrs Purfoy, wrote about her purchases which for mundane items of furniture were from a local auction,[145] whereas she sent orders to London for special or particular items.

Auctions were also a common way of disposing of stock, particularly in the event of a death or bankruptcy. A famous example was conducted on 17 March 1766, when the *Public Advertiser* published details of an auction sale planned to realise the assets of the partnership of Chippendale and Rannie. Amongst the items the advertisement listed were:

> a great variety of fine mahogany and tulip wood cabinets, desks, and bookcases, cloaths presses, double chests of drawers, commodes, buroes, fine library, writing, card, dining and other tables . . . fine pattern chairs and sundry other pieces of curious cabinet work.[146]

Although these items were perhaps aimed at retailers or the general public, the sale of other parts of the business stock, including quantities of timber board, veneer and feathers, were clearly more attractive to trade buyers. In a similar vein were sales of cabinet-makers' stocks-in-trade. The detail of these sales can give a picture of the quantities of objects in stock at a furniture-making establishment and as an example it is worth quoting fully. The advertisement for the sale of Francis Croxford's stock-in-trade:

> To be sold . . . several fine walnut-tree, mahogany, mehone, and other desks and bookcases with glass doors, and several fine mahogany clothes chests ornamented with brass, mahogany, walnut-tree and pigeon-wood quadrille tables, fine mahogany dining tables of all sizes, and dressing glasses and dressing tables of several sorts, walnut-tree, mahogany and other desks, fine walnut-tree chests upon chests and about one hundred dozen chairs of several sorts.[147]

The large quantities may give rise to a suspicion about the genuine nature of the sale. Merchants have often been known to encourage sales by offering time-limited inducements. Indeed, the case of the strange repetition of advertisements for the sale of cabinet-maker James Faucon's long list of household goods and works, from 16 February 1731 to 26 September 1732 is unexplained, but may have been simply another business ploy.

With all this competition, it is not surprising to find some singular methods of sales promotion which were sometimes quite ingenious. One unusual method was raffling. In 1699, John Renshaw, a London cabinet-maker offered an 'exceedingly fine desk and bookcase of fine mahogany with embellishments of tortoiseshell and brass'. By buying a raffle ticket for 2*s*. 6*d*. (12½ p) one had a single chance to acquire the article.[148]

These sorts of promotions raise an interesting question. Did cabinet-makers use the growing demand for a range of ordinary objects to provide capital for the production of spectacular one-offs, or was it the other way round, whereby the spectacular pieces drew custom from the less wealthy who would purchase inexpensive products? Both would have provided routes to prosperity for the cabinet-maker. The well-known example from the ceramic industry of Josiah Wedgwood certainly seemed to demonstrate the value of promotion. Wedgwood was keenly aware of the sales value of supplying unique or special orders for the royal family and nobility; the advertising value of this type of patronage was then used to promote his goods in all the other classes.[149] There is reason to think that some furniture-makers realised the same ideas as Wedgwood or certainly saw the successful results of his methods and followed suit to some degree. Although advertisements for specific brands or even individual items of furniture are rare in the eighteenth century, the advertising that was carried out usually referred to a retail outlet or a specific sale of stock.

As London was recognised as the centre for the dissemination of taste, it is not surprising to find the influence of London being used as a selling point for provincial businesses. Examples include cabinet-makers who puffed their connections through their journeymen's relations with London masters, or others who told that they had recently been to London and returned with the latest fashions. In an advertisement in the *Newcastle Courant* (19 May 1792), John Dobson pointed out that not only was he a master of the fashionable French and Turkish modes of furnishing but that he 'assures his friends, the least change of fashions cannot take place, but he will have it sent down immediately'.[150] At the beginning of the century, the same phenomenon is found in Edinburgh. The *Edinburgh Courant* (29 December 1708) noted that 'there is lately come from London to this place, an Upholsterer who mounts all kinds of Beds after the Newest Fashions'.[151] The phenomenon existed in America as well. Montgomery quotes an advertisement by Thomas Elfie from 1751 which states that 'having now a very good upholsterer from London [he, Elfie] does all kinds of upholsterer's work in the best and newest manner'.[152]

Rather more permanent were the trade labels that were affixed to furniture in the period. In advertising terms these agents of trade can be interpreted as being a reminder which would bring a customer back to the particular shop for another item, or they might act as a recommendation to another customer.[153] This may be the case in visually-accessible labels, but there must be another explanation for the hidden ones.

Transport

The movement of goods around the country in raw, semi-finished, and finished states was an essential element of the growing economy. Sea transport remained important for much of the century, and a system of rivers, estuaries, and later canals, enabled movements to be easily organised to inland areas.

Transport of stock for retail sale, as well as customers' own purchases made up this trade. The movement of quantities of finished goods of 'London quality' is exemplified in the promotion of looking glasses 'made in London' but offered for sale in Edinburgh.[154] It seems as if these were either job lots of stock or they were superior to anything available in Edinburgh.

In the case of individual purchases, delivery methods varied. Elizabeth Shackleton records how a new table arrived from Gillows in 1779:

> It came quite safe and well, not the least damage or scratch. It is in 3 parts. The middle a square and 2 ends which are half-rounds – all put together make an elegant oval. The wood very handsome. 16 feet all very strong and made neat, it cost, the table only £5 5*s*., packing 3*s*. 6*d*., in all £5 8*s*. 6*d*.[155]

This delivery had to cross the Pennines, so some form of road transport was involved. In another very different example, Parson Woodforde recorded that a sideboard ordered from Norwich some ten miles from his home was 'brought on the Men's Shoulders all the way and very safe'.[156]

The successful transportation of furniture always involved careful packing and special materials for its protection. Damage to goods in transit was both costly and wasteful, therefore many furniture suppliers took great pains with this part of the process. Chippendale, commenting on a shipment to the Earl of Dumfries in Ayrshire noted that, 'the goods had been sent by boat in a glew'd case to prevent any damage by water. The contents of each case with proper directions are given to the person who goes to put up the furniture.'[157] Gillows were also very careful with packing goods for dispatch. For example, in 1780 they noted that 'the feet of the firescreen are sent loose to save expense of packing and damages of breaking but may soon be glued on'.[158] The packaging processes could be quite costly as Gillows explained: 'it is not the box and matts only that constitute the value, we are obliged to employ experienced packers, we also pay high for straw line etc.'.[159]

The most vulnerable objects were likely to be mirror glasses. The glass company often arranged to reduce the cost if the client ran the risk of breakage, but were canny enough to want payment before delivery.[160] Much of this good practice was usefully codified by Sheraton in his *Cabinet Dictionary* which devoted over two full pages to detailed instructions on packaging, with information on sizes of battens, special cases for chairs and glass, as well as more general instructions.[161].

Imports and exports

Although the degree of interference in trading was meant to be limited, there were in fact a number of examples of government actions that were taken, either to encourage exports, or discourage imports of luxury goods. In 1701 for example, an act was passed which imposed duties on imported manufactured cabinet work from the East Indies.[162] This was in response to a petition from London cabinet-makers, joiners and japanners who had complained that this trade was not only hurting home business, but was also hurting the export trade:

> The large quantities of japan'd goods expected shortly to be brought form the Indies, will not only tend to the ruin of the japan-trade here in England, but will also obstruct the transportation of our English lacquer to all Europe, which is a considerable advancement to His Majesties Customs, whereas the Indian lacquer being exported from hence draws back the custom.[163]

Attempts to direct parts of the trade and by implication to protect English businesses is nowhere better seen than in the English attitude to the North American colonies. The Commissioners of Trade were informed in 1732 that

> the people of New England being obliged to apply themselves to manu-
> factures more than other of the Plantations, who have the benefit of a

better soil and warmer climate, such improvements have been lately made there in all sorts of mechanic arts, that not only scrutores, chairs, and other wooden manufactures . . . are now exported from thence to the other plantations, which if not prevented, may be of ill consequence to the trade and manufactures of this Kingdom.[164]

By using improvements in the mechanic arts, the colonists were not only supplying their own needs, but establishing an export trade to other parts of the Americas. No doubt the plentiful supply of materials and ease of transport offset the high labour costs which were in themselves commuted by the mechanisation of parts of the process.

It also seems that some colonists were not anxious to own imported goods of the latest London taste. This is evident in contemporary records:

This man lives well; but though rich, he has nothing in or about his house but what is necessary. He hath good beds in his house but no curtains; and instead of cane chairs, he hath stools made of wood.[165]

Nevertheless the middle classes of the American trading cities retained a taste for English goods. Even as late as 1794, Henry Wansey's description of William Bingham's house in Philadelphia clearly shows that fashionable taste was still being dictated and furnished from London:

I found a magnificent house and gardens in the best English style, with elegant even superb furniture. The chairs of the drawing room were from Seddon's in London, of the newest taste; the back in the form of a lyre, adorned with festoons of crimson and yellow silk.[166]

The taste for English designs and for furniture made from them was also fashionable in Europe. The successful marketing of English products abroad was partly based on matching the objects to the clientele. In Spain and Portugal there was a specific taste for japanned work, and in particular, colours were chosen that were deemed to suit the climes of the Peninsular.[167] Giles Grendey is a well-known example of one successful specialist maker who dealt with this trade.[168] Such understanding of the domestic requirements of the export markets was also clear in the example of Seddon who exported painted furniture to Norway.[169]

Other sources of export sales were venture cargoes and emigrants. Venture cargo was offered to merchants or sea captains by firms advertising their goods for export.[170] Upon arrival in a foreign port, the stock would be advertised for sale, often on the quay side, and when sold, any profits would have been divided between the merchant and the maker. For emigrants, other makers offered to fit ships with furniture (sometimes folding or collapsable) that could later be used on arrival, and some even guaranteed climatic stability for the furniture they supplied.

On the other hand, furniture imports were connected to the supply of fashionable objects that were exotic or superior to English models. The demand for Oriental or French *objets d'art* and furniture was high and therefore profitable. In the case of French furniture the importation of finished and semi-finished items was a regular occurrence, as the following advertisement shows:

> Mayhew and Ince respectfully announce that they have an Assortment of French furniture, consign'd from Paris, for immediate Sale, very much under the original Cost, which may be seen at their Warehouse, Broad Street, Soho.[171]

To satisfy the demand for products and to avoid excise duty at the same time, smuggling of furniture became big business.

Smuggling

The smuggling of furniture into England to avoid duty was clearly a lively trade by the mid-eighteenth century. Although smuggling conjures up an image of secret coastal rendezvous and clashes between pirates and excise officers, furniture smuggling was much less glamorous. The two main methods used were either to declare the items for a lower value as lumber, or to use the services of a diplomat who brought furniture into the country through the 'diplomatic bag'.[172]

The avoidance of duty by declaring a lesser value was a trick that did not always work. In 1761 Chippendale tried to avoid duty on imports by declaring them below their true value. He was challenged, and on this occasion the customs officers took advantage of the regulations and only paid the declared worth to Chippendale. This was of course much less than their true cost, so that Chippendale incurred a large loss, whilst the excise department disposed of the goods at the true market value and made a profit.[173]

The other method, which used the diplomatic bag, was first made public in 1772 by a petition of Masters and Journeymen

Cabinet-makers of London and Westminster, who complained that the system was allegedly disrupting the employment and livelihood of English cabinet-makers. This plea was not successful and in 1773 there was another attempt to involve Parliament in the problem. This time it was considered and a committee was appointed to report on the matter.[174]

Their report showed that goods which were not for personal use were often imported in the diplomatic bag. The case of Baron Berlindis, the Venetian Resident proved the point.[175] Goods imported under his name were found in three different cabinet-makers' shops,[176] the most famous being Cobb, of the Vile and Cobb partnership.

Clearly the attraction of French furniture was such that even highly reputable firms were willing to resort to devious methods to obtain the latest fashions from Paris, presumably in the knowledge that they would have a ready and profitable sale for such objects. No doubt due to the high value, the importation of mirrored glass was an area particularly developed by smugglers.[177]

During the eighteenth century, furniture distribution began to develop an infrastructure that was to be the basis for later developments. The growth of shops, the separation of workshops from showrooms, and the rising role of the retailer as a specialist adviser, meant that the nature of purchasing changed. In addition, the development of support services such as import-export merchants, transport facilities, finance, advertising and promotion meant that retailing and distribution began to take on a prime economic role. All these developments confirm the results of a demand-led furniture industry.

Notes

1 See P. Kirkham, *The London Furniture Trade 1700–1870* (Furniture History Society, 1988), p. 57. She devises and develops the concept of a comprehensive manufacturing firm which acted as an entrepreneur and organised the work of many of the subsidiary trades.

2 P. Kirkham, 'The Partnership of William Ince and John Mayhew 1759–1804', *Furniture History*, x (1974).

3 For a discussion about the practice of the upholsterer see J. Fowler and J. Cornforth, *English Decoration in the Eighteenth Century* (London, Barrie and Jenkins, 1974), chapter 4.

4 *A General Description of all Trades* (1747).

5   H. C. Mui and L. H. Mui, *Shops and Shopping in Eighteenth-Century England* (London, Routledge, 1989), pp. 62–3.

6   P. Kirkham identifies this group as 'the comprehensive manufacturing firm'.

7   C. Williams (trans.), *Sophie in London 1786* (London, Cape, 1933), pp. 173–5.

8   *Ibid.*, p. 174.

9   G. Hughes, 'George Seddon of London House', *Apollo*, LXV (1957), pp. 177–81.

10 J. Collyer, *The Parent's and Guardian's Directory and the Youth's Guide in the Choice of a Profession or Trade* (London, 1761), p. 86.

11 T. Mortimer, *The Universal Directory* (1763), p. 11.

12 This section acknowledges the work of Pat Kirkham and her definitions of the comprehensive manufacturing firm in *London Furniture Trade*.

13 P. Kirkham, 'Samuel Norman: a study of an eighteenth-century craftsman', *The Burlington Magazine*, CXI (August 1969), pp. 500–11.

14 P. Kirkham, 'The careers of William and John Linnell', *Furniture History*, III (1967).

15 C. Gilbert, *The Life and Work of Thomas Chippendale* (MacMillan, London, 1978), p. 23.

16 W. Cotton, 'The North Country chair-making tradition: design, context and the Mark Chippindale deposition', *Furniture History*, XVII (1981).

17 Inventory of Paul Saunders, 1760. See Kirkham, 'Samuel Norman', p. 513. For other examples see details in various price books.

18 See J. R. Kellett, 'The breakdown of gild and corporation control over the handicraft and retail trade in London', *Economic History Review*, X (1958), pp. 381–94; also Kirkham, *London Furniture Trade*, chapter 11.

19 For the upholders' company see J. F. Houston, *Featherbedds and Flock Bedds, Notes on the History of the Worshipful Company of Upholders of the City of London* (Three Tents Press, Sandy, 1993).

20 For a full discussion of apprentices and apprenticeship in the furniture industry, see Kirkham, *London Furniture Trade*, pp. 40–56.

21 P. Kirkham, 'Furniture-makers and trade unionism. The early London Trade Societies', *Furniture History*, XVIII (1982).

22 S. Pryke, 'A study of the Edinburgh furnishing trade taken from contemporary press notices 1708–1790', *Regional Furniture*, III (1989), p. 61.

23 C. Montgomery, *American Furniture. The Federal Period* (New York, 1966), p. 22.

24 J. Stabler, 'English newspaper advertisements as a source of furniture history', *Regional Furniture*, V (1991), pp. 97–8.

25 Kirkham, 'Furniture-makers and trade unionism', p. 4.

26 G. Wills, *English Furniture 1760–1900* (London, Guinness Superlatives, 1969), pp. 132–3.

27 J. Collyer, *Parent's and Guardian's Directory*, p. 86.

28 J. F. Hayward, 'A further note on Christopher Fuhrlohg', *The Burlington Magazine*, CXIX (July 1977), pp. 486–9.

29 P. Kirkham, 'Inlay, Marquetry and Buhl workers in England *c*. 1660–1850', *The Burlington Magazine*, CXXII (June 1980), p. 416.

30 From the nineteenth century, Kelly's trade directory listed over 250 sub-divisions or associated suppliers to the furniture trade.

31 M. Sturmer, 'An economy of delight: court artisans of the eighteenth century', *Business History Review* (Winter 1979), p. 518.

32 C. Hummel, *With Hammer in Hand. The Dominy Craftsmen of East Hampton, New York* (University Press of Virginia, Charlottesville, 1968).

33 Information on the Linnell firm is taken from Kirkham, 'Careers of William and John Linnell', pp. 28–42.

34 M. Sturmer, '"Bois des Indes" and the economics of luxury furniture in the time of David Roentgen', *The Burlington Magazine*, CMIX (December 1978), p. 799.

35 *Ibid*.

36 Gilbert, *Chippendale*, pp. 11–15.

37 See Kirkham, 'Partnership of Ince and Mayhew'.

38 Montgomery, *American Furniture*, p. 23.

39 *Ibid*.

40 S. Stuart, 'Prices for workmen in Lancaster – the earliest surviving cabinet-makers price list', *Regional Furniture* (1988), pp. 19–23.

41 C. Gilbert, 'An early cabinet and chair work price list from York', *Furniture History*, XXI (1985).

42 C. Gilbert, 'London and provincial books of prices comment and bibliography', *Furniture History*, XVIII (1982).

43 C. Gilbert, *English Vernacular Furniture 1750–1900* (New Haven and London, Yale University Press, 1991), p. 25.

44 Montgomery, *American Furniture*, p. 20.

45 M. Weil, 'A cabinet-maker's price book', Ian Quimby (ed.), *American Furniture and its Makers, Winterthur Portfolio*, XIII (1979).

46 Montgomery, *American Furniture*, p. 20.

47 Charles Pryor had a manufactory in Paradise Row Chelsea, and his shop at 96 New Bond Street, and from 1790 at 472 The Strand.

48 D. Defoe, *The Complete English Tradesman* [1727] (New York, Kelley, 1969), Preface, p. xiii.

49 See J. L. Oliver, *The Development and Structure of the Furniture Industry* (Oxford, Pergamon, 1966), p. 6.

50 G. B. Hughes, 'Furnishers of Georgian Mayfair', *Country Life* (19 November 1964).

51 R. W. Symonds, *Furniture-making in Seventeenth and Eighteenth-Century England* (London, Connoisseur, 1955), pp. 130–1.

52 Gilbert, *Vernacular Furniture*, p. 17.

53 P. Legg, 'The Bastards of Blandord', *Furniture History*, XXX (1994).

54 C. Saumarez-Smith, *Eighteenth-Century Decoration* (London, Weidenfeld and Nicolson, 1993), pp. 19–22.

55 See Helena Hayward and Sarah Medlam, 'The Continental context; Germany', in C. Gilbert and T. Murdoch, *John Channon Brass-Inlaid Furniture 1730–60* (New Haven and London, Yale University Press, 1993), and L. Boynton, 'The Moravian Brotherhood and the migration of furniture-makers in the eighteenth century', *Furniture History*, XXIX (1993), pp. 45–59. See also T. Murdoch (ed.), *The Quiet Conquest: the Huguenots 1685–1985* (London, Museum of London, 1985).

56 See for example, Spanish *varguenos* from the sixteenth century onward. The superior joiners who made the luxurious cabinets of the late sixteenth and seventeenth centuries in Europe were given the name of their creations, hence cabinet-makers.

57 The French term for cabinet-maker, *ébéniste* (*c.* 1650s), refers to the early use of ebony as a furniture-making material that was only suitable in veneer form, confirming that cabinet-making methods had to be used.

58 Although evidence shows that the term (cabinet-maker) was used as early as 1660 in England. See Adrian Bolt's petition to be re-admitted to the office of cabinet-maker which he had held in the reign of Charles I: State Papers Domestic, 1660, quoted in R. Edwards, *The Shorter Dictionary of English Furniture* (London, Country Life, 1964).

59 Sturmer, 'Economy of Delight', p. 516.

60 J. Evelyn, *Account of Architects* (1664).

61 Quoted in R. W. Symonds, 'Craft of the cabinet-maker', *Connoisseur* (May 1940), p. 201.

62 A cursory analysis of A. Heal's *The London Furniture-Makers, from the Restoration to the Victorian Era 1660–1840* (London, Batsford, 1953), reveals at least sixteen French names and five Dutch names between 1690 and 1760. See also Kirkham, *London Furniture Trade*.

63 See H. Hayward and S. Medlam, 'The Continental context: Germany', in Gilbert and Murdoch, *John Channon*, for further discussion of Roentgen's movements and other exchanges between craftsmen. Also for discussion about influence of English design in Europe, p. 30

64 H. Huth, *Roentgen Furniture* (London, Sotheby, 1974).

65 G. Beard and C. Gilbert (eds), *Dictionary of English Furniture-makers* (Furniture History Society, 1986), p. 411.

66 Mortimer, *Universal Directory*, p. 11.
67 B. Langley, *City and Country Builder's and Workman's Treasury of Designs* (1740).
68 See Kirkham, *London Furniture Trade*, Chapter 3, for a useful discussion about craft training and apprenticeships.
69 Collyer, *The Parent's and Guardian's Directory*. This description is very similar to that published by Campbell in 1747.
70 R. Campbell, *The London Tradesmen* [1747] (Newton Abbot, David and Charles, 1969), p. 171.
71 Examples taken from newspaper reports in Heal, *London Furniture-makers*. Other well-known examples would include Cobb and Hallett. See Kirkham, *London Furniture Trade*, p. 90.
72 Campbell, *London Tradesmen*, p. 171.
73 See Defoe, *Complete English Tradesman*, for many examples of the difficulties facing anyone setting up in business.
74 Quoted in Huth, *Roentgen Furniture*, p. 58.
75 A. Smith, *Wealth of Nations* (London, Methuen, 1961), Book 1, chapter 3, p. 20.
76 For example see Kirkham, 'Furniture-makers and trade unionism', *Furniture History* (1982). See also introductory article by Gilbert, 'London and provincial Books of Prices'.
77 For a more detailed analysis see 'The business of cabinet-making' in Montgomery, *American Furniture* (1966).
78 Campbell, *London Tradesmen*, p. 174.
79 *Ibid.*, p. 172.
80 Collyer, *Parent's and Guardian's Directory*.
81 *Ibid.*
82 T. Sheraton, *The Cabinet Dictionary* (London, 1803), pp. 135–6.
83 Campbell, *London Tradesmen*, p. 108.
84 *Ibid.*
85 Heal, *London Furniture-makers*, p. 49, who refers to him as Jean Dominique. According to Kirkham he was a specialist water gilder (*London Furniture Trade*, p. 28)
86 W. Chambers, *Cyclopaedia or Universal Dictionary of Arts and Sciences*, 2 vols (London, 1728), p. 501.
87 Heal, *London Furniture-makers*, p. 102.
88 *Ibid.*, p. 92.
89 *Ibid.*, p. 19. Other examples might include Christopher Gabriel who appears to have made up stringing and marquetry shells and other decoration in bulk. See W. Goodman, 'Christopher Gabriel His book', *Furniture History*, XVII. Also note that the *London Book of Prices*, 1793, lists a separate charge for letting in shells and stringing into tea caddies.

90 Kirkham, *London Furniture Trade*, pp. 17–19.
91 Montgomery, *American Furniture*, p. 40. Montgomery saw this as significant for the identification of regional differences in furniture by analysis of the marquetry designs.
92 *Ibid.*, p. 36.
93 Sheraton, *Cabinet Dictionary*, p. 257.
94 *A General Description of All Trades* (1747), p. 57.
95 Sheraton, *Cabinet Dictionary*, p. 145
96 See for example William Gardner of St Paul's Churchyard who advertised that 'he maketh and selleth cane chairs couches and cane sashes at reasonable rates of dry wood', Heal, *London Furniture-makers*, p. 61.
97 See Kirkham, *London Furniture Trade*, pp. 21–2.
98 *Ibid.*
99 *Ibid.*
100 Collyer, *Parent's and Guardian's Directory*, p. 96.
101 Campbell, *London Tradesmen*, p. 170. For a different interpretation see, B. Jobe, 'Boston upholstery trade' in E. S. Cooke (ed.), *Upholstery in America and Europe from the Seventeenth Century to World War I* (New York, Norton, 1987), p. 76.
102 Campbell, *London Tradesmen*, p. 170.
103 *Ibid.*
104 Kirkham, *London Furniture Trade*, p. 35.
105 Campbell, *London Tradesmen*, pp. 169–70.
106 For a summary of this role, see P. Clabburn, *The National Trust Book of Furnishing Textiles* (Viking, London, 1988), pp. 71–3.
107 *Ibid.*, p. 175. See also Collyer's description in *Parent's and Guardian's Directory*, p. 96.
108 Campbell, *London Tradesmen*.
109 *Ibid.*, p. 172.
110 *Ibid.*, p. 174.
111 Gilbert, *English Vernacular Furniture*, chapter 2.
112 Legg, 'The Bastards of Blandford', pp. 15–42.
113 For examples see C. Hutchinson, 'George Reynoldson, Upholsterer of York 1716–1764', *Furniture History*, XII (1976). Also C. Gilbert, 'Wright and Elwick of Wakefield 1748–1824. A study of provincial patronage', *Furniture History*, XII (1976).
114 The following list was extracted from Heal: Arabella Beard, Elizabeth Bell, Ann Buck, Elizabeth Gumley, Barbara Gunter, Elizabeth Hawkins, Elizabeth Hutt, Catherine Means, Catherine Naish, Mary Osman, Mary Smith, Elizabeth Stent, Elizabeth Swain, Esther Tomkins, Elizabeth Watson, Anne Wraughton, Mrs Savage, Mrs Wyat.

115 Allen (1704) listed in Heal, *London Furniture-makers*.

116 Kirkham, *London Furniture Trade*, p. 4.

117 I. Caldwell, 'Working women in the eighteenth century', *Antique Collector* (October 1985), p. 79.

118 Kirkham mentions royal joyners: Elizabeth Price (1685), Catherine Naish (1759), and upholsterers – Sarah Gilbert (1759), Hanah Framborough (1773) and Lucy Gilroy (1783).

119 There are some well-known and documented exceptions: for example, the inventory of the Linnell workshops, Chippendale's fire insurance policies, as well as others mentioned elsewhere in this book.

120 The records of the Gillow company are a probably unique exception. The work of Pat Kirkham in her *London Furniture Trade*, has opened many avenues of research, and many of her interpretations are as useful as can be hoped for at the moment. I will not therefore replicate her findings, rather try to examine the overall part played and contextualise the distributive processes.

121 Mui and Mui, *Shops and Shopping*, pp. 44–5.

122 Trade Card in Heal, *London Furniture-makers*. See also Charles Pryor, a cabinet-maker and upholsterer who sold retail from premises at 472 The Strand in 1763 (see Heal) and from his manufactory in Paradise Row, Chelsea.

123 *General Description of All Trades* (1747). The term 'engrossing' would indicate some kind of wholesale function as well as a retail one.

124 Collyer, *Parent's and Guardian's Directory*, p. 286.

125 Hayward and Kirkham, *William and John Linnell*, p. 45.

126 Heal, *London Furniture-makers*, p. 33.

127 *General Description of All Trades* (1747), quoted in E. Joy, *The Connoisseur's Complete Period Guides* (London, Connoisseur, 1968), p. 544.

128 Dedication in The First Edition of *The London Cabinet-maker's Book of Prices* (1788).

129 Mui & Mui, *Shops and Shopping*, p. 244. This form of trading still irritates established retailers.

130 Heal, *London Furniture-makers*, p. 201.

131 *Ibid.*, pp. 160, 209.

132 Richard Steele, *The Lover*, 13 May 1715, quoted in R. Edwards and M. Jourdain, *Georgian Cabinet-makers c. 1700–1800* (London, Country Life, 1955), p. 41.

133 Heal, *London Furniture-makers*; Hodsons Trade Card, p. 80.

134 The Gillow records include numerous examples of special orders with details of the customer, the materials used and so on.

135 See S. Pryke, 'Pattern furniture and estate wrights in eighteenth-century Scotland', *Furniture History*, xxx (1994).

136 R. H. Randal, 'Templates for boulle singerie', *The Burlington Magazine*, cxi (September 1969), pp. 549–53.

137 Williams (trans.), *Sophie in London*, p. 237.

138 Edwards, *Dictionary of English Furniture*.

139 A. Vickerey, 'Women and the world of goods: a Lancashire consumer and her possessions, 1751–81', in J. Brewer and R. Porter (eds), *Consumption and the World of Goods* (London, Routledge, 1993), p. 281.

140 Saumarez-Smith, *Eighteenth-Century Decoration*, pp. 233–6.

141 P. Thornton, *Authentic Decor. The Domestic Interior 1620–1920* (London, Weidenfeld & Nicolson, 1984), p. 150.

142 Gilbert, *Chippendale*, p. 33.

143 K. M. Walton, 'Eighteenth-century cabinet-making in Bristol', *Furniture History*, xii (1976).

144 Heal, *London Furniture-makers*, p. 116.

145 Saumarez-Smith, *Eighteenth-Century Decoration*, pp. 133–4.

146 Quoted in G. Wills, *English Furniture 1760–1900* (London, Guinness Superlatives, 1969), p. 14.

147 *Daily Post*, 12 July 1733, quoted in Edwards and Jourdain, *Georgian Cabinet-makers*.

148 Gilbert and Murdoch, *John Channon*, p. 18

149 For a full description and analysis of Wedgwood's methods see N. McKendrick, J. Brewer and J. H. Plumb, 'Josiah Wedgwood and the commercialisation of the potteries', *Birth of a Consumer Society* (Bloomington, Indiana University Press, 1982), pp. 99–145.

150 J. Stabler, 'English newspaper advertisements as a source of furniture history', *Regional Furniture*, v (1991), p. 96.

151 Pryke, 'Study of the Edinburgh furnishing trade', p. 53.

152 Montgomery, *American Furniture*, p. 12.

153 M. Lovell, '"Such furniture as will be profitable". The business of cabinet-making in eighteenth-century Newport', *Winterthur Portfolio*, xxvi (1991), p. 44.

154 Pryke, 'Study of the Edinburgh furnishing trade', p. 54. Pryke's examples cover the period from 1748 to 1787.

155 A. Vickery, 'Women and the world of goods', in Brewer and Porter, *Consumption and the World of Goods*, p. 287.

156 The Diary of a Country Parson, 1924–31, J. Beresford (ed.) Quoted by Joy in *Connoisseur's Complete Period Guides*, p. 834.

157 Gilbert, *Chippendale*, p. 132.

158 S. Stuart, *Gillow Chairs and Fashion* (Exhibition Catalogue, North West Museums Service), 1991–92.

159 *Ibid.*

160 A. Coleridge, *Chippendale Furniture* (London, Faber, 1968), p. 163.

161 Sheraton, *Cabinet Dictionary*, pp. 279–81.

162 12 and 13, Will, c. 41.

163 'The case of the japanners of England, 1710', *Tracts on Trade*, 13:1.

164 R. W. Symonds, 'Export trade of furniture to colonial America', *The Burlington Magazine*, MCLXXVII (November 1940), pp. 152–60.

165 *Ibid*, p. 154.

166 Henry Wansey, *Excursion to the United States of North America in the Summer of 1794* (2nd edn) p. 123. Quoted in Montgomery, *American Furniture*, p. 42.

167 R. W. Symonds, 'English eighteenth-century furniture exports to Spain and Portugal', *The Burlington Magazine*, LXXVIII (February 1941), pp. 57–61.

168 C. Gilbert, 'Furniture by Giles Grendey for the Spanish trade', *Antiques*, XCIX (April 1971), pp. 544–50. S. Jervis, 'Giles Grendey 1693–1780', *Country Life*, CLV (6 June 1974), pp. 1418–19.

169 Hughes, 'George Seddon'.

170 See for example, Heal, *London Furniture-makers*, Luke Young Trade Card and others.

171 Quoted in Wills, *English Furniture*, p. 68.

172 G. Wills, 'Furniture smuggling in eighteenth-century London' *Apollo*, LXXXII (August 1965), pp. 112–17.

173 E. Joy, 'Chippendale in trouble at the customs', *Country Life*, CX (24 August 1951), p. 569.

174 *Journals of the House of Commons,* vol. 34, p. 297; Report and Appendix, pp. 349–55.

175 The items brought in under his name included seventy-six chair fronts, twenty-four marble slabs, eighteen arm'd chairs, nineteen cabriole chairs and many other assorted chair parts.

176 The three involved were Wall and Riley of Gerrad Street, Cullen of Greek Street, and Cobb of St Martin's Lane. Further details can be found in Wills.

177 W. Rieder, 'Furniture smuggling for a Duke', *Apollo*, XCII (September 1970), pp. 206–9. See also W. A. Cole, 'Trends in eighteenth-century smuggling', *Economic History Review*, 2nd Series, X (1958), pp. 395–409.

3   Materials and techniques

The matrix of material culture is held together by the substances and manipulating processes that enable the craftsman to transform raw materials into the desirable objects demanded by their customers. This chapter will discuss and examine the materials and processes used in the productions of the eighteenth-century furniture trade. By following the manufacturing processes in a sequential way, combined with the close evaluation of the materials, techniques, and technology that were used in the period, a view of the changes and choices that occurred in response to the supply or demand will be traced.

Before looking at these developments, it will be useful to define three particularly significant features of the period that relate to materials and technology. First, the total range of products increased, both as a response to the wider selection of raw material supplies, as well as a reaction to the demand for choice, style and novelty. This development was due to the combined efforts of merchants, importers, dealers, and retailers, who were keen to introduce new ideas to the market.

Second, the wider dispersal of technical know-how meant that new or improved processes became available to a larger audience. One result of the decline of guild controls of the 'mysteries' of trade which had occurred since the seventeenth century in England, was that skilled craft secrets were more easily and more widely known. In America, were there was no guild tradition, there was a continuing demand for widely-skilled workers who could turn their hands to a variety of jobs in a community.

This movement of skills was due in part to apprenticeship schemes, in part to a more fluid labour force, and in part to the dissemination of printed guides and encyclopedias. Whichever way the process moved, it meant that by the end of the century it was quite common for provincial furniture-makers to be versed in many of the skills that were once the preserve of the fashionable London makers.

The third feature was a demand for imitations of high-style objects which meant that inventors and makers had to devise and supply substitute materials to take the place of expensive originals. This factor should not be taken to mean makeshift techniques or merchandise, but rather the opposite. It has been suggested that in the eighteenth century, 'imitation was then seen not as compromise but as opportunity'.[1] Indeed, with the growing demand for sophisticated-looking goods, as well as an interest in new techniques and technologies for their own sake, there was both a need for, as well as a fascination with, imitations. The instance of oriental lacquer is clearly the most attractive (see below), but there were many other examples.[2]

The development of responses to changes in demand, whether by imitation or progression, can be divided into three parts. First, it could be a completely new item or technique; second, it could be a series of small changes that accrued over time, and third, it could be the use of existing materials in new forms. All these will be considered in this chapter using a selection of examples. However, as tools were essential to any furniture business these must be the first to be discussed.

Tools

A valuable early discussion about woodworking tools and their uses is found in a source that was not designed as a record of trades. In Johann Amos Comenius's book of Latin grammar, *Orbis Sensualim Pictus* (translated by Charles Hoole in 1685), descriptions of carpentry, cabinet-making, and turning may be found which are valuable for their detail,[3] for example the description of the box-maker (cabinet-maker):

> smootheth hewen boards with a plain upon a work board, he maketh them very smooth with a little plain, he boarth them thorow with an augre, carveth them with a knife, fasteneth them together with glew, and cramp-irons and maketh tables, boards, chests &c.

In this account, the kit of tools, which includes planes, augers, glue and cramps, clearly indicates a cabinet-maker rather than a joiner working in solid wood.

A little later, an inventory from an American cabinet-maker working in Boston in 1717, gives a list of tools and materials that were in his shop at the time.[4] The list includes a variety of planes designed for particular parts of the cabinet-making process including block, smoothing, rebating and toothing versions. Chisels and files, as well as drills and bits, along with a variety of saws, augers and gimlets were also to be found. These tools have much in common with the trade of the joiner; it is only when the 'finering hammer and pincers', the 'fine saw', 'walnut fenere', 'eighty pounds of lead', 'nus skin', glue and beeswax are also accounted for that the inventory clearly indicates a cabinet-maker rather than a joiner.

The growing range of tools and the increasing reliability of the metal components used during the century enabled cabinet-makers to have a degree of flexibility and application to individual circumstances, as well as increasing certainty as to the quality of the end product.[5] Although high quality results could be obtained with simple methods, the need for continual production of goods at an acceptable standard meant that semi-skilled artisans had a better chance of achieving regular quality with particular tools that would achieve an accepted and certain result. The quality of tools was therefore important to the final end product. As it was customary for tradesmen to provide their own tools, it is not surprising to find that they were highly regarded. The production of a personal tool chest was not uncommon, nor was the taking out of insurance as a precaution against loss.[6]

Sophie von la Roche suggested that it was the calibre of tools that helped to make the superior products of Seddon and Company. She was so impressed that she recommended 'see[ing] the tools with which they [Seddon's cabinets] are made, manufactured in Birmingham; for I handled some of them here, and regarded them as most valuable and beneficent inventions'.[7] It was in fact in Sheffield that a new, harder, cast steel was produced by Benjamin Huntsman which had brought improvements to cutting tools amongst other articles, but this would have soon been known in Birmingham.[8]

Timber and processing

In terms of furniture, the eighteenth century has often been misleadingly labelled the Age of Mahogany.[9] It is true that enormous quantities of mahogany were used in the period, but considerable amounts of other timbers were also part of the furniture-maker's repertoire. The continuing fashion for walnut in the first half of the century is well-known, as is the introduction of satinwood, rosewood and other exotic timbers during the later part of the century. In addition, the large amount of vernacular furniture that was produced using indigenous timbers, especially oak, elm, beech, and fruit woods, should not be forgotten.

An idea of the range of timbers available in the middle of the century is indicated by a description of a typical London timber merchant's stock.[10] He was 'furnished with deal from Norway; with oak and wainscot from Sweden; and some from the counties of England; with Mahogany from Jamaica; with Wall-nut tree from Spain'.[11] Presumably this was the inventory of a general timber merchant, as the example of the timber stocks of a specialist cabinet-making business in 1760 demonstrates a more eclectic selection. Samuel Norman's timber store included a variety of sizes of Wainscot, 11,986 feet of inch Mahogany, 914 feet of inch Lime Tree, 306 feet of inch Virginian Walnut Tree,

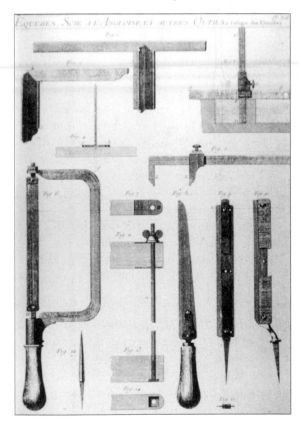

12 As cabinet-making grew in complexity, the range of tools also developed. This selection of French cabinet-makers' tools dates from *c.* 1772.

146 foot of inch Cherry Tree, 416 feet of inch Pear Tree and a quantity of Black Ebony. In addition were double deals, single deals, and yellow deals.[12]

At the end of the century, another high-style maker, Chippendale the Younger, had his timber listed for a bankruptcy sale:

> very valuable old Jamaica, Spanish, Cuba and Honduras Mahogany in plank and boards; choice Satin, Rose and Kingswood, Cedar in logs, Walnut-tree, American Birch; and a selection of the most beautiful veneers of extraordinary dimensions and very scarce.[13]

Both these listings indicate that fashionable cabinet-making houses held a wide stock of timbers designed to meet the varying needs of the exclusive clientele they dealt with. Despite these examples, Sheraton pointed out that for many makers 'the inconvenience of keeping a large stock of seasoned wood . . . meant that the pressing necessities of some tradesmen oblige them to work up wood unfit for use'.[14] The ability to hold stocks of fine timbers indicated a sophisticated and established business, contrary to the jobbing makers who seem to have obtained timber, or were supplied with it, as and when the jobs were offered.

However, for all makers, timber supplies were subject to the vagaries of economic circumstances. The example of walnut is instructive, as is the case of mahogany (see below). The French ban on the export of walnut to England to try and hinder the manufacture of rifle butts, and the well-known severe winter of 1709[15] contributed to a decline in the use of French walnut and accounted for a growth of walnut imports from other European countries.[16] The English Parliament encouraged the American colonies to export Virginian Walnut in increasing quantities. Indeed, the Naval Stores Act of 1721 and its amendments promoted the import of timber carried in English ships from the colonies, by removing the import duty completely.[17] Whatever the economic changes were that affected the choice of timber at any particular time, it is clear that fashion was an equally, if not more important factor in the wood selection decisions. The skill of the entrepreneur cabinet-maker or indeed of the timber importer, in selecting timbers, could affect his fashionable standing and hence his economic success.

Notwithstanding the opening remark of this section, the importance of mahogany must not be underrated. It is the most well-known of the eighteenth-century hardwoods used in furniture, and was clearly one of the most popular with makers as well as users. A hard, heavy, durable wood with a close grain, it was ideal for cabinet-making as well as being workable in both solid and veneer forms, and often being available in large board sizes.[18] One of the reasons for its popularity with cabinet-makers from early in the eighteenth century onward, was succinctly recorded by Nicholson (1826): 'logs of mahogany may be cut into planks of such amazing breadth as to afford table tops of immense width'.[19] For consumers, its strength, its ability to take a high polish, its light red colour which deepened on exposure, as well as its exotic connotations satisfied many of their needs. A contemporary remarked on this taste for exotic timbers:

> My Lords contemptuous of his Country's Groves,
> As foreign Fashions foreign Trees too loves:
> Odious! upon a Walnut-plank to dine!
> No – the red-veined Mohoggony be mine!
> Each Chest and Chair around my Room that stands
> Was Ship'd thro' dangerous Seas from distant Lands.[20]

Mahogany was not simply an eighteenth-century wood. It was apparently first used for woodwork in San Domingo Cathedral around 1514 and it was later employed in the furnishing of Madrid's Escorial palace which was completed in 1584. In the English-speaking world it was certainly known of by the seventeenth century. An unusual example of its use was a chair from Aberdeen dated 1661,[21] whilst in 1671 mahogany was listed in John Ogilby's record of the botanical species of the New World in his *America*.[22] Its first recorded use in England was apparently in the fitting out of Nottingham Castle in the 1680, and by 1692 the intrepid diarist, Celia Finnes, had noted mahogany in panelling and furniture.[23] A clear indication of its growing economic importance was the beginning of the government's collection of mahogany import statistics in 1699.

The commercial introduction of mahogany as a viable business proposition rested upon the abolition of import duties in 1722.[24] Mahogany soon developed into an important timber as the import figures show: in 1720 the value of imported mahogany was £42 13s 0d, in 1721 it was £155 13s 0d, and by 1724 it was £1220 5s 6d. It had reached £6430 in 1735, and by 1750 was almost £30,000.[25] The mahogany trade had become so important that by 1770 another

Act[26] was passed which extended the freedom from duty to include all American timbers because mahogany 'had become very useful and necessary to cabinet-makers'. Although not directly intended to, the change inevitably assisted the cabinet-maker in his search for novelty.[27] The reason for this freedom was not completely altruistic. It was thought that the increase in inexpensive timber supplies would assist exports of furniture from England.[28] In 1792 the value of mahogany imports had risen to £79,554 which represented well over 7,000 tons of timber.

The types of mahogany employed also changed during the century. Initially supplies came from Jamaica and it was known as Jamaica wood. By the late 1740s this source of timber had been substantially worked out. Spanish or Cuban (Havana) mahogany became more popular after 1750 as it provided superior veneers with a fine range of figures, whilst that from San Domingo provided a mahogany with little figure, a hard texture and straight grain, which was ideal for construction, as well as for crisp carvings. By the latter part of the century, Honduras mahogany (from Yucatan, according to Nicholson) had supplanted the West Indian varieties to a great degree. Popularly known as baywood, it had a deep reddish-brown colour, a uniform grain and a softer texture than West Indian varieties, although it paled after exposure.[29]

The continual use of mahogany alongside other woods that moved in and out of popularity is revealing. It is an example of the establishment of particular timber types that were recognised as being appropriate to a particular item, room or use. In the case of mahogany, it was especially destined for the dining room (although examples of most furniture types can of course be found which use the same timber). Indeed, by the nineteenth century, dining tables were referred to generically as 'the mahogany'.[30]

The establishment of the superiority of mahogany was ultimately based on commercial considerations. Once mahogany was available at £8 (average) per ton compared to £40–£50 per ton for walnut, there was little contest in much of the furniture retail market. Perhaps it also helps to explain initial design decisions which used mahogany in the solid, rather than in veneer form as was the case with walnut.[31]

Although the latter part of the seventeenth century has often been labelled the Age of Walnut, it is again misleading, as walnut was used through much of the following century. In many ways walnut was an ideal timber for furniture as it was easily worked, had an even grain, and was strong though relatively light in weight. A very varied grain pattern obtained from burrs and veneers made it even more desirable.

Although used as a constructional timber, walnut was most successful as a veneer. Desirable cuts were made to expose a dark striated figure which sometimes originated from the roots or burrs of the tree, hence burr-walnut. The varieties of walnut available in the eighteenth century give another indication of the international nature of the timber trade, as well as confirming a continuing taste for this wood. At varying times, sources included North America, Europe (especially France), England and Circassia. American Black Walnut (Juglans Nigra), also known as Virginia walnut, supplemented the lighter European varieties and was also highly regarded. John Evelyn praised the American walnut, saying: 'had we store of this material, especially of the Virginian, we should find an incredible improvement in the more stable furniture of our houses'.[32]

The use of American walnut to improve English furniture did not materialise as Evelyn had hoped, Sheraton gave a clue to its demise in furniture-making when, in 1803, he commented that 'the black Virginia [walnut] was much in use for cabinet work about forty or fifty years since in England, but it is now quite laid aside since the introduction of mahogany.'[33] English walnut's decline was also recorded (with a different emphasis), in the 1776 edition of Evelyn's *Sylva*: 'Formerly the walnut tree was much propagated for its wood, but since the importation of mahogany and the Virginia walnut it has considerably decreased its reputation'.[34]

Although mahogany continued to be a popular wood, by the last quarter of the eighteenth century, satinwood[35] was being recognised as the fashionable timber for high-style veneered furniture. Sheraton described it thus: 'It has a cool, light, and pleasing effect in furniture on which account it has been much in request among people of fashion for about twenty years past'.[36] It was originally imported in the 1760s from the West Indies, and then from the East Indies from about 1780. The distinction between the two as far as cabinet-makers were concerned, was important: 'The West India was considered more valuable than the East India because of its breadth and general utility.'[37]

The use of rosewood is also worth recording, although its high point of popularity was not reached until the early nineteenth century. Two varieties were used by furniture-makers, one from South America, the other from the Indian sub-continent. The earliest use of rosewood seems to have been in the late seventeenth century when it was imported by the East India Company and employed to make cabinets, and it continued to be used for small works during the eighteenth century. The Rio or South American version was imported in the last quarter of the eighteenth century and is distinguished by black streaks which form patterns when cut as veneer.

For much of the veneered furniture of the period, especially that which was being made to a price, it was essential to have an inexpensive but suitable substrate.[38] 'Deal' was perfect for this job. Deal is a common name for varieties of pine softwood. It was originally a measure of timber, but by 1804 it was referred to in the generic way: 'Deal is the wood of the fir tree, and is chiefly brought from Sweden, Norway and other European countries . . . The Norway fir produces the whiter deal commonly used by carpenters . . .'[39] Unlike the white pine, the yellow, and later the red, were used extensively for carcases for veneered work as they were generally freer of knots and easier to work, indeed deal was considered most suitable for curved forms such as commode fronts or *bombé* shapes. In France, the use of oak was more common as a substrate for cabinets but it can also be found in some English cabinet work.

At the end of the century (1796) it was beech timber that took the limelight. Much used for fancy chair frames, it was also apparently popular with cabinet-makers:

> The cabinet-makers chief woods are Mahogany and Beech, next to these follow Dutch Oak, Deal and Elm . . . In some country places a considerable quantity of English Oak is worked up into tables, chairs, drawers, and bedsteads: but in London, Beech is almost the only English wood made use of at present, by the cabinet- and chair-makers.[40]

It would not be of any advantage to discuss in further detail the many other timbers used for either solid or decorative purposes by furniture-makers during the eighteenth century.[41] It is worth noting, however, that common home-grown timbers, i.e. ash, elm, oak and pine, were used extensively by woodworkers to produce furniture, often in imitation of the high-style items made with imported timber.

One thing they all had in common was that (with the exception of green timber construction), any timber that was to be used had first to be seasoned. But even before this, the initial task was to convert a tree log into manageable timber boards.

Preparatory processes

The original method in England of timber conversion from log to boards was pit-sawing.[42] Indeed this was the most common method in England until the early to mid-nineteenth century when steam- powered sawmills were fully developed. The technique was labour-intensive and time-consuming as it was a purely human-powered operation, the top sawyer having the responsibility to keep to the sawing line, whilst the bottom man supplied the muscle power.[43] In mainland Europe it was more common to use large trestles to support the timber to be cut above ground, or indeed to employ water-powered sawmills.

The growth of the trade in the export of timber from Europe and North America meant that as early as the seventeenth century, the value of sawmills, operated by running water and built near stands of timber, was well established. Indeed, it was the only practicable way of supplying the increasing demand for pre-cut boards, bearing in mind the cost of labour.[44] As pine and oak timbers were mostly imported in board form into England, it seems clear that Europe employed a large number of sawmills.[45]

Even though England was not in the forefront of sawmill developments, there were some attempts to mechanise the process and the earliest recorded patent that tried this in England, is from 1629, 'for an engine for cutting timber into plank or board'.[46] In 1683 another patent was taken out for an 'engine for sawing timber and boards without the aid of wind or water',[47] with yet another following in 1703.[48] It seems safe to assume that these were aimed at the requirements of primary converters and bulk users such as ship and house builders, rather than the furniture trade specifically. However, the 1731 inventory of John Bastard of Blandford, Dorset, a business whose interests covered building, joinery, and furniture-making, specifically lists 'The Engin and wheel for sawing'.[49] Although it is likely that this was a vertical frame saw, as it was housed in a shop which listed large quantities of deals and 'square stuff', there is no evidence to suggest that it was based on designs by any of the patentees mentioned above.

Further serious consideration of the problem did not come again until 1761 when the Society of Arts awarded a premium to James

Stansfield for a plan of a sawmill. This was subsequently built by Charles Dingley at Limehouse using wind vanes to power it. The vested interests of the pit-sawyers prevailed over innovation; they envisaged the mill putting their livelihoods at risk and so burned it.

Most sawmills built in the seventeenth century were based on attempts to replicate the reciprocal (i.e. back and forward) motion of the human arm and hand saw. A more successful idea, and a precursor of the mechanised processes, was the invention by Samuel Miller of Southampton, who devised a saw with a circular blade. He was granted a patent for his machine in 1777.[50] In 1781 it was recorded that William Taylor was using circular saws[51] 'which proved of ineffable use in expeditiously cutting timber for any purpose, particularly lignum vitae shivers to an exact thickness'.[52] Barely twenty years after the pit-sawyers' action at Limehouse, the Society of Arts could report that in 1782 sawmills were well established in England.[53]

Development was rapid from there on, although once again the spur did not come from the cabinet-making trade but was a result of naval requirements. Samuel Bentham[54] was commissioned by the government to tour the Baltic countries to investigate their power-sawing processes, and upon his return he patented his own ideas and began to produce various woodworking machines. In 1791 Bentham developed the principle of saw segments mounted on a circular disc, which enabled sawing to be carried out more speedily and efficiently. In 1805, another engineer, Marc Isambard Brunel, took out a patent for very large circular saws,[55] particularly associated with veneer cutting, and in 1807 further developed the mechanical saw, in association with naval block-making machinery.

These developments did not directly affect the eighteenth-century furniture trade, although the possibility of regular control over timber purchase and conversion was clearly useful to high-quality makers. In fact, at least one major company had their own full facilities. Sophie von la Roche commented upon Seddons of London, who 'had their own saw-house too, where as many blocks of fine foreign wood lie piled, as firs and oak are seen at our sawmills.[56] Other quality makers, Linnell for example, are recorded as having saw-pits in their yard, whilst others only had drying rooms and store rooms, the assumption being that timber had been already cut elsewhere. However the timber was prepared, the need to season it was essential to the quality of the final pieces made.

13 A water-driven saw-mill using the vertical saw for converting logs to planks, *c.* 1670.

Working with wood in the eighteenth century was never an exact science, it was not even an inexact science. However, the increasing demand for fine workmanship and high quality products, as well as a demand for larger quantities of more middling ranges of furniture, meant that all the processes of conversion and manufacture would have been scrutinised at various times during the century. Some understanding of timber technology and the necessity for seasoning to prevent warping and cracking was clearly comprehended, although not necessarily brought to any high degree of refinement. The traditional methods of seasoning by using smoke kilns or by charring were certainly used for shipbuilding work, but no references have been found that directly relate to furniture-making. With cabinet-making the moisture content is critical in relation to veneer stability, so cabinet-makers must have been interested in the problem to some extent. In 1720 a patent was acquired by John Cumberland for a method which involved placing timber planks into wet sand and heating it until the 'juices were extracted'.[57] Richard Neve (1726) discussed the various seasoning processes and the choice of options available at the time. The main method was open-air seasoning in plank form, but other possibilities existed which were positively bizarre. These included the placing of the timber in running water, burying it in the earth, drying it by burning the outside of a pile of timber, or covering a timber pile with dung.[58]

From this rather eccentric list it would seem that the open-air process was the most satisfactory as it still exists as part of a seasoning process today. As methods of seasoning were only adequate, and in no real sense controlled, the making process itself often called for additional seasoning processes. As the main aim of seasoning was to reduce the risk of timber movement and the ensuing damage that would occur, it is not surprising to find prepared parts being treated further. For example, when table tops were jointed up, Sheraton recommended that 'the tops should stand to shrink as much as possible before they are glued for good'.[59]

Once the raw material was prepared, but before the final construction or assembly took place, other preparatory processes were required.

The processes of shaping, fitting and finishing are all associated with the most versatile of furniture-makers' tools, the plane.[60] For much of the eighteenth century a wide variety of hand planes were used in the traditional manner to give a varying degree of smoothness to wooden surfaces. If the surfaces were exposed they would require further attention to create a flat surface, but if they were hidden they often reveal the undulating dressing marks left by the operation of the tool.

In response to the growing demand various improvements and developments occurred which increased speed and accuracy, but it was not until 1776 that the first mechanical planer was invented and patented by Leonard Hatton.[61] In the same way as saws, planing machines had been developed by simply trying to replicate the reciprocating human action. In 1791, Bentham again improved upon the original scheme, first with a reciprocating plane and then with one based on the rotary principle. By 1802, Joseph Bramah, an engineer who had been trained as a cabinet-maker, had developed the planing machine further by introducing a transverse motion mechanism.[62] Like the saws, they were also designed to assist large-scale users rather than being supplied to cabinet workshops. This meant that timber mills were often in a position to supply prepared timber that was planed ready to work, rather than rough boards. This was clearly an advantage to the small-scale maker who bought nominal amounts of raw material to make up and sell on a cyclical basis.

Eighteenth-century furniture-makers were completely pragmatic about the options available to them. If processes had worked well in the past, then there was no need to change them; if an improvement suggested itself and it assisted productivity or profitability, then it might be adopted. In this case the change would be assimilated into existing processes and did not necessarily encourage any revision of existing designs. One process that was based on simple technology was that of wood-bending.

The bending of timber was clearly a common practice in furniture-making if Sheraton is to be believed. He devotes many lines to technical descriptions of the various bending processes, but ultimately he confirms that bending was a difficult process which was best done in conjunction with steam and pressure.[63]

The early history of bentwood furniture can be traced at least to the eighteenth century with the Windsor chair-makers using simple techniques to achieve bow backs for their chairs. The difficulty with bending solid wood was due to the uneven tensions in the wood fibres. On the outside of a curve the wood might split; on the inside the fibres often compressed and buckled. Early attempts at overcoming the problem were made. The Windsor chair back bows had the bark removed from the inside of the bend only. This had the effect of stabilising the 'outer' part of the timber to a degree. Although difficult to confirm, some authorities have suggested that the bent bows were steamed and left to cool in a primitive clamp.[64]

More precise technology was applied to trades such as shipbuilding and wheelwrighting, both of which used curved wood sections in their products. A patent for bending wood was first taken out by John Cumberland in 1720,[65] but it took another seventy years before John Vidler patented another wood-bending process in 1794.[66] This probably applied to cabinet-makers as well as shipwrights as it used a series of 'concaves and convexs' (or formers) with weights and balances to bend the wood to shape.[67] Whilst bending was mainly associated with chair-making, in the case of carcase work, to achieve the effect of bent wood sections, or indeed to build strong curved sections, it was often most successfully attained by using laminations.

Laminations are simply wood veneers, slivers or even sections that are glued together with the grains running either in parallel or at right angles to each other.[68] Although the technique was of ancient origin, it was not until 1793 that the inveterate inventor, Samuel Bentham, devised a mechanical method of 'giving curvature to wood' by dividing it into thicknesses.[69] A few years later, around 1802, the Belgian *ébéniste*, Jean-Joseph Chapius, used quarter-inch thick wood slats which, when glued together, bent and then shaped, made semi-circular legs for chairs.[70] In this case the technology was completely subservient to the neo-classical design and can really only be seen as a means to an end.

Where the laminating process really came into its own was in the making of pierced galleries for table tops and other stands. Eighteenth-century cabinet-makers used this unself-conscious adaption of the technique to achieve a certain end-result which was typical of the pragmatic approach already identified. The laminating process had the effect of increasing the strength of the timber and therefore allowing a more intricate piercing than would have been achievable with solid wood.[71] The same procedure was used for chair splats. For other shaped parts (especially curves), they were often made with coopered joints or made in a built-up construction process (see below).

Although turning was an ancient art by the eighteenth century, and to some extent had its hey-day in the late seventeenth century, it remained part of the repertoire of the furniture-maker. The operatives were generally a separate trade who made all sorts of turned wood products.[72] In many cases it would seem that they offered a sub-contracting service to furniture-makers, which was useful as many designs of the period did not require turned components. However, in some cases, cabinet-makers had turning equipment on their premises, perhaps indicating a degree of self-sufficiency. It was recorded in 1764 that Paul Saunders, who had a well-established cabinet and upholstery business, had '2 Turners leaths [lathes] with coller and mandrels the one a foot wheel the other a large hand wheel with screw box chucks'.[73]

The turning lathes were of three types: pole-, wheel- or pedal-operated. The pole lathe was simply operated by a line fixed to a springy sapling (or ceiling-mounted spring board), which was threaded round the work and then fixed to a treadle below the bed of the lathe.[74] The disadvantage of this type was that the operator could only cut on the down stroke, and so was not able to produce a continuous cut; however, this does not seem to have been considered much of a brake on productivity. The advantage of the pole method was that it could be set up either in a workshop or in a clearing of a stand of trees. The figure of the bodger[75] working in the beech woods of the Chilterns is not particularly fanciful; the origins of the great nineteenth-century chair business in High Wycombe were rooted in this tradition.[76]

For busy workshops, the wheel lathe was operated by a powered large wheel which was linked by a continuous cord to the lathe itself. By rotating the wheel continuously, via human or natural power, the lathe could turn both large and heavy components. The pedal lathe method was similar to the wheel but was on a smaller scale, using a pedal fixed under the bed to propel a wheel which turned the lathe.

Although the turners did not find continuous work from high-style cabinet-makers in the eighteenth century, they were clearly responsible for a whole range of common chairs for various uses, as well as enormous quantities of treen and turnery.

The application of decorative mouldings to carcase furniture, ranging from a simple cock bead to a drawer front, through to an elaborate built-up cornice, meant that techniques of producing mouldings changed during the eighteenth century. They were often cut separately and then applied to the surface so that they could be worked beforehand, rather than being cut into solid members as previously. This change in process was a minor example of the sub-division of some parts of the making process.

Mouldings were usually applied in two forms. In one case they were built up on a backing of inferior wood; alternatively they were produced as a composite of several simpler moulded shapes, thus offering a large variety of decorative possibilities relatively simply. Indeed, the range of choice could be further extended by adding carving, contrasting veneer, tracery, inlay or even marquetry to the moulding surface. This is another simple example of the way cabinet-makers could offer choice without great inconvenience to themselves.

The moulding tools were initially made by the cabinet-maker himself but as the demand grew, specialist moulding plane-makers set up in business.[77] The planemaker was usually able to make any profile of cut to a customer's requirements, whilst the home-made scratch stock continued to be used for the more simple mouldings. The standardisation of moulding planes occurred around 1770,[78] but this did not mean a limiting of variety. Examples quoted by Humell indicate that some American woodworking shops had as many as 180 varieties of plane in their tool collection.[79]

An early attempt at mechanising what was essentially a hand process was the wave-moulding machine. It mechanically produced an undulating reeded band that resembled the natural wave motion, but supplied a regularity which would have been difficult to produce with hand tools. This particular moulding was often executed in ebony or ivory or stained sycamore. Diderot's *Dictionnaire* has a full description and illustration of such a machine.[80] Despite this example, most mouldings were struck by hand tools until the nineteenth century, when machines were devised to cut them 'by the yard'.

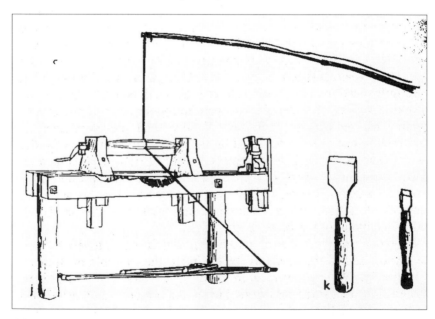

14 A schematic diagram of a pole lathe showing the simple principle of its set-up and operation.

Although these various developments in the techniques of bending, turning and moulding do not seem to have been outstanding in their application of machinery, by the turn of the eighteenth century concern was being expressed about the influence of the machine in terms of the abuse of labour and the denigration of design. In 1807, Thomas Hope warned against the debasement of furniture design and production 'through the entire substitution of machinery for manual labour'.[81]

This alarmist comment should not be taken too seriously, as most furniture continued to be fabricated with hand tools well into the nineteenth century and in some cases beyond.[82] The employment of these preparatory processes was quite varied and the choice and particulars of usage were dependent on the nature of the demands put upon particular furniture-makers. The same may be said of the construction methods .

Construction

The process of quality furniture-making in the eighteenth century was the result of the combined efforts of a number of craftsmen who were often specialists in various fields. However, the fundamental construction of the carcase remained the basis of the furniture upon which the decorative treatments would be added. Changes in furniture-making were influenced by a more sophisticated demand, better tools, and the increased variety of materials that were introduced during the seventeenth and eighteenth centuries. Fundamental developments in construction had already occurred in the seventeenth century with the use of veneers, dovetail jointing and improved drawer construction. Therefore the aim of many of the changes that occurred in the construction techniques of the eighteenth century was to meet the opposing demands of an increasingly cost-conscious market on the one hand, and to maintain high quality on the other.

To explain this process of refinement which was attuned both to the market and to the needs of the business, the example of drawers is instructive. In the seventeenth century, drawers were made with rebated sides that fitted into front panels, the bottom was rebated into the front and nailed to the bottom of the sides. To allow this drawer to work simply, a groove was cut into the exterior side of the drawer up to half an inch deep, so it was necessary that the drawer sides were made from relatively thick timber. The grooves accommodated wooden runners which were fixed inside the carcase to support the operation of the drawer.

Although improvements in the late seventeenth century incorporated the dovetail joint, there was no progress on reducing the chunky drawer frames until a new support system was devised. Side drawer runners became obsolete as soon as the drawer was so arranged as to run on a wooden platform; this meant that base boards had to be fully rebated and glued to avoid nail damage and it was also possible to construct drawers with daintier narrow sides. By the eighteenth century, this resulted in drawer bottoms that were rebated about an eighth of an inch with the result that the side bottom edge projected. This was strengthened by a fillet, half to three quarters of an inch thick, which created a slide for the drawer.

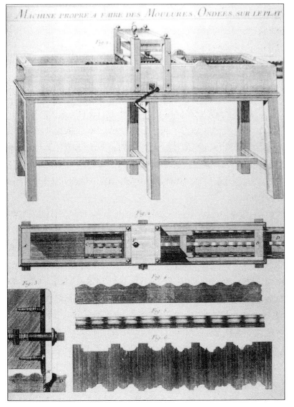

15 A moulding machine designed to make regular and repetitive multiple wave-shaped mouldings, 1772.

Drawers also helped to maintain the carcase stability, and are therefore an indicator of quality. Cheaper cabinets allowed for the drawer divisions to be dovetailed into the carcase side while the drawer supports were often nailed to the side panel in the manner of the previous century. This method created a problem, as the rails acted as battens and hindered the movement of the carcase panels, thus causing splitting. Conversely, on expensive work, it has been known for the drawer bottoms to be made on the 'frame and panel' method, to completely avoid splitting.[83] This process of drawer refinement was one example of the cabinet-makers' need to produce differentiated furniture which was seen to be of a particular quality, when viewed in relation to other makers or styles.

Regardless of the question of merit, the change from working with solid wood using joinery techniques to refined cabinet-making skills and the use of veneers, meant that most methods of making were altered to some degree. For example, prior to the introduction of veneering, table frames and tops were usually pegged together. When the top surfaces were to be veneered, other procedures clearly had to be developed. The simple procedure was the technique of holding tops on with blocks, which were glued and fitted to the top board and side rails. Further changes, perhaps related to poor adhesion problems, meant that by the 1740s gouged recesses were being made to accommodate screws which held tops to frames. These were not universal methods by any means. Recent research has shown that a wide range of fixing methods were used in the same furniture type.[84] The examples simply demonstrate the continuing pragmatic approach to construction that occurred during the century.

It is sometimes the case that developments which were extremely important, had little to do with high-style construction methods. The satisfactory result derived from a process of evolvement assisted by effective problem-solving, is nowhere better seen than in the development of the Windsor chair. This is an example of a product that shows a degree of sophistication in design, combined with a masterly use of materials and techniques which produced a type form. The choice of straight-grained beech for the supports, rugged elm for the seats and supple yew for the curved sections showed a remarkable degree of discrimination in matching materials to performance requirements.

As the Windsor chair was essentially a functional chair which was often produced in batches, a 'reductivist' approach to its manufacture was sensible in terms of both cost and quality control. For example, the use of bent sections reduced the number of components and joints particularly in the case of armchairs; its one-piece solid seat avoided jointing and upholstery, and the often-used wedged construction simplified the assembly. It is not surprising that this 'unsophisticated' process of component supply was exploited in the latter part of the eighteenth century and onwards as a cottage industry, aiming to provide bulk supplies for both urban and rural use.

Naturally this analysis was not appropriate for higher status goods where function was less important than image. In these cases, the quality of a piece of furniture was judged on two counts: the interior construction and the surface decoration. The client was often paying for the 'hidden' quality, and in some cases this had to be explained, since the fine construction details were not immediately apparent. Regarding luxurious furniture, Sheraton explained that

> it is difficult to ascertain, in many instances, the true value of furniture by those who are strangers to the business. On this account gentlemen often think themselves imposed upon in the high price they must give for a good article.[85]

An example of this hidden quality could be the relatively simple matter of attaching base mouldings. In quality work, mouldings were glued to secondary wood blocks which were in turn glued to the base so that any movement was limited to stresses in the main frame of the secondary wood.[86]

It is to be expected that techniques of construction used by quality makers were partly aimed at avoiding the pitfalls arising from the use of solid wood. Built-up framing, either in plies or blocks, was clearly evident in much of the superior work of the century. Due to the fine quality demanded by some jobs, components were made up from blocks of timber that were jointed and then cut to size to create curved and shaped parts. In terms of cost and function it was a most satisfactory way of producing *bombé* or curved shapes. A prestigious piece such as the Channon writing commode benefited from such workmanship.[87]

Built-up curved work was usually made in four ways.[88] First, solid sections could be cut into small curves and then jointed together edge to edge. Second, small blocks were shaped and then built up like brickwork. Third, laminates of wood were vertically aligned; and finally, kerfs were cut into a rail or skirt allowing them to be bent to a curve. These various techniques all demonstrate a variety of solutions to a design problem, aimed at achieving a particular stylistic interpretation within certain parameters.

Examples abound of these various techniques. Drawer fronts were often made from built-up timbers, especially useful in the case of shaped fronts for commodes for instance. Some card tables produced in the 1760s to 1770s had their tops formed from cross members framed by shaped muntins, the flush under-surfaces supported by a central strut and the shaped friezes built up in three layers.[89] It was not only friezes and drawer fronts that were built up. The natural use of laminates was another example of a practical design decision.

16 The Windsor chair – a fine example of the development of a type form in furniture design.

Sheraton explained how card table tops, which need to be as flat as possible, were to be made. His jointing method was remarkably similar to some modern boards: 'I take it to be the best to rip up dry deal or faulty mahogany, into 4 inch widths, and joint them up. It matters not whether the pieces are whole lengths, provided the jump joints be crossed.'[90] Mahogany lippings were then tongued into the ends of the tops, and slips were glued to the sides, so once veneered, they created the appearance of solid mahogany.

The built-up system was not limited to fancy shapes or card tables. Sheraton suggested it as a general expedient to counteract movement. In his design for a Universal table he advised that 'the bed panels [for the top] are sometimes glued up in three thicknesses, the middle being laid with the grain across, and the other two lengthways of the panel to prevent warping'.[91] The underframe of the Universal table was to be made 'of faulty mahogany or of wainscot veneered'.[92] Round surfaces were also treated in a similar manner. Arch tops were glued up in thicknesses round a caul,[93] while curved doors were either framed and panelled or 'glued up in narrow slips of inch mahogany and clamped'.[94]

These techniques, based on trial and error, were realistic solutions to particular problems. Some of the results however, could be very ingenious. An eighteenth-century method of turning pilasters demonstrates this.[95] Because pilasters were attached after the carcase was made, it was necessary to turn the columns first. They were initially planed square then rebated to the angle of fixing. This angle was then fitted with a fillet of deal that was lightly glued in for easy removal after turning, thus keeping the rebate intact. The piece was then turned to shape and could easily be fitted when finished. A workmanlike solution to a problem.

These practical techniques were not limited to English work. In America, an ingenious method of creating a cabriole leg effect was achieved by cutting a wedge out of the front of the leg above the foot. The lower piece of timber was then bent forward to achieve the shaped effect; it could then be glued and finished off by shaping tools.[96] In Germany, Roentgen's use of a patchwork of veneer is a clear demonstration of a practical solution to a construction problem. The underside of panels were veneered in this way, aiming to counteract the potential warping that might be caused by his mottled top veneers.[97]

It was not just cabinet-makers who adapted processes to object requirements. Chair-makers also developed particular methods to simplify making or to solve problems. For example, chairs with drop-in seats had frames made with rebates in thin side rails which were combined with a simple wooden corner block or brace. Seats that were designed to be over-upholstered had thicker rails and larger braces to accept the tension of the webbing. Stiles and centre splats were tenoned into top rails but often left loose in the shoe to allow for movement. Armchairs, which required stability, had the arms screwed to seat rails and into back stiles, while stretchers were tenoned into legs.

Having pointed out that the construction processes were the result of considerations of function and material use, it must be said that considerations of profit and loss were also a priority for makers. As was seen in the discussion on pricing and price books, the costing of construction processes was a well-established practice in many workshops. Indeed, customers' bills often included details of the materials used, from which a later onlooker can infer the making process. The following 'Note of prime cost of a Desk and a Bookcase veneered with Broom [wood] for The Hon. John Murray Esquire' included the labour cost of 210.5 working man days at a cost of £12 3s. 0d. as well as the following materials:[98]

To locks brasses and hinges etc.	£1 5s. 6d.
To Sundries green cloath	12s. 6d.
To Glew 8/2, Oil 10d., fir and rushes 3/6	12s. 6d.
To sundries Wainscot	£1 19s. 6d.
To fir 4/4, Walnut-tree 9/6	13s. 9d.
To Mahogany 4/2, Glasses 3/6	9s. 8d.
To sundries 2d., and etc. 4d.	6d.

The above example gives a good indication of the scrupulous costing process of one cabinet-maker who accounted for all his labour and materials.

Having dealt at some length with the question of interior cabinet construction, it is now worth looking at surface decoration in some detail.

Veneering and marquetry

Veneering, like turning, was already an ancient art by the eighteenth century, but its revival and use by cabinet-makers in continental Europe during the seventeenth century, meant that amendments to the ways of making furniture were required. The old frame and panel process for constructing the carcases was unsuitable for surfaces that were to receive veneers or marquetry. Instead techniques used by wooden case-makers were employed to make a rigid carcase suitable for flush veneering.

Fundamentally, veneering is simply the placing of a thin slice of exotic timber over a less valuable base, thus providing an interesting and attractive finish. Therefore one of the skills that had to be developed was the cutting of thin slices of timber, about 3mm thick (approximately 8 to the inch).

Although veneering seemed an ideal candidate for a mechanical process, it is surprising to find that little success could be achieved with mechanical methods of cutting or application until the early nineteenth century. However, there were attempts; the earliest recorded patent for the machine-cutting of timber into scales or veneers was in 1635.[99] The results were undeveloped and the process explained in Chambers' *Cyclopaedia* (1728) changed little over the century. This description showed how timber was held in a vice and cut to the thickness of a line. The vice was a simple press which held the timber baulk steady, whilst two men sawed the wood into slices.[100]

Once the veneer was ready to apply, it was glued to the base board and then the finished component was put under another board on a bench. The pressure required to bond the two parts might be obtained by 'go-bars' which Chambers describes as pieces of wood or poles which are tensioned between the board (with the veneered panel below) and the ceiling.[101] If the veneered parts were shaped, sand bags or lead weights were used to hold down the veneer to the base or if it was a large piece, the use of specially shaped cauls might be required.[102]

Whatever method was used, veneering was highly successful and did not seem to have been a derogatory term until the nineteenth century, although it is revealing to find Sheraton describing veneering in the following terms: 'Sometimes the object of veneering is cheapness and sometimes appearance. In most cases however, the ground, glue and extra time are equivalent to the expense of solid wood'.[103] Clearly it was the resultant appearance that was the main selling factor in the use of veneers.

A particular technique of veneering named after its most famous exponent, André Charles Boulle, was one of the most desirable decorative treatments of the period, as it involved using a variety of materials in veneer form in conjunction with each other, to create a spectacular effect. These could include fine timber veneers, or metals such as brass and pewter, as well as mother-of-pearl, turtle or tortoiseshell.

Boulle work is best known for its use of sea-turtle shell. The production of this decorative method has its own history and technology which gives an insight into the lengths that were taken in order to supply especially desirable objects. The preparatory processes included boiling and clamping the shells into moulds and allowing them to settle to produce a flat area. As many shell-plates were quite small, it was common practice to fuse them together to create larger surfaces,[104] whilst in lesser quality work the plates were often simply abutted together. Almost all shell was painted on the back to provide a coloured background, which was then covered with thick paper to disguise any joins.

The process of cutting the shell, timber or metal, either as a sandwich or individually, has caused some confusion. The materials needed to produce the design could have been cut individually or as a complete sandwich of the various parts. Gillian Wilson (1972) has shown that the brass and tortoiseshell of early Boulle work were not cut together, as tracings of brass work on seemingly identical drawer fronts reveal small differences.[105] She has, however, suggested that sandwich cutting was in fact used in the latter part of the eighteenth century to speed up the process. Furthermore, she considers that printed templates of designs were used in each case of cutting.

Richard Randall (1969) has suggested that the existence of two full Boulle design sheets indicated that whilst one was used pasted down on the surface of the brass, the other was pasted onto the tortoiseshell, thus producing *premier* and *contre partie* veneers. The use of actual prints rather than tracings suggests that the expense of the material required the most exact registration possible. Randall suggests that using prints does not in itself deny the idea of multiple cutting of a sandwich of design brass and tortoiseshell, it just seems to make it easier.[106]

However, by the early nineteenth century, Peter and Michaelangelo Nicholson were clear about the method:

In joining this ornament with that to which it is to unite, the part for the ornament and that for the ground must be glued together, drawn upon the one, and laid upon another such piece joined in the same manner, but placed in reverse order; then the design being drawn upon the one, and the whole substance making one thickness, is cut by means of a fine bow saw, thus producing four parts joined in twos reversed to each other.[107]

It seems that as the process developed from a very limited and high quality market to a slightly wider and less demanding clientele, small adjustments were made to ensure that a sensible balance remained between costings and retail prices. One of these would be multiple cutting, designed to save time, whilst paradoxically appearing to produce a better register of design.

The success and desirability of Boulle work made its imitation inevitable. The tortoiseshell material itself was a prime candidate for

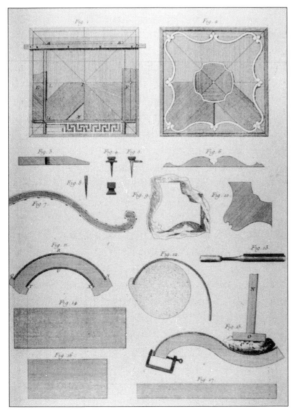

17 Examples of part of the veneering process. The use of the sandbag to give weight and allow the veneer to follow contours is clearly shown.

imitation and methods of doing so were well-known in the eighteenth century. As early as 1688, Stalker and Parker had published recipes for the counterfeiting of tortoiseshell.[108] These procedures were based on paint techniques which copied the effects of tortoiseshell backed with silver foil. It is difficult to judge these effects now, but they would surely have created the desired image in candle-lit eighteenth-century interiors.

Tortoiseshell could also be imitated in a more solid form. Interestingly, it is in Plumier's *Art of Turning* (1749) that the process of producing imitation shell is described in detail. By softening horns to a pulp in a lye[109] wash, one was then able to mould them into flat plates. They were then covered in a mix of quicklime, litharge[110] and lye so that they would develop the distinctive partly opaque, partly transparent effect of real tortoiseshell.[111] Even this process was complicated in comparison to a less intensive method which involved dipping wire mesh into a bath of fish glue and allowing a film to build up by repeated dippings. When varnished it was apparently quite adequate as imitation horn.[112]

An interesting variant of Boulle work, which could hardly be considered as imitation, was the work of the firm of Coxed and Woster. In the first quarter of the eighteenth century, they were producing furniture in the style of Boulle work, which used burr-elm timber, stained to resemble tortoiseshell, which was then cross-banded with kingwood and inlaid with pewter stringing.[113]

The attraction of combinations of materials meant that many other makers produced marquetry furniture throughout the century in various mixes, including wood veneers, brass and mother-of-pearl.[114]

The marquetry process[115] which had been developed in conjunction with veneering in the seventeenth century, was still popular in the early eighteenth century. The method involved laying a variety of wood veneers of differing colours and sizes onto a ground to build up a picture. This could be laboriously done using individual cuts, but was soon made easier. The process was described in Chambers' *Cyclopaedia* of 1728. The selected veneers and the chosen pattern were put together in a sandwich form. The practice of sandwiching the selection of veneers that constituted the design was devised to save time and to avoid splintering. The sandwich was then placed into a vice with two jaws or chaps, one fixed and one moveable. The latter jaw was operated by a cord fixed to a treadle, so that the sandwich could be held tight whilst the pattern was being cut by saw.[116]

To heighten a three-dimensional effect, various methods were used. Different coloured timbers produced major contrasts, whilst smaller sections were dipped into hot sand to produce a graduated shaded effect. During the first quarter of the eighteenth century the pictorial designs, made up from small sections of various coloured woods, were often of floral or seaweed styles with the fine detail being achieved by thin saw cuts in the veneers. By the latter part of the eighteenth century (from the 1760s) the detailed effects of the mainly neo-classical and symbolic images were accomplished by finely engraving the surface of the marquetry.

The question as to whether there were specialist marquetry workers during the century has been addressed in recent years.[117] The actual process of cutting and assembling was within the scope of a professional cabinet-maker, so it is unlikely that a particular craft developed completely separately to produce this form of decoration. However, there is evidence to suggest that some makers specialised in this form of decorative treatment, and in some cases supplied others with ready-made marquetry parts.

Finishing processes

The staining and polishing of the surfaces of furniture must have taken a high place in the cabinet-making process. It was the finish that reflected the quality of the piece either in appearance or in reality, by imitating or truly achieving the required effect. The processes therefore resulted in a piece of furniture that was both protected and enhanced decoratively. As a protective measure, finishing was intended to keep the surface usable and practical, whilst for improving the apparent quality of an object many recipes were devised. In view of the demand for high-style objects at all levels, it is not surprising to find that methods were devised to give an inexpensive timber the look or colour of a higher quality one. In addition to this form of disguising, the colouring or dyeing of different woods was legitimately used to produce a colourful marquetry or inlay pattern. In either circumstance, the process often took place on pale-coloured timbers, such as holly, pear and beech that were relatively easy to acquire and able to take the colour well.

Dyes and stains were therefore important in the cabinet-makers repertoire, the distinction between them being that stains colour the surface, whilst dyes penetrate the material and effect a change due to chemical reaction. In either case the choice of substances for achieving colour change was immense. The more commonly used dyes were alkanet, logwood, verdigris, copperas and barberry root, whilst archil, dragon's blood and brazil-wood were regularly used as stains.[118] Contemporary guides offered recipes for rosewood and ebony colours which were relatively straightforward, but for a mahogany effect a fearful process was suggested which involved rubbing the wooden surfaces with dilute *aqua fortis* and then covering the article with hot sand and placing it in an oven. As with other processes, the resourcefulness of the cabinet-maker or his supplier was sometimes the only limitation on developments in the field.[119]

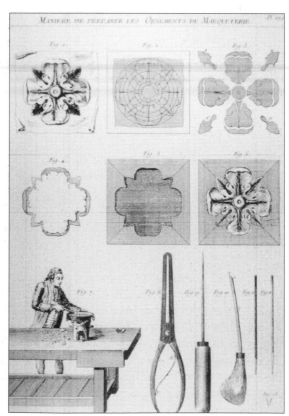

18 Part of the marquetry process. Note the process of shading of small sections of veneer in hot sand to change the colour.

Once an item had been through the various staining and colouring processes, the final effect was provided by polishing. Again this appears to have been a labour-intensive process. Stalker and Parker (1688) discussed the procedure of applying a clear varnish to olive wood and walnut:

> After applying ten to twelve coats of seed-lac varnish (with the top removed for later use), dried between each coat and polished with rushes, apply the top part of the varnish in six coats. After three days standing, apply powdered tripolee and rub till it acquires a gloss.[120]

Quite an involved process, but essential if the cabinet-maker was to bring out the beauty of the timber and provide a degree of surface protection.

If varnish was not used then either of the older methods of oiling or waxing would be applied. Although considerably overstated, Neve (1726) indicated the beneficial preservative effects of linseed oil: 'It was experimented with in a walnut-tree table, where it destroyed millions of worms immediately.'[121]

Wax finishes were illustrated by Diderot showing the process of rubbing liquid beeswax onto a surface with a rag bundle, which then forced the wax into the pores of the wood. The waxing process was also recommended in England: 'After it has been sufficiently scraped, then polish it with the skin of a sea-dog, wax with a brush or polish with shave grass.'[122] This would seem to have produced a less glossy finish than the varnish mentioned above, and it was still recommended for interior woodwork in Sheraton's *Dictionary*.[123] The enhancement of timber surfaces naturally occurred with wax polishing which not only built up a protective surface but also created a patina. This patina was not particularly admired in the eighteenth century as it was associated with the old and out-of-date.[124]

Some finishing processes were very resourceful. In the papers of John and William Myers of Wheldrake, Yorks (1778) the following method is recorded:

> To polish mahogany doors oyle it over with linseed oyle over night then in the morning take sum brick dust put it into a silk stocking or anything that is fine then dash it over the door and take a piece of new carpitt or any woolon cloth and rub it. Oyle coats after another with brick dust and oyle until you make a glow till you can see youre self in it.[125]

This practice was clearly quite common: indeed Sheraton noted that 'the general mode of polishing plain cabinet work is . . . with oil and brick dust'.[126] It is quite clear that a glossy finish which produced a mirror-like shine was a statement of pride in ownership, which was intended to be noticed. A French visitor commented that 'the tables and chairs . . . have a brilliant polish like that of finely tempered steel'.[127]

Part of the polishing process involved abrasives, and the wide variety of rubbing materials, ranging from sea-grass to brick dust, again testifies to the ingenuity and resourcefulness of the cabinet-maker. The use of certain fish skins as an abrasive forerunner to sandpaper seems to have been common.[128] For example, Samuel Norman's inventory of 1760 included forty-one fish skins and five dozen fins and some scouring paper, as well as six rubstones.[129]

The processes discussed so far have mainly related to wooden surfaces. Other decorative finishing processes assumed importance at various times and two of the most fashionable treatments were lacquering and japanning.

Explaining the reasons for the establishment of a lacquer industry in England, Hans Huth (1971) wrote: 'Toward the end of the seventeenth century there was an urge among artisans to introduce new techniques or combine old ones to create new effects based on experiment rather than theory.'[130] Developments like this were clearly an off-shoot of the continuing curiosity in natural science and philosophy that was to find its high point in the intellectual climate of the Enlightenment, and was to become manifest in the interest in scientific and natural phenomena that extended even as far as furniture. As has been seen above, the taste for exotic timbers and ingenious mechanisms confirms this, as well as illustrating a desire to enjoy the environment in which one lived. The techniques of lacquering and the resulting furniture are fine examples of both attitudes.

From the late-sixteenth century, the West had developed a fascination with the lacquer-work of the Orient. Although imported lacquer-work initially met the taste, it was soon clear that the demand was to greatly exceed the supply. In addition, less expensive copies were widely sought after. A class of japanners were therefore established who were to pioneer imitative techniques. As the essential ingredient of oriental lacquer, the resin, *rhus vernicifera*, was not available in the West, imitations had to be made from other gums or resins. By the latter part of the seventeenth century, substitutes were known in England and Italy, and by the end of the century most of Europe was smitten with the lacquer phenomenon.[131] Activity in England was hectic: Edward Hurd and James Narcock petitioned for a patent for lacquering in 1692. In 1695 a 'company of patentees for lacquering after the manner of Japan' was established who successfully lobbied Parliament for an increase in import duties on foreign lacquer-work.[132] By 1697 the patentees were offering cabinets, secretaires, tables, stands, looking glasses and tea tables 'after the manner of Japan'.[133]

The development of decorative lacquers in France was particularly successful and these products set the standard for the rest of Europe. The Martin Brothers obtained a *Privelège* for lacquer manufacture in 1730, renewed it in 1744, and again in 1753. An indication of their importance is that 'vernis Martin' has become a generic name for French lacquer-work of this period. Indeed its success in its own time was such that Voltaire is quoted as saying, 'Ces cabinets ou Martin, A surpassé l'art de la Chine'.[134]

The French superiority in lacquer-work, urged the Society for the Encouragement of Arts, Manufactures, and Commerce in London to offer a prize for an equivalent result to the French product.[135] The prize was eventually awarded to Stephen Bedford in 1763.

The fact that the European lacquer process was an imitation did not indicate that it was inferior, but inevitably as demand outstripped supply, some took advantage of the situation. Although Robert Dossie could say 'by japanning is to be understood the art of covering bodies by grounds of opake colours in varnish: which may be either afterwards decorated by painting or gilding or left in a plain state',[136] he also pointed out that practitioners had started to omit undercoats or priming which had always been used in 'traditional' work. As the demand increased, the practice of japanners who reduced their quality was seemingly a natural response to market forces. In contrast, one French example gave directions that included an initial coating of the frame with six coats of gesso, followed by eighteen lacquer coats of one colour, six of a second, and fifteen of clear varnish. These were to be applied over a two-month period or even longer.[137] As with all methods there was a place for the highest quality as well as the meanest.

Even though the European lacquer was not authentic, the designs were mostly based on Oriental images, either real or imaginary. The

19 Designs suggested for lacquering and japanning drawer fronts. Their resemblance to true Oriental examples is unhampered by veracity.

mid-eighteenth century therefore saw an encouragement of oriental styles through the publication of books such as William Halfpenny's *New Designs for Chinese Temples* (1750), Lock and Copland's *New Book of Ornaments* (1752), and Edward's and Darly's *New Book of Chinese Designs* (1754). In addition to these, Jean Pillement produced engraved designs of Chinese subject matter in London between 1757 and 1764. All this visual wealth meant that not only were skilled cabinet-makers supplied with designs, but also that there was a craze for 'do-it-yourself' lacquering by amateurs. The publication by Robert Sayer, of *The Ladies Amusement or the Whole Art of Japanning Made Easy* (1762) confirms this, and there are examples of wealthy families paying for daughters to be trained in the art, which seems to have been something of a social accomplishment.

105

Although the craft of lacquer-working was separate from furniture-making, the supply of finished lacquer items was often a part of the furnishers' normal trade.[138] For example, while Daniel and Joseph Mills traded specifically as japanners and cabinet-makers at the *Japan Cabinet and Cistern* in Vine Street between 1768 and 1777,[139] other leading firms were quietly meeting the demand as and when required. Well-known cabinet-making businesses which produced and sold lacquer-work included those of Jensen, Grendey and Belchier.

Full-scale lacquering gradually declined in popularity and it began to be replaced in the latter part of the century by varnishing processes laid over painted decoration. This new fashion was noted by Hepplewhite (1788) who said that japanning was 'the new and very elegant fashion . . . arisen within these few years'. The idea was to finish chairs 'with painted or japanned work, giving a rich and splendid appearance to the minuter parts of the ornaments, which are generally thrown in by the painter'.[140]

The uses of japanning and varnishing processes were not always designed to imitate oriental products. In many cases the finish was an imitation of another more valuable material such as tortoiseshell. John Baskerville took out a patent for a 'new method of making and flat-grinding thin metal plates', which once fabricated, were japanned and varnished to produce 'fine glowing mahogany colour . . . or an imitation tortoiseshell'. They were designed to be 'applied to the frames of paintings and pictures of all sizes, looking glass frames, the front of cabinets, buroes, . . . and every other sort of household furniture'.[141] Other methods using metallic bases included figure paintings that were made on copper panels and tole or tin-painted panels which were often let into the surface of cabinets.[142]

In America lacquering was a Boston tradition which was no doubt due as much to the city's successful commercial position as to the taste of its inhabitants.[143] Unlike most European products, their process used maple or pine as the base wood, which being denser, did not require a gesso foundation for the lacquer surface. The pattern could be built-up directly onto the wood.

The trade of japanning was never far away from other techniques like painting, and it is sometimes the case that the two trades were carried on in one business.[144]

Painted finishes for furniture have been known for thousands of years, so it is no surprise to find them being used in both high and vernacular styles in the eighteenth century. Within any discussion of painted furniture there are distinctions which should be made between a small amount of fine painted decoration added to a cabinet, an all-over paint finish, and other combinations thereof. It should also be recognised that japanners were usually responsible for the ground, and decorative painters provided the finishing details.

In the vernacular tradition, painted finishes served to disguise poor quality timber and provided an opportunity to introduce some much-needed brightness into a room. The variety and styles of these finishes extend beyond the scope of this chapter but their importance in enhancing common furniture with attractive patterns, simulations of high-quality materials (e.g. tortoiseshell, marble, fine timber, etc.), or simply with a plain colour, are a necessary reminder that nearly all social groups wanted to enjoy attractive surroundings.[145]

From the 1770s, in the high-style markets, a taste developed for furniture made in light tones and sometimes featuring delicate colourings, which, in some cases were especially designed to integrate into a particular interior. Painted motifs, sometimes in combination with marquetry, supplied the correct degree of delicacy, whilst the chosen designs often reflected the architectural features of a particular room.

Again there were degrees of painted finish. In some cases paint would be applied onto veneer to create simple border designs, or in other cases the whole piece might be finished with a paint decoration. Clearly, the use of painting techniques on furniture enabled decorators such as Adam to achieve the unification of complete interior schemes very accurately.

Gilding was yet another ancient method of decorating furniture that found favour in the eighteenth century. It was often subject to the vagaries of taste and its popularity changed over the century, but with the propensity towards display and self-aggrandisement in the eighteenth century, gilding was often considered as representative of status, wealth and even taste.

Initially connected with the massive Kentian manner of the early part of the century, gilding was soon assimilated by the rococo designers such as Thomas Johnson, who was particularly associated with the carving trade. There was a close link between the two crafts of gilding and carving, and during the eighteenth century there was a tendency towards the amalgamation of the two. This was in part due to the cyclical nature of the trade whereby taste for gilding or carving fluctuated, thus causing potential loss of earnings. Indeed Campbell's *London Tradesmen* noted that there was little work available for gilders who were not also able carvers.[146]

By the third quarter of the century, tastes for gilding had begun to change and even Adam was being accused of being 'all gingerbread and filigraine', a derisory reference to his particular taste for gilding. Regardless of particular styles, it was the techniques of colouring and application of the gold leaf that made distinctions between the quality of work.

The techniques were divided between dry, water, and oil gilding. The terms refer to the medium of application and the distinction is important as they produce differing results. In eighteenth-century furniture, oil gilding was chiefly used for finishing hardwood cabinet work, whilst water gilding was used on softwood items such as chairs, side tables and picture frames.[147] Water gilding is recognised as having 'the advantage of oil gilding, but is attended with much more trouble and expence'.[148] The process was undoubtedly involved. Coats of white gesso, a mixture of chalk and glue heated to make a paste, would be applied to bare wood, and the surfaces would be smoothed and any carving re-cut as necessary. This surface was then sealed and coloured by adding a surface finish of bole mixed with glue, the colour of which varied from the usual Armenian bole, which is a purplish red-brown, to an orange or pinky-brown, or blue depending on the colour of gold leaf being used.[149] The gold leaf was then applied to a wetted surface and allowed to dry. The final burnishing was carried out by agate stone.

Accessories and other materials

Although much furniture was destined to be left with a plain polished, or patterned wood finish, there were numerous cases where additions were intended either as a convenience or as decoration. Whatever the case, the manufacture of these components was often undertaken by a specialist, skilled in metalwork, glass-working, or ceramics. The introduction of castors in England at the end of the seventeenth century is a case in point.[150] The use of the castor demonstrates how furniture-makers reacted to and reflected social needs. When there had been few items, mostly designed to remain in one specific place, there had been no need for easy movement. Changing lifestyles meant that more furniture was required to be moved about at certain times (often daily), and in addition, precious carpets and floors needed some protection from scuffing. So, for most of the century, castors remained a utilitarian part of furniture accessorising and were simply a convenience. Originally made with wooden or leather rollers, by the end of the century there were many varieties, mainly made from metals. These were often quite elaborate, sometimes being combined with decorative foot mounts, thus making a distinctive decorative feature from a necessity.[151]

Other decorative metalwork that featured in the design of a piece of furniture was clearly subject to the vagaries of fashion far more than were the simple accessories. From the discreetly inserted brass stringing, to the extraordinary chased and gilded mounts, the century saw the whole gamut of designs and styles interpreted in metal, often in combination with other exotic materials. Highly esteemed furniture, using metal combined with exotic timbers, had a long pedigree. The continuing fascination for, and influence of Boulle work beyond its own boundaries meant that there was a small, though steady demand for metal, especially brass, inlaid items. Recent scholarship on this furniture type has begun to make some revealing connections,[152] which confirm the interdependence of various trades. For example, there seems to be a connection between silversmithing and the engraved work executed upon metal mounts, as well as the specialist parts of the engraving trade such as heraldic engravers, and those who worked on gun stocks.[153]

Another example is Campbell's (1747) description of the process of mercury gilding under the heading of a sub-division of the goldsmith's work.[154] However, in certain special circumstances cabinet-makers too involved themselves in these specialised processes. The example of Seddon who apparently employed 'girdlers – who mould the bronze into graceful patterns', was worthy of comment by Sophie von la Roche.[155]

Less exotic, though important in their own right, were drawer handles. These underwent many mutations; for example, from 1715 to 1735 they were based on slender drop loops on a shaped back plate, from 1740 the drop loop became stouter and by the 1750s two small plates had been substituted for the single back plate.[156] The growing pressure for these metalwork items, not only in terms of quantity but also in variety, meant that mechanical processes were developed to meet it. The demand prompted three patented processes within the space of five years.[157] These techniques developed the stamping method of forming which would have seemed particularly appropriate for them, but cast-working remained the most popular method for the production of brass sundries.[158]

In small specialist divisions of furniture-making there appears to have been a regular degree of sub-contracting. In other circumstances furniture-makers had to rely on outside suppliers or sub-contractors, for all their requirements. One example of this trading is the supply of screws.[159] These were handmade by smiths for much of the century. Initially they were small, made from brass and hand-filed with an irregular thread; there was little taper to the shaft and the end was cut square with an irregular slot. By the 1720s screws were in general use but still expensive due to the laborious processes involved.[160] A break-through came in 1760, when J. and W. Wyatt patented a device for machine-making them,[161] and from then on lathe-made screws with a clearer diminishing spiral could be used for fixing hinges and securing tops. In 1776, the Wyatt brothers set up a factory but it was not until 1798, when Henry Maudsley devised a lathe to mass-produce the screw that they became widespread. The establishment in 1823 of the Nettlefolds company meant that the business of machine-cut screws became fully established.[162]

Despite supply problems, screws were apparently common in some workshops if the 1760 inventory of the Samuel Norman workshop can be a reliable guide: 'one and a half gross of three-inch screws, one hundred and five gross of screws of various sizes'.[163]

Apart from the screw-makers, tool-makers, nail-makers and brass-workers, furniture producers relied on other parts of the metalworking trades. This field of expertise was called upon when metal parts were required for fitting into furniture. These components could range from the iron brackets used in press beds, to sophisticated control mechanisms for articulated furniture. They were often used in conjunction with patent or metamorphic furniture for special movements and operating parts. One example might be Day Gunby's patent for springs designed to fit desks, tables, chairs, etc.,[164] which allowed sections to be raised or lowered on counter balances. In these cases the invention of the mechanism was based on a general principle which could be adapted to a variety of styles and furniture types; for example, Seddon and Co. used the Day Gunby system in a series of tables.[165]

Although English cabinet-makers were competent enough to produce intriguing mechanical furniture[166] it was in France and Germany that the greatest exponents of the art practised. Jean-François Oeben and his techniques of designing furniture with hidden drawers and single locks for sets of drawers and roll tops is a fine example of the genre.[167] The other famous name in this field is David Roentgen.[168] His collaboration with clockmaker, Peter Kinzing, produced many inventive mechanisms which allowed secret drawers to be opened with springs, or writing slides and roll tops to simultaneously open.

Mirrors and glass

Throughout the eighteenth century mirrors were considered an essential in any well-furnished house, but the desirability of glass as a glazing material as well as the basis for mirrors has a long history.[169] From c. 1500 the manufacture of glass plates was combined with the tin-mercury process of 'silvering'[170] which created the mirror, thus establishing the basis of most mirror making for the next 400 years.

The Venetians had established a lead in the supply of glass mirrors from the early sixteenth century. This was due to the technical development of the 'broad' or Lorraine process of glass-making which involved blowing a tube of glass until it reached the appropriate size, when it was then sliced lengthwise and afterwards flattened within an annealing chamber.[171] Clearly this process was limited to the finished sizes that could be made, but this did not deter market growth. The high value placed on glass and mirrors was due to the expense and limited availability caused by the manufacturing process, which made ownership desirable due to their value as functional pieces and as status symbols.[172]

Indeed, the marketable value of glass and mirrors was not lost on English entrepreneurs. In 1621, Sir Robert Maunsell petitioned the King for the right to develop a looking glass factory. His business employed 'strangers from foreign parts to instruct natives not only in making Crystalline Morano glasses but also looking glass plates and theyre foyling'.[173]

There continued to be limitations on the size of glass sheets until the development of cast glass. Put simply, this was a process of pouring molten glass onto an iron plate covered with sand, which was then made smooth before the annealing process. This practice was devised by Bernard Perrot in the 1680s and developed at St Gobain in Picardy. From then on the prestige of French mirror glass was established throughout Europe.[174]

Although there was an industry in England, such was the quality and prestige of French mirrors that they were imported in quantity. The mirror glass was often imported in an unfinished state and it was necessary to further process it in England. This is the sort of work that might have been carried out by furniture businesses which had glass rooms and employed grinders and polishers.

As glass-mirror finishing involved grinding, polishing, silvering and cutting to size, the specialist glass grinder was often employed. He 'fixes plate glass horizontally and rubs it backward and forward upon a plane, on which sand and water are constantly running. The glass being thus on both sides ground perfectly true is afterward polished with emery and putty'.[175] Often the glass grinder was also responsible for silvering the back to make mirror glass. Such is the case of James Welch, who offered for sale a 'great variety of peer [sic], chimney, or sconce glasses, fine dressing glasses, coach, chariot or chair glasses'.[176]

Other specialists were also employed in mirror making, the main one being the frame-maker. Campbell described this sub-group as 'a set of joiners who make nothing but frames for looking-glasses and pictures and prepare them for the carvers'.[177] The work apparently involved the simple joining up of a frame ready for the carver to finish.

It is not surprising to find that businesses engaged in carving and gilding work were also involved in the mirror framing and supply business. The example of Joseph Cox is one such enterprise. He described himself as a 'frame-maker and gilder' who made and sold 'all sorts of carved and gilt frames for looking glasses . . . likewise old glasses new silvered and put into the newest fashion gilt sconces'.[178] It is fascinating to see that the refurbishment of mirror glass was a cost-effective way of keeping up with fashionable taste.

By the mid-eighteenth century, the techniques of glass-making had improved sufficiently enough to create extraordinary mirror sizes. According to contracts made by Chippendale, the size of 243 × 117 cm (96 × 46 inches) was not unusual, and his company were even able to supply mirrors of 289 × 228 cm (114 × 90 inches), but this was undoubtedly exceptional.[179] The ability to produce large plates reflects a desire to lessen the importation of French glass and keep the trade national.[180] Sheraton confirms the change when he mentions that pier glasses could be made in London in sizes from 91 × 152 cm (36 × 60 inches) up to 190 × 297 cm (75 × 117 inches).[181]

In the context of the eighteenth century, the use of looking glasses was twofold. They were used in a practical manner for enhancing the decoration and lighting of rooms that mainly relied on candle-power for illumination. In a quite different sense, mirrors provided the physical access to view the self within one's particular surroundings, thus confirming the owner's self-status.

This status message of mirrors (alongside other items such as books, clocks and pictures) becomes clear through the research undertaken by Lorna Weatherill (1988).[182] She has shown that between 1675 and 1725 ownership of mirrors (based on the inventory samples analysed) rose from 58 per cent to 80 per cent in London, whilst in provincial towns the rise was from 36 per cent to 74 per cent. It is not surprising to find that it was the gentry and high-medium status tradesmen and merchants who registered the greatest rise in ownership of these desirable objects. It is legitimate to suggest that this process of acqui-sition continued throughout the eighteenth century and continued to filter through many sections of society.

As with many consumer goods, once they had reached down to a certain level, variations were presented to re-introduce a degree of exclusivity at the high levels. Mirrors were no exception. The enormous variety in the range of frames were the greatest asset in this instance, but even the glass itself could be specially treated to provide distinction. In the early eighteenth century the *verre églomisé* process was an example of this.

Simply put, this is the technique of engraving on gold applied to glass. The name is derived from Jean-Baptiste Glomy, an eighteenth-century designer and framer, who apparently made frames for prints with this type of decoration. Although it has this later appellation, the method of decoration was known to the ancient Romans, and was revived in fourteenth-century Italy by Cennino Cenninni. The working method involved the following process: upon the chosen glass, a layer of glair (white of egg and water) was laid as a base for the design. This was then covered by gold (or silver) leaf. When the whole was dry it was finely engraved, the background removed and the surface was then painted in colour.

An alternative recipe is found in the *Dictionarium Polygraphicum* (1751) which called for the design, cut into paper, to be placed on a previously varnished glass surface. When the varnish was dry the paper was moistened and removed. The design was then filled with colour and backed by silver leaf.[183]

Upholstery

Along with the growing desire for personal display and symbols of status and rank, there was another altogether different demand. This was the search for designs which would support the body and allow

20 An example of a carved mirror-frame closely resembling the pattern design in figure 23.

a relaxed posture, and that could be used in the more intimate and private rooms that were being developed. It could be argued that 'being at ease' was in fact a manifestation of status, since a high degree of comfort was only available to those who could afford it.

The early methods of support both in beds and upholstery were often quite crude. They usually consisted of some types of lattice or webbing, made of ropes, string, cane or webs, but in every case they were inflexible and non-resilient to any noticeable degree, intended simply to provide support. Even with the arrival of upholstery systems, the degree of resilience was initially poor.

Upholstery systems are deliberate attempts at building up a support from the base through to the suspension, filling, undercover and finally the top covers. The early techniques of upholstering were simple but workmanlike. An account of the process published in 1688 demonstrated the systematic but basic technique:

> Girth it with webbing drawn and crossed. Canvice it by nailing canvice onto the frame over the web. Rowle it by putting rowls [rolled pads] on the top edges. Stuffing follows with hay, wool flocks or feathers. It is assumed that the cover goes on at this time. Fringing follows by nailing around the sides. Backing is to fix the back on the chair. Garnishing is to finish with brass nails.[184]

By the mid-eighteenth century the procedure followed a similar pattern: webbing was stretched to form an interlaced support over which was fixed hessian. Curled hair was laid onto this, and stitched through to the webbing to prevent excessive movement. A roll edge was made by fixing a tube of stuffing material to the front rail to maintain the shape at this wear point. A layer of linen was fixed over the hair and then the final top covering was close fitted. Loose seats and backs were upholstered in the same way.

In these systems the quality of the filling was important for success. Hay, wool and hair were common, but there were also various attempts to develop alternative fillings. The ideas ranged from feather cushions to pigs' bladders filled with air.[185] The air-bags are an unknown quantity, but Edward Joy (1965) has shown that feathers were clearly a success story. The feather import figures show the valuations in 1700 as £600, in 1750 as £1086 and in 1800 as £23,810.[186] In the 1730s, Samuel Grant, a Boston upholsterer, charged between three and four shillings per pound for feathers. The cost of some items of upholstered furniture would therefore be expensive. If a complete bed required sixty pounds of feathers, the charge would have exceeded ten pounds. When this is compared to the bed-frame cost of about three and a half pounds, the expense is put into perspective.[187]

A technical development, which was originally meant to stabilise the fillings, soon turned into a design feature. This method was tufting. The process used cords that were inserted through the thickness of the pad and held by a bunch of threads that stopped the cord being pulled through the pad, but held the fillings firm and level. This technique, introduced in England and America in the mid-eighteenth century, suited the flatter, squarer design of their chairs rather than the more fashionable domed squab seats favoured in France.

One of the most tantalising questions in eighteenth-century upholstery is that of springing. Commonly thought to have been a nineteenth-century innovation, there is evidence of earlier use. The initial demands for springs appear to have come from two sources. The first came from coach builders and the second from furniture-makers. Coach builders were seeking to improve the ride of vehicles as well as to improve upon the interior comfort of seats for the passengers. Most of their efforts were directed towards leaf springs which were generally unsuitable for transfer to upholstery.[188]

A patent was granted as far back as 1706 to a Henry Mills for springs to be used in coaches and chaises.[189] However, as Dorothy Holley (1981) has noted, there was no specific reference to the essential of an early upholstery spring, namely the coil, in this patent.[190] Further patents associated with springs were taken out during the course of the eighteenth century. In 1724 Thomas Rogers took out a patent for a steel-worm or rolling spring to be used in coaches etc.[191] A little later, in 1762, Richard Treadwell was granted a patent for an 'iron machine for moulding and setting all kinds of springs for hanging coaches'.[192] Treadwell also received five other patents relating to springing between 1759 and 1766. The first mention of spiral springs appears to be in a patent taken out in 1769 by a Joseph Jacob for the 'construction of wheel carriages, by application of united spiral springs, hoop wheels and leather boxes'.[193]

The connection between carriage springs and upholstery may seem tenuous but it should be remembered that blacksmiths produced metalwork for carriage-makers as well as cabinet-makers and upholsterers, so there would be an inevitable exchange of ideas across crafts.

Initially, furniture-makers' interest in spring technology seems to have been connected to making health-related items. The first known sprung furniture appears to be eighteenth-century chamber horses, designed for indoor exercise. Edward Pinto (1955) mentions examples and describes these sprung horses in some detail.[194] Pinto noted that the earliest reference to these objects appears to be 1739, when Henry Marsh of Clare Market advertised himself as the inventor of the chamber horse. Other examples quoted by Pinto included two chamber horses supplied to the Royal household of George III which were made with a 'mahogany frame and spring seats'.

It is not until Sheraton's *Drawing Book* that a contemporary source is able to give details of the making process.[195] Having outlined the construction particulars of the framing, Sheraton then gives a very clear description of the spring-making process: 'strong wire is twisted round a block in regular gradation, so that when the wire is compressed by the weight of those who exercise each turn of it may clear itself and fall within each other'. It is evident from this description and the illustration accompanying it that the springs were waisted-helical in shape. The springs were mounted onto wainscot boards and were effective as an exerciser but there was no intention of imparting comfort. Indeed, the top of the horse was simply a board upholstered with hair or similar material. The use of springs in chamber horses continued well into the nineteenth century with the 1823 edition of the *London Chair-maker's Book of Prices* listing the details of how to make a chamber horse and including the cost of 'turning the springs' for it.[196]

It can be inferred from this description of making chamber horses (above) that it is likely that the production of springs was often in the upholsterers' own hands. Indeed, there are examples of the Gillow factory quoting for chamber horses and estimating the quantity of wire required for making the springs.[197]

The English chamber horse was not the only example of the use of upholstery springing in the eighteenth century. In fact, the idea of introducing springs into seat upholstery may well have come from Germany. Some accounts propose that a German blacksmith was responsible for the invention of the coil spring and suggest that it was first used in making sprung bed bases.[198] Mattresses were indeed made with interior springs but it is difficult to show whether they preceded upholstered chairs or vice versa. Further examples come from Stengel (1958), a German historian, who noted the use of upholstery springing from the third quarter of the eighteenth century.[199] Stengel claims that he had located a reference to a spring sofa dated 13 November 1766. He also noted a chair-maker named Funke who advertised an upholstered sofa with carving, springs, and gilding. Further, Stengel noted a bill of 1772 for an upholstered chair with springs as part of the total costings.[200]

France can also claim some part in the early promotion of springs in upholstery. One of the first references to spring upholstery can be found in the *Memoirs of Mme Campan*.[201] Mme Campan was the friend of Louis XV's daughter, Mme Victoire. In a delightful sequence she describes how she first met the princess, and goes on to say how the princess showed her the 'bergère a ressorts' (a sprung chair) in which she was reclining. The story goes that the King's other daughter, Louise, decided to retire to a convent and Mme Campan begged Victoire not to follow suit. She replied: 'I would never have Louise's courage. I love life's comforts too much. Without this chair here I would be lost'. A classic sign of the demand for comfort that springs obviously satisfied. Although these two examples are based on European sources, they do indicate a knowledge of springing that surely must have been known in England.

Whilst fully upholstered furniture continued to be in favour throughout the century, another seating system suffered first a decline and then a revival in taste. An alternative to cloth upholstery and padding was the caning of chair frames for backs and seats. In England it was popular from the Restoration in 1666 until the 1730s. The success of the product can be witnessed by the development of the specialist cane chair maker; equally, the decline is witnessed by the extinction of the specialist trade. Later in the century it enjoyed a revival both in England and France especially in conjunction with japanned or painted finishes.[202]

Other materials

The use of marble or stone slabs as table tops (or sometimes for commodes) was a fluctuating fashion throughout the century. Initially, Italian exports were used in eighteenth-century interiors as slabs for

CHAMBER HORSE

21 Sheraton's illustration of the springing method for an exercise or chamber horse.

table and commode tops. Gilbert (1978) has suggested that most marble or scagliola slabs used for table tops would have been purchased from merchants, although clearly some owners purchased abroad and had the slabs fitted to a frame in England.[203]

Like other materials mentioned, marble was also subject to imitation. The cost of real marble, along with the need to be selective about the nature of the colours, led architects to call for an imitation version for their interiors. Scagliola was the answer. Of Roman origin, its manufacture was revived in the seventeenth century. It was made from a variety of recipes but was essentially finely ground plaster of Paris, isinglass, colouring matter and marble chips. According to Sir William Chambers, the best scagliola products in England were made by Richter and Bartoli of Newport Street. They do seem to have had a serious interest in the business, as John Richter took out a patent in 1770 for inlaying scagliola into marble or metals to imitate birds and flowers.[204]

With the establishment of reliable suppliers in London, its popularity apparently continued apace. Vincent Bellman started a manufactory in London in 1790, and in 1808 George Smith recommended its use in his *Household Furniture*.[205] Scagliola was essentially an imitative process and one of many that were developed in the eighteenth century.

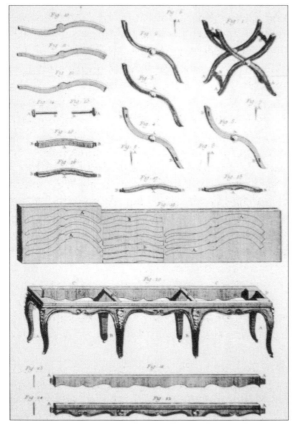

22 A cutting plan for the woodwork of a French upholstered bench.

Imitation processes

As has been noted above, the increasing demand for fashionable items, as well as the opportunity to emulate high styles in less expensive materials, led to a variety of attempts to provide imitative processes and materials.

One of the earliest was in Stalker and Parker's 1688 publication which offered a recipe on how to mould carved work for frames. Interestingly, they acknowledged it to be of no use to 'those persons who want frames [who] lived at London, or had any commerce with and conveyance from that City; because carved work is there done very cheap and well'.[206] Their plaster process was complicated and still required the use of tools to carve and shape the plaster, hence it offered little real savings in time or money.

Efforts to mechanise the carving process itself go back further than 1845 when Thomas Jordan patented his machine; indeed Jordan acknowledges this fact himself. According to the *Art Union Monthly Journal* (1848), one of the first machines to achieve true carving as its objective was invented by James Watt, in the latter part of the eighteenth century.[207] Sir David Brewster suggested that Watt wanted to patent his machine in conjunction with another inventor who had been working on the same idea. In the event, the idea was lost as Watt was unable to patent the invention because he was so concerned with improvements to the steam engine. However, it was alleged that there were some examples of the machine carving executed by Watt in his home at Heathfield Hall. Apparently, the important furnishing firm of Seddon purchased an example of Watt's copying (carving) machine in the 1780s.[208] This would appear to be a rare example of a large enterprise experimenting with savings in time and labour, which seems to have gone unnoticed by the rest of the trade.[209]

Even if mechanical carving was not a success, there were plenty of other attempts at introducing novel decorative processes. In 1638, William Billingsley patented a method of printing furniture with liquid gold and silver,[210] which appears to be the earliest attempt to register a process like this.

Over 100 years later in 1769, John Pickering developed a process of chasing cabinet-work in metals.[211] According to Hughes (1957), the cabinet-makers Seddon and Co. used Pickering's machine for stamping out parts.[212] Rather more exotic were three patented ideas which seem quite fanciful, but give an indication of a potential taste. In 1774 Joseph Jacob patented a method of furniture decoration using tin-foil, lead or pewter, beaten or rolled into sheets for application to cabinets and other articles.[213] Twelve years later, Thomas Rogers, a glass cutter, patented a process using coloured, stained and clear glass to produce decorations for furniture and looking glasses.[214] That year also introduced a patentee named John Skidmore, who devised a process for ornamenting furniture with 'foil stones, Bristol stones, paste and all sorts of pinched glass, and every other stone glass and composition used in, or applicable to, the jewellery trade'.[215]

All these examples indicate an interest in devising methods of producing decoration that supplied magnificent decorative effects easily; whether any of the processes were commercially successful is unknown.

The archetypal imitative material that was used in the eighteenth century was papier mâché. The origins of papier mâché can be traced to India, and other parts of the Orient. But the earliest mention of the material in England is in Robert Boyle's essay, *Of Man's Great Ignorance of the Uses of Natural Things* published in 1672.[216] In this work Boyle refers to the use of papier mâché as suitable for 'frames of pictures and divers pieces of embossed work and other curious movables'. In 1693 a patent was taken out for a similar material: 'making a composition with wood to run liquid into moulds; useful for beautifying rooms and embellishing cabinets'.[217] However, there is little evidence that either papier mâché or artificial wood was much used before the mid-eighteenth century. In 1749 William Duffour of Soho claimed to be the original maker of papier mâché, and Pat Kirkham (1988) has suggested that his French surname may give some credence to the suggestion that the craft of papier mâché manufacture in Europe was first established in France.[218] Other evidence also supports this assertion. Eighteenth-century commentators like Robert Dossie, in his work *The Handmaid to the Arts* of 1758, refer to French snuff boxes made from papier mâché, and in 1763, Peter Babel a papier mâché worker, refers to his raw material as 'an invention of modern date, imported by us from France and now brought to great perfection'.[219]

The person credited with producing papier mâché goods, including furniture, on a commercial scale in England is Henry Clay. Clay was an apprentice of John Baskerville, a famous paper-maker and japanner from Birmingham. In 1772 Clay took out a patent for making in paper 'high varnished panels, for rooms, doors, cabins of ships, cabinets, bookcases, screens, chimney-pieces, tables etc. . .'.[220] The fashionable acceptance of Clay's work can be seen in the *Description of Strawberry Hill* published in 1784. It specifically mentions a Clay-ware table, highly varnished with a Gothic design by Paul Sandby, and also a 'Tea-chest of Clay-ware painted with loose feathers'.[221] His success can also be gauged by a fascinating description written in 1791 by the traveller Edward Clarke which gives a clear impression of the manufacturing process employed by Clay:

> A number of sheets of paper are pasted together and dried; they are then carried into a room, resembling a little timber yard, contiguous to which is a very large workshop: cabinet-makers form every article as it is required, sawing it out of paper and planing it with the greatest exactness. It is then japanned and polished and this is always done by hand.[222]

Both the Strawberry Hill items and the description above show that furniture had a long association with the repertoire of the japanner's trade, and it was not a Victorian invention. However, the cyclical nature of the business is indicated by the suggestion that at one time Clay was alleged to have employed 300 hands but by 1802 the number had diminished to less than 100.[223] Whereas Clay's process was mainly concerned with making japanned paper panels and finished furniture items, the patent of John Pickering (1773) was designed to make ornaments with paper that resembled wood carvings suitable for fixing to furniture,[224] another example of specialist sub-contractors planning to make ready-made parts for the trade.

The growing range of choices in materials, as well as developments in the processing of them, meant that the trade was able to meet the burgeoning consumer demand for variety, choice and style. Although the pressure for these changes came from the consumer, by careful selection of materials, increasing control over techniques and a handle on the management, marketing and economics of a business, the furniture-maker of the eighteenth century was well placed to handle the demands made upon him.

Notes

1 R. Benhamou, 'Imitation in the decorative arts of the eighteenth century', *Journal of Design History*, IV (1991), pp. 1–14.

2 For example, the patent by John Richter, No. 978, 28 December 1770, whose subject was the 'art or method of inlaying scagliola or plaster upon marble and metals to imitate flowers, birds, etc.'.

3 Quoted in P. Welsh, *Woodworking Tools 1600–1900, Contributions from the Museum of History and Technology, United States National Museum Bulletin,* No. 241 (Smithsonian Institution, 1966), p. 183. It should be noted that through much of the eighteenth century there was a fascination with the techniques and tools of trades generally and many encyclopedias give comprehensive details on the tools used. For example, D. Diderot, *Dictionaire raisonne des sciences des arts et des metiers, 1751–1772* (1793). J. Moxon, *Mechaniks Exercises or the Doctrine of Handy Works etc.* (1677) (Praeger reprint, 1970); A. C. Roubo, *L'Art de Menuisier* (Paris, 1772).

4 Inventory of William Howell, quoted in B. Forman, *American Seating Furniture, 1630–1730* (New York, Norton, 1988), p. 49. The reference to finering (veneering), the use of weights to hold veneers, and the polishing equipment (skins and wax), all point to the conclusion.

5 See J. M. A. Gaynor and N. L. Hagedorn, *Tools Working Wood in Eighteenth-Century America* (Colonial Williamsburg, 1993).

6 The well-known case of Chippendale employees' loss of tools through fire is a case in point. See C. Gilbert, *The Life and Work of Thomas Chippendale* (London, Macmillan, 1978), pp. 10–11.

7 C. Williams (trans.), *Sophie in London* [1786] (London, Cape, 1933), p. 175.

8 Huntsman set up a steel works in Sheffield, which used the crucible process to burn away impurities and produce a fine steel ideal for edge tools.

9 This term seems to have been coined by P. McQuoid who published *The Age of Mahogany* [1906] (reprinted, Woodbridge, Antique Collectors Club, 1987).

10 For further discussion on the eighteenth-century timber trade see John Cross, 'The changing role of the timber merchant in early eighteenth century London', *Furniture History*, XXX (1994).

11 R. Campbell, *The London Tradesmen*, [1747] (Newton Abbot, David and Charles, 1969) p. 167.

12 P. Kirkham, 'Samuel Norman, a study of an eighteenth-century craftsman', *The Burlington Magazine*, CXI, pp. 500–11 (August 1969), Appendix, p. 506.

13 W. T. Whitley, *Artists and their Friends in England 1700–1799* (1928), Vol II, pp. 262–3, quoted in R. Fastnedge, *Sheraton Furniture* (London, Faber, 1962), p. 40.

14 T. Sheraton, *The Cabinet Dictionary* (London, 1803), p. 117. The 'pressing necessities' being financial pressures.

15 J. C. Loudon, *Arboretum and Fruticetum Britannicum* (London, Longman, 1844), vol. II, p. 1426.

16 I gratefully acknowledge Adam Bowett and his work on timbers of the period. See his 'The commercial introduction of mahogany and the Naval Stores Act of 1721', *Furniture History*, xxx (1994). Bowett points out that even the punitive 50 per cent duty on French walnut did not stop the trade in this timber. According to Loudon the Dutch bought as much walnut as they could and profited by the scarcity and rising prices.

17 *Ibid.*

18 Sheraton quotes sizes of Honduras mahogany boards as being up to 14 feet in length and on average 2 to 4 feet wide. *Cabinet Dictionary*, p. 254.

19 P. and M. Nicholson, *Practical Cabinet-maker and Upholsterer* (London, 1826).

20 Thomas Wharton, *Poems on Several Occasions*, 1748, quoted in R. W. Symonds, *Furniture-making in Seventeenth- and Eighteenth-Century England* (London, Connoisseur, 1955).

21 D. Learmont, 'The Trinity house chairs, Aberdeen', *Furniture History*, xiv (1978).

22 Quoted by B. Latham, *Timber. A Historical Survey of its Development and Distribution* (London, Harrap, 1957), p. 156.

23 *Ibid.*

24 8, Geo. 1, c. 12, See E. Joy, *The Connoisseur's Complete Period Guides* (London, Connoisseur, 1968), p. 582. Also see Bowett, 'Commercial introduction of mahogany'.

25 These figures are from Bowett and from Joy (1968).

26 11, Geo. 111, c. 41.

27 The main reasons for abolishing import duties on mahogany and other timbers from the Colonies were economic. Prior to this change it was not viable to import timbers which were bulky, relatively light and were subject to duty at a rate of 20 per cent. By abolishing the duty, the Government enabled a return trade from the West Indies that had an element of profit in it for the shipper. This whole matter is explained in Bowett, 'Commercial introduction of mahogany'.

28 Joy, *Connoisseur's Complete Period Guides*, p. 825.

29 The principal kinds of mahogany in use by cabinet-makers at the end

of the century according to Sheraton, *Cabinet Dictionary*, p. 254. The usefulness of this sort of classification is open to debate.

30 J. Gloag, *A Social History of Furniture Design* (London, Cassell, 1966). The Oxford English Dictionary suggests a date of 1840. See also Sheraton, *Cabinet Dictionary*, p. 184.

31 Bowett has suggested that mahogany became a 'levelling agent' in terms of furniture design and making. Once timber imports through the provincial ports grew to a sufficient level, and when they were combined with the re-distribution of timber via London, the provincial cabinet-maker had the same standard of timber at roughly the same price as London makers. This meant that with equality of material, this benefit only needed to be matched with similar standards of design to level the field.

32 Forman, *American Seating Furniture*, p. 31.

33 Sheraton, *Cabinet Dictionary*, p 331.

34 J. Evelyn, *Sylva, a Discourse of Forest Trees* (1776 edition), quoted in R. Luff, 'The craftsmanship of English walnut furniture', *Antique Collector* (June/July 1972), p. 151.

35 Also known as yellow wood and recognised since the seventeenth century. See F. L. Hinckley, *Directory of Historic Cabinet Woods* (New York, Crown, 1960).

36 Sheraton, *Cabinet Dictionary*, p. 314.

37 *Ibid*.

38 For examples and analysis of carcase construction and substrate material see L. Wood, *The Lady Lever Art Gallery Catalogue of Commodes* (London, HMSO, 1994).

39 *The Book of Trades or Library of Useful Arts* (London, 1804), p. 49.

40 W. Marshall, 'Planting and rural ornament' (1796), quoted in Symonds, *Furniture-making in Seventeenth- and Eighteenth-Century England*, p. 31.

41 These would include for example, Sabicu, Thuya, Sycamore, Tulipwood, Holly, Yew, Kingwood. Refer to Hinckley, *Directory of Historic Cabinet Woods*, and J. Gloag, *Dictionary of Furniture*, for further details.

42 For this topic see W. Linnard, 'Sweat and sawdust, pit-sawing in Wales', *Folk Life*, xx (1981–2), pp. 41–55.

43 The resulting kerfs were parallel and straight but slightly angled. They often show variety in their depth and angle and are therefore evidence of the process used.

44 See B. Forman, 'Mill-sawing in seventeenth-century Massachusetts', *Old Time New England*, LX (Spring 1970), pp. 110–30.

45 Sheraton, *Cabinet Dictionary*, p. 62.

46 Hugh Bullock, Patent No. 45, 2 January 1629. The main interest in new timber conversion techniques came from ship-builders rather than

cabinet makers, but the latter benefited from the technology spin-off. This benefit process has been a feature of the furniture business ever since.

47 John Booth, Patent No. 230, 27 November 1683.
48 George Sorocold, Patent No. 369, 1 January 1703.
49 P. Legg, 'The Bastards of Blandford', *Furniture History*, xxx, 1994.
50 Samuel Miller, Patent No. 1152, 11 April 1777.
51 W. Sims, *200 years of History and Evolution of Woodworking Machinery* (Burton Lazars, Walders Press, 1985), p. 3.
52 P. d'A. Jones and E. N. Simons, *The Story of the Saw* (Newman Neame for Spear and Jackson, 1961), p. 42.
53 Latham, *Timber. A Historical Survey*, p. 210.
54 At that time Inspector General of Naval Works.
55 M. Brunel, Patent No. 2844, 7 May 1805.
56 Williams (trans.), *Sophie in London*, p. 175.
57 Patent No. 427, April 1720.
58 R. Neve, *The City and Country Purchaser's and Builder's Dictionary* (1726) (reprint, Newton Abbot, David and Charles, 1969), p. 260. The latter method was known to the Romans.
59 T. Sheraton, *The Cabinet-maker and Upholsterer's Drawing Book* (1793).
60 For details of the many sorts and their uses see, R. A. Salaman, *Dictionary of Tools used in the Woodworking and Allied Trades 1700–1970* (London, Unwin Hyman, 1975).
61 Patent No. 1125, 21 May 1776. An engine for planing boards and fluting wood for columns.
62 I. McNeill, *Joseph Bramah, a Century of Invention, 1749–1851* (Newton Abbot, David and Charles, 1968).
63 Sheraton, *Cabinet Dictionary*, p. 46
64 G. B. Hughes, 'Windsor chairs in palace and cottage,' *Country Life*, cxxxi (24 May 1962), pp. 1242–3.
65 John Cumberland, Patent No. 427, 14 April 1720.
66 John Vidler, Patent No. 2020, 5 November 1794.
67 In cabinet-making terms these weights and balances are related to cauls.
68 The distinction between the various types can be simplified by saying that parallel grains produce laminations, cross grains make 'plywood'.
69 Samuel Bentham, Patent No. 1951, 23 April 1793.
70 P. Kane, 'Samuel Gragg: his bentwood fancy chairs', *Yale University Art Gallery Bulletin*, xxxiii, No. 2 (Autumn 1971), p. 31
71 Derek Ostergard has suggested that in at least one example, there may be evidence of early plywood being used in this form of furniture. He cites a pair of candlesticks that have a distinctive light-dark pattern in

the five laminates used. See D. Ostergard (ed.), *Bentwood and Metal Furniture 1850–1946* (University of Washington Press, 1987), p. 15.

72 For background and history see R. Champness, *The Worshipful Company of Turners of London* (London, Lindley-Jones and Brother Ltd, 1966).

73 Kirkham, 'Samuel Norman', p. 506.

74 Salaman, *Dictionary of Tools*, p. 489.

75 The term 'bodger' has unfortunate connotations and many possible derivations. In this instance I tend to favour the one that describes the bodger as one who makes part of an object; to be exact, it describes a person who prepares turned parts for the chair-maker to assemble.

76 See J. L. Mayes, *History of Chair-making in High Wycombe* (London, Routledge, 1960).

77 For plane-makers see W. L. Goodman, *British Plane-makers from 1700*, 3rd edn, 1993 (Roy Arnold, Needham Market, 1993).

78 Salaman, *Dictionary of Tools*, pp. 238–42.

79 This may have been exceptional but 40 or more seems to have been quite common. If a mixed selection of mouldings are used the variations are enormous. See C. Humell in P. Kebabian and W. Lipke, *Tools and Technologies: America's Wooden Age* (Vermont, University Press, 1979), p. 49–50.

80 Diderot, *Dictionnaire*, Ebenisterie-Marqueterie, plate IX.

81 T. Hope, *Household Furniture* (London, 1807), p. 5.

82 For the history of the nineteenth-century furniture trade and its methods see C. Edwards, *Victorian Furniture* (Manchester, Manchester University Press, 1993).

83 See C. Gilbert and T. Murdoch, *John Channon and Brass-inlaid Furniture, 1730–1760* (New Haven and London, Yale University Press, 1993), p. 54, for a brief discussion of the continental influence that many have encouraged this method of drawer-making.

84 Wood, *Catalogue of Commodes*, which refers to reciprocal rebates, dovetails, tenons, dowelling, and tongue and groove joints all variously used to fix tops.

85 Sheraton, *Cabinet Dictionary*, p. 117.

86 W. B. Gusler, 'Variations in eighteenth-century casework', *Fine Woodworking*, XXIII (July/August 1980), pp. 50–3. An example of a customer complaint might be the 'walnut tree chairs [which] were made of rotten worm eaten wood the holes filled up with saw dust and glue . . .' 1753, S. Pryke 'The extraordinary billhead of Francis Brodie', *Regional Furniture*, IV (1990), p. 87.

87 Information from Philip Astley Jones of Hatfields Ltd.

88 See B. Hewitt, P. Kane and G. Ward, *The Work of Many Hands, Card*

Tables in Federal America 1790–1820 (New Haven, Yale University Press, 1982).

89 C. Streeter, 'Marquetry tables from Cobb's workshop', *Furniture History*, x (1974).

90 Sheraton, *Drawing Book* (1793), Appendix, p. 17. The similarity to blockboards is noticeable.

91 *Ibid.*, p. 356.

92 *Ibid.*, p. 358.

93 *Ibid.*, p. 383.

94 *Ibid.*, Appendix p. 19.

95 *Ibid.*, p. 404.

96 Ostergard, *Bent Wood and Metal Furniture*, p. 19.

97 G. H Himmelheber 'The craftsmanship of David Roentgen', *Connoisseur* (September 1976), pp. 17–21.

98 A. Coleridge, *Chippendale Furniture* (London, Faber, 1968) p. 159.

99 Sara Jerom and William Webb, Patent No. 87, 31 October 1635. Oddly Sara Jerom took out another patent in 1638 for a similar machine.

100 See Diderot, *Dictionnaire*, for illustration of the process in a French workshop *c.* 1770.

101 W. Chambers, *Cyclopaedia or Universal Dictionary of Arts and Sciences* (London, 1728), p. 291. Go-bars were still in use in woodworking workshops until at least the 1970s.

102 A caul was a solid wooden shape made to fit the piece being made. Once heated and greased it was applied to the veneer so that the heat and pressure would bind the veneer and substrate together. Were they indicative of a batch production process?

103 Sheraton, *Cabinet Dictionary*, p. 328.

104 G. Wilson, 'Boulle', *Furniture History*, vIII, 1972.

105 *Ibid.*

106 R. H. Randall, 'Templates for Boulle singerie', *The Burlington Magazine*, cxI (September 1969), pp. 549–53. Two printed templates the full size of a table top are preserved in Boston.

107 Nicholson, *Practical Cabinet-maker*.

108 J. Stalker and G. Parker, *A Treatise of Japanning and Varnishing* (1688), pp. 81–2.

109 Lye is a strong alkaline solution, achieved by percolation through vegetable ashes.

110 Litharge is a red crystalline form of lead monoxide.

111 Benhamou, 'Imitation in the decorative arts', p. 7

112 *Ibid.*

113 R. Edwards and M. Jourdain, *Georgian Cabinet-makers c. 1700–1800* (London, Country Life, 1955), p. 91. See also J. Ward, 'The work of

Coxed and Woster in Mulberry wood and Burr Elm', *Apollo*, LV (November 1941), pp. 104–6.

114 For example, Frederick Hintz, see Edwards and Jourdain, *Georgian Cabinet-makers*, p. 100. See also Gilbert and Murdoch, *John Channon*, pp. 2–9 and passim.

115 Described in some detail in R. Edwards, *The Shorter Dictionary of English Furniture* (London, Country Life, 1964).

116 Diderot's *Dictionnaire* mentions *anes* (donkeys) as part of the marqueteur's tools. These are simply small seat-benches with the same holding method as Chambers described in the 1720s, and marqueteurs still use this method.

117 See P. Kirkham, *The London Furniture Trade, 1700–1870* (Furniture History Society, 1988), pp. 17–18, especially footnote 87.

118 For further descriptions of these dyes and stains see Gloag, *Dictionary of Furniture* and S. New, 'The use of stains by furniture-makers 1660–1850', *Furniture History*, XVII (1981).

119 For a discussion of the various stains used in the eighteenth century see New, 'The use of stains'. See also R. D. Mussey, 'Old finishes and early varnishes', Fine Woodworking Techniques 6, *Fine Woodworking* (March/April 1982), pp. 71–5.

120 Stalker and Parker, *Treatise of Japanning*, p. 18.

121 Neve, *City and Country Purchaser's and Builder's Dictionary*, p. 262.

122 J. Barrow, *Dictionarium Polygraphicum* (London, 1758), vol II, p. 350, and see Chambers, *Cyclopaedia*, p. 291.

123 Sheraton, *Cabinet Dictionary* (1803), p. 289.

124 See chapter 5. Patina is now considered a valuable asset to any old furniture.

125 C. Gilbert, *English Vernacular Furniture, 1750–1900* (New Haven and London, Yale University Press, 1991), p. 18.

126 Sheraton, *Cabinet Dictionary*, p. 289.

127 F. de la Rochfoucauld (S. C. Roberts trans.), *A Frenchman in England 1784* (Cambridge, Cambridge University Press, 1933), cited in Gloag, *Dictionary of Furniture*, p. 530.

128 Some fish skins have derma-dentils which are on the skin: they act like tiny teeth and abrade the wooden surface.

129 Kirkham, 'Samuel Norman', Appendix, p. 508. Rubstone is a stone used for rubbing or sharpening.

130 H. Huth, *Lacquer of the West. The History of a Craft and Industry, 1550–1950* (Chicago, 1971).

131 The well-known publication, *A Treatise of Japanning and Varnishing* by Stalker and Parker was published in 1688.

132 *Lacquer: an International History and Collector's Guide* (London, Bracken Books, 1989), p. 181.

133 Edwards, *Dictionary*, p. 328.

134 Quoted in J. Whitehead, *The French Interior in the Eighteenth Century* (London, Laurence King, 1992), p. 192.

135 Benhamou, 'Imitation in the decorative arts', p. 9.

136 R. Dossie (1758), quoted in Edwards, *Shorter Dictionary*, p. 327.

137 C. Plumier, *The Art of Turning*, quoted by Benhamou, 'Imitation in the decorative arts'.

138 Linnell and the Badminton bed, and Chippendale and the Nostell Priory commission, are two well-documented products.

139 A. Heal, *The London Furniture-makers, from the Restoration to the Victorian Era 1660–1840* (London, Batsford, 1953).

140 A. Hepplewhite and Co., *The Cabinet-maker and Upholsterer's Guide* (1788).

141 Huth, *Lacquer of the West*, p. 174.

142 See Wood, *Catalogue of Commodes*, No. 30, a commode with painted copper top.

143 See M. Hecksher and Frances Gruber Safford, 'Boston japanned furniture in the Metropolitan Museum of Art', *The Magazine Antiques*, CXXIX (May 1986), pp. 1047–59.

144 The business of Thomas Johnson in Boston supplied engravings, paintings and japanned work. Sheraton's *Cabinet Dictionary* discusses japanning under a general topic title of Painting.

145 See examples in Gilbert, *English Vernacular Furniture*. For other painted furniture see C. Kinmonth, *Irish Vernacular Furniture 1700–1950* (New Haven and London, Yale University Press, 1993). For American furniture see D. Fales, *American Painted Furniture, 1660–1880* (New York, Dutton, 1972).

146 Campbell, *London Tradesmen*, p. 108.

147 For full technical descriptions see Stalker, and Parker, *Treatise of Japanning*, and Sheraton, *Cabinet Dictionary*, who devotes ten pages to the topic.

148 Sheraton, *Cabinet Dictionary*, p. 227.

149 Bole is a clay-like substance (hydrous aluminium silicate) that varies in colour and composition depending on its origin. It is available in red, blue or yellow tones which are used for particular effects.

150 According to Edwards, *Shorter Dictionary*, there is evidence that by 1690 the trade was distinct, for in the *London Gazette* [359/4] a Charles Mansell is listed as a castor-maker.

151 See Sheraton, *Cabinet Dictionary*, pp. 138–9.

152 Gilbert and Murdoch, *John Channon*.

153 *Ibid.*

154 Campbell, *London Tradesmen*, p. 144.

155 Williams (trans.), *Sophie in London*, p. 173. An example of the specialist worker might be William Miers of the Strand who from 1802 traded as an 'Ormolu worker and miniature frame maker', Heal, *London Furniture-makers*, p. 117.

156 See Goodison, 'The V & A metalwork pattern books', *Furniture History*, XI (1975).

157 John Pickering, Patent No. 920, 7 March 1769; Joseph Jacob Junior, Patent No. 1065, 14 February 1774; John Marston and Samuel Bellamy, Patent No. 1165, 1 August 1777.

158 See Goodison, *Ormolu, the Work of Matthew Boulton* (London, Phaidon, 1974), p. 65. For the distinction between French mercury gilt-bronze and English ormolu alloy see P. Hunter-Steibel, 'Exalted hardware the bronze mounts of French furniture', *Antiques*, CXXVII (January 1985), pp. 236–45.

159 For a broad discussion of screws see R. C. Brooks, 'Origins, usage and production of screws: an historical perspective', *History and Technology*, VIII (1990), pp. 51–76.

160 The firm of John Bastard of Blandford, Dorset, listed three gross of wood screws in his 1731 inventory and it is noticeable that they also had a smith's shop on their premises, Legg, 'Bastards of Blandford', p. 31.

161 J. and W. Wyatt, Patent No. 751, 1760.

162 The modern gimlet-point screw dates from *c.* 1851.

163 Kirkham, 'Samuel Norman', Appendix, p. 508. Nails were however available in far greater quantities.

164 Day Gunby, Patent No. 2248, 6 July 1798.

165 See 'G. Hughes, Day Gunby's Patent Furniture', *Country Life* (21 February 1957), pp. 330–1.

166 See for example rising tables, harlequin tables, dining tables, travelling items and cabinets with secret compartments, etc.

167 R. Stratmann, 'Design and mechanisms in the furniture of Jean-François Oeben', *Furniture History*, IX (1973), pp. 110–13.

168 Himmelheber, 'The Craftsmanship of David Roentgen', pp. 17–21.

169 For mirrors see G. Wills, *English Looking Glasses: a Study of Glasses, Frames and Makers, 1672–1820* (1965); S. Roche, G. Courage, P. Devinoy, *Mirrors* (Paris, 1956; London, 1985).

170 This tin-mercury process stuck thin tinfoil onto the glass by using a mercury medium. For details see Per Hadsund, 'The tin-mercury mirror: its manufacturing technique and deterioration process', *Studies in Conservation*, XXXVIII (1993), pp. 3–16.

171 In comparison the crown process produced circular sheets which were too thin for grinding.

172 R. W. Symonds, 'English Looking glass plates and their manufacture', *Connoisseur*, May 1936, pp. 243–9, and July 1936, pp. 9–15.

173 Quoted in B. Schweig, *Mirrors* (London, Pelham Books, 1973), p. 22.

174 For a overview of this history see P. Thornton, *Seventeenth-Century Decoration in England France and Holland* (New Haven, Yale University Press, 1978), pp. 74–80.

175 Collyer, *The Parent's and Guardian's Directory and the Youth's Guide in the Choice of a Profession or Trade* (London, 1761), pp. 57, 149.

176 Symonds, *Furniture Making in Seventeenth- and Eighteenth-Century England*, p. 155. Heal notes that Welch advertised himself as a glass-grinder and looking glass maker in Blackfriars.

177 Campbell *London Tradesmen*, p. 174.

178 Heal *The London Furniture-makers*, pp. 32, 40.

179 Gilbert, *Chippendale*, p. 44.

180 This attitude, along with the certain profitability of glass-making, encouraged the establishment of the British Cast Plate Glass Co. in St Helens during the second half of the eighteenth century.

181 Sheraton *Cabinet Dictionary* (1803), p. 230.

182 L. Weatherill, *Consumer Behaviour and Material Culture in Britain, 1660–1760* (London, Routledge, 1988).

183 Barrows, *Dictionarium Polygraphicum*, pp. 50–2.

184 Forman, *American Seating Furniture*, p. 207.

185 P. Thornton, *Authentic Decor. The Domestic Interior 1620–1920* (London, Weidenfeld & Nicolson, 1984), p. 155.

186 E. Joy, 'The overseas trade in furniture in the eighteenth century', *Furniture History*, I, 1965.

187 B. Jobe, 'The Boston upholstery trade', in E. Cooke (ed.), *Upholstery in America and Europe from the Seventeenth Century to World War I* (New York, Norton, 1987), p. 71.

188 But see S. Giedion. *Mechanisation Takes Command* (New York, Oxford University Press, 1948), pp. 401–2, where he describes and illustrates a patent rocking chair which used wagon leaf springs and is defined as a health vehicle.

189 Henry Mills, Patent No. 376, 12 April 1706.

190 D. Holley 'Upholstery springs', *Furniture History*, XVII (1981).

191 Thomas Rogers, Patent No. 470, 24 October 1724.

192 Richard Treadwell, Patent No. 768, 1762.

193 Joseph Jacob, Patent No. 932, 13 July 1769.

194 E. Pinto, 'The Georgian Chamber Horse', *Country Life* (20 October 1955), p. 846.

195 Sheraton, *Drawing Book.*
196 *London Chair-makers' Book of Prices* (1823), p. 68.
197 Holley, 'Upholstery springs'.
198 J. Deville, *Dictionaire du Tapissier de L'Ameublement Français* (Paris, 1878–80), p. 179.
199 W. Stengel, *Alte Wohnkultur in Berlin und der Mark im Spiegel der Quellen des 16–19 Jahrhunderts*, quoted in Thornton, *Authentic Decor*, p. 102.
200 Quoted in Thornton, 'Upholstered seat furniture in Europe, seventeenth and eighteenth Centuries' in Cooke (ed.), *Upholstery in America and Europe*, p. 38 n. 11.
201 H. Havard, *Dictionnaire de l'Ameublement et de la Decoration* (Paris, 1890–94) p. 326.
202 For details see A. C. Roubo, *L'Art Menuisier* in Forman, *American Seating Furniture*, p. 373–9 [translation].
203 Gilbert, *Chippendale*, p. 46. Although the workshops of Linnell held such slabs in stock: see H. Hayward and P. Kirkham, *William and John Linnell, Eighteenth-Century London Furniture-makers* (London, Studio Vista, 1980), p. 51.
204 John Richter, Patent No. 978, 28 December 1770.
205 Edwards, *Shorter Dictionary.*
206 Stalker and Parker, *Treatise of Japanning*, p. 61.
207 'On the applications of Science to the fine and useful arts', *Art Union Monthly Journal* (1848).
208 G. Hughes, 'George Seddon of London House', *Apollo*, LXV (1957), pp. 177–81.
209 A carving machine would have been beneficial to a large organisation such as Seddon. Even in the 1760s a business like the Linnell's had twenty-four plaster heads and thirty-three assorted busts in the carving shop. Kirkham and Hayward, *William and John Linnell*, p. 48.
210 William Billingsley, Patent No. 121, 10 December 1638.
211 John Pickering, Patent No. 920, 7 March 1769.
212 Hughes, 'George Seddon', pp. 177–81.
213 Joseph Jacob, Patent No. 1065, 14 February 1774.
214 Thomas Rogers, Patent No. 1568, 7 November 1786.
215 John Skidmore, Patent No. 1552, 5 August 1786.
216 Quoted in McQuoid and Edwards, *Dictionary of English Furniture*, vol. 3, p. 24.
217 Marshall Smith and Thomas Puckle, Patent No. 317, 7 March 1693. An artificial wood was again patented in 1772 by William Whitlock and William Hodgson, Patent No. 1011.
218 Kirkham, *London Furniture Trade*, p. 117.

219 Mcquoid and Edwards, *Dictionary of English Furniture*, p. 14.
220 Henry Clay, Patent No. 1027, 1772. Also another patent on 20 November 1792, No. 1918.
221 Quoted by McQuoid and Edwards, *Dictionary of English Furniture*, p. 14.
222 E. Clarke, *A Tour Through the South of England, Wales and Parts of Ireland Made During the Summer of 1791* (London, 1793).
223 W. Aitken, 'Papier mâché manufacture' in S. Timmins (ed.), *Birmingham Resources and Industrial History* (1866), p. 567.
224 John Pickering, Patent No. 1058, 20 December 1773.

4   Design and design processes

Initially, design may be referred to in two ways. On one level, design may be said to represent a system of taste that a society, or part thereof, has embraced to define its own aims; on another level, it might be simply a self-conscious device used by a crafts-person to attain a particular end. In the eighteenth century both roles were considered to be invaluable as Diderot (1748) explained:

> Design is not only of interest to the architect, for under this name in general is comprehended form [and] ornament . . . It ought to enter into the place of all education; for men of the first order, in order to acquire taste, of which design is the soul; for all well-born men for their personal use, and for artisans in order that they may advance and distinguish themselves in their professions.[1]

The pattern books published by furniture designers and others in the second half of the century clearly show this dual appeal. The title of Chippendale's work, *The Gentleman and Cabinet-maker's Director* (1754), could not define his intended audience more clearly.

In addition to Diderot's definition, design also represented three other factors which need to be recognised.[2] First, it was a tool to assist economic prosperity, in an attempt to equal the success of foreign makers of decorative arts and also to meet the demand for an ever-growing range of differentiated products at home. Second, design represented an aspect of the intellectual environment of the time which embraced a national consciousness, a feeling of the dawning of a new age guided by persons of taste and sensibility. This was combined with an intellectual interest in methods of production, as well as an understanding that design, being an analytical and problem-solving skill, related well to the rational thinking of the time. Third, the multitude of published designs was an outward symbol of the extraordinary growth in printed visual sources for commercial and private use.

From any point of view, the first of these roles was crucially important to a trading nation such as Britain. In Robert Dossie's *The Handmaid to the Arts*, 1758 (which was dedicated to the Society for the Encouragement of Arts, Manufactures and Commerce), the preface clearly states the mercantile design perspective:

> that the national improvement of skill and taste in the execution of works of design is a matter of great importance to any country, not only on account of the honour which is derived to civilised nations by excelling in the polite arts, but likewise of the commercial advantages resulting from it.[3]

The 'commercial advantages' of design no doubt referred to the potential results that would accrue from dislodging France from its role as taste arbiter of Europe. Dossie saw that French superiority lay in the organisation of design within that country:

> It must be with regret therefore we see that the French have got greatly the start of us in this very material pursuit [cultivating trade in tasteful goods] and that the encouragement given by the Government, together with the opportunities afforded by a well-intentioned academy has diffused such a judgement and taste in design among all classes of the artisans as to render France at this time the source of nearly all inventions of fashions.[4]

Although academies and design schools had been established in England prior to Dossie's writing, it seems that their influence was limited, certainly in the first half of the century. Successful products required quality designers, therefore the need to train was linked to the establishment of schools which specialised in this area. In 1735 Bishop Berkeley considered 'whether France and Flanders could have drawn so much money from England for figured silks, lace and tapestry, if they had not had academies for designing?'.[5] The same thought could just as well refer to furniture. Thirty years later a similar sentiment was being expressed by William Sleater. In 1767, he pointed out the value of training designers.

> Silks, Tapestries, Velvets, Carpets, Carving, Gilding, Gardening, and Architecture owe the greatest part of their price to one branch or other of design. Nay, it gives value even to toys. We see what sums the French extract from this article. Now tho' few could excel as liberal Artists, yet they might influence the form and fashion in some of the above works.[6]

This acknowledgement that England might be better at producing artisan/designers, rather than artists, had important implications. While France was the acknowledged supplier of artistic luxury goods, England was becoming well-known for its range of tasteful, practical goods which were popular in both Europe and North America, as the Weimar *Journal des Luxes und der Moden* (1786), explained:

> English furniture is almost without exception solid and practical; French furniture is less solid, more contrived and more ostentatious. England will undoubtedly maintain its position of dictating taste in this sphere for a long time to come.[7]

The spread of an anglicised taste in furniture was also aided by the publication of English pattern books abroad. French was the international language of polite society so it is not surprising to find, for example, Ince and Mayhew's *Universal System* (1759–62), Chippendale's *Director* (1754), and Adam's *Works in Architecture* (1778) all published with editions in French, or supplied with sub-titles.

However, before looking at the furniture pattern books in detail, some other aspects of eighteenth-century furniture design need to be discussed.

Nature of design

Alongside the changes in the character of design already mentioned, other developments were taking place. The growth in demand, and the need for techniques that began to ensure some regularity and standardisation, became part of the remit of the designer. David Pye (1968) has suggested that developments in craftsmanship and tool use are reflected in a change from items whose end results illustrate the risks attendant on hand-working, to those items that can be produced with varying degrees of certainty as to the final results.[8] The changes, although affecting workmanship in the main, clearly had a bearing on design. For example, to establish regularity and control in high-style furniture, the use of measured drawings, templates and models etc., were essential to achieve uniformity. This meant that these design tools would assist in achieving a more certain result. In contrast to the use of design as a control mechanism was the well-established system of the workmanship of habit and its attendant risks.

Originally, the maker was a design adapter, a craftsman who did not and often could not draw his plans, nor could he give reasons for his design decisions. The form of a craft-based object was often modified by many failures and successes in a sequential way. The weakness of this process was that usually only one change at a time was developed, rather than taking the opportunity to review the whole process. Thus the object was a cumulative store of information that became the form itself, made from existing patterns, memories, etc.[9] It could be argued that this process developed a category of 'type forms' long before the idea was consciously formulated in the early twentieth century.

This unselfconscious tradition, which continued through the eighteenth century, is best exemplified by vernacular cabinet and chair-making. The process was one of gradual adjustment which either took high-style developments and adapted them to their known tradition, or developed models from simple origins. Examples might include the making of bureau bookcases in a once fashionable shape but using solid oak rather than veneered walnut or mahogany, or in the latter case, the development of the vernacular Windsor chair from simple stools.

With the tendency towards conscious design, the planning process was based on a wider perceptual span and was combined with a 'formal language' of arrangement which could result in objects (and their divided parts) being easily represented.[10] This seemed to require some specific training in comprehending the formal language as well as being able to take an overview of a project. Many pattern books and manuals addressed this by providing sections on patterns and draughting techniques. However, the essence of these developments was that the separation of thinking about designs from the execution of them made it possible to sub-divide production, as well as offering the possibility of separating the designer from the maker.

The separation of the designer and maker

The conscious design processes mentioned above meant that the detached designers needed to be trained both in the formal language and in the design method. Demands for proper training in drawing skills that could be applied to trade as well as, or rather than, fine art were becoming more vocal. The reasons were quite clear. Campbell (1747) in his *The London Tradesmen* indicated not only the problems coming from a misguided reliance on French patterns, but more importantly stressed an emphasis on drawing to create novelty as a prerequisite for success in the furniture business itself.

> In the case of the cabinet-maker a youth who designs to make a figure in this branch must learn to draw; for upon this depends the invention of new fashions, and on that the success of his business: He who first hits upon any new whim is sure to make by the invention, before it becomes common in the trade; but he that must always wait for a new fashion till it comes from Paris, or is hit upon by his neighbour, is never likely to grow rich or eminent in his way.[11]

The rise in interest in design and its teaching resulted in demands for academies and, perhaps more effectively, produced a crop of drawing masters who advertised their services and taught from their own homes.[12] In some cases, these individuals had been practising cabinet-makers, whilst others came from a fine art background. Intentionally perhaps, one of the most well-known of these drawing schools was established close to a London furniture-making centre in the 1730s.

The Academy in St Martin's Lane,[13] was founded by William Hogarth in 1735 and was a nursery for the English interpretation of the rococo style. Although founded and run by English artists, it is not surprising to find European designers employed: two of the more important being George Michael Moser and Hubert Gravelot. Both had connections with the furniture trade. In 1732 Gravelot arrived in London from Paris, having been trained under Boucher. He brought French forms, idioms and patterns for all manner of design work: 'besides his designs for engravings, he was much employed to make drawings for monuments and other antiquities and to design for cabinet-makers, upholsterers etc.'.[14] Moser moved to London from Germany in about 1721, and was initially employed by the cabinet-maker John Trotter as a chaser of furniture mounts. He later went on to be the manager of the St Martin's Lane Academy.

The connection between the Academy and the furniture trade is also recorded in the attendance of John Linnell,[15] and it is probable that Thomas Chippendale and Matthias Lock were also members.[16] The close proximity of the Academy to a furniture-working area was also likely to encourage cross-fertilisation between designers and makers.

Following on from the apparent success of the Academy, in or about 1740 Batty and Thomas Langley established a School of Architecture in nearby Soho, which encouraged artisans in the art of drawing, particularly in the rococo style.[17] Others followed suit: in the late 1740s, for example, the designer and illustrator, Matthias Darly, invited tradesmen and students to attend his evening classes in St Martin's Lane.[18]

By 1754, William Shipley had established the Society of Arts with the express purpose of offering premiums to promote improvements in the 'Liberal Arts, Sciences Manufactures etc.'. He also organised his own drawing school nearby, which he clearly saw as one route towards the improvements that he sought. Shipley specifically explained that it was commerce as well as fine art that was to benefit from drawing lessons. It is interesting that he particularly saw the benefits of drawing for the furniture trade. Shipley was 'earnestly solicitous to produce among the boys, ingenious mechanics, such as carvers, joiners, upholsterers, cabinet-makers, . . . etc.'[19]

The financial rewards accruing from drawing schools seemed to have encouraged some craftsmen to give up the trade to concentrate on training furniture draughtsmen and designers. The examples of Thomas Malton and Thomas Sheraton will be discussed below, but the case of Edward Edwards, who had originally been apprenticed with the Hallett business, illustrates the point. He opened a drawing school in which he offered evening classes specially for those who would 'qualify themselves to be cabinet or ornamental furniture-makers'.[20]

Clearly not all cabinet-makers were to become competent designers, even if they attended drawing schools. Perhaps one example of an attempt to cover this deficiency, but also to keep up to date, was the craftsman's compilation of scrap-books of designs.[21] At the other extreme of this design training were architects who had a professional interest in furniture and interiors.

The role of the architect

The key role of the architect and his interest in furniture in the eighteenth century was his consideration of the interiors as well as the architectural shell. Taken to its extreme, this resulted in an interior, furnishings and a building that were integrated into one complete whole. This is not surprising, as the concepts of taste in the eighteenth century were often based upon ideals of harmony and integration which could be more easily achieved by a single coordinating mind.

Some architects had been involved in this comprehensive designing during the seventeenth century, with the main exponents being the French court architects and Daniel Marot,[22] but it was not until a larger client base became established that the integrated interior could become truly popular.

As the eighteenth century progressed, the architect changed from an educated amateur with an interest in antiquities and building to a professional businessman. As far as furniture was concerned it appears that architects' interests ranged from a passing acquaintance to a full-scale design practice for objects that were intended to furnish their rooms. Amongst those with a known interest in designing furniture for integrated interiors were Robert Adam, Sir William Chambers, James Gibbs, William Kent, James Stuart and James Wyatt.[23]

In particular circumstances, that is the building or re-furbishing of a house, the architect considered himself to be in overall charge of the project. Even if this did not include prescribing the furniture selection, the architect often had a hand in the purchasing decisions. Christopher Gilbert (1978) has recorded how the York architect, John Carr, visited cabinet-making establishments with his client John Spencer: 'Mr Car went with me . . . to Cobbs, Chippendale's, & several others of the most eminent Cabinet-makers to consider of proper furniture for my drawing room'.[24] This relationship between the client and his architect seems to have been one of adviser and selector for furnishings suitable for the rooms being created.

The ensuing association between architect and craftsman was not always a happy one, as it appears that some craftsmen felt themselves quite capable of giving sound advice on furniture selection. In an oft quoted passage, Sir William Chambers, working at Melbourne House in the 1770s, wrote to his client asking that *his* opinion be sought before final decisions about furnishings were made:

> Chippendale called upon me yesterday with some designs for furnishing the rooms which upon the whole seem very well but I wish to be a little consulted about these matters as I am really a very pretty connoisseur in furniture . . .[25]

The discord between the craftsman-entrepreneur and the architect was perhaps increased by economic considerations, particularly in respect of the costs of supplying drawings. Whilst the cabinet-maker responsible for making the goods provided drawings as part of the price of manufacture, the architect charged separately for them. With the growing distribution of architectural and furniture pattern books, the advantage of ordering direct from the maker seemed clear.

The developments in the delineation of architectural designs for rooms is a useful indicator of changing attitudes towards interiors.[26] In the early part of the century, drawings were usually cross-sections of the house, with little in the way of moveable furnishings shown. By the middle of the century, representations included 'exploded' model rooms and individual wall plans often complete with furnishings. By the end of the century, the designs were often based on three-dimensional, water-coloured, perspective drawings, which represented a room as it might actually be seen. These changes show not only the growing desire to ensure that interiors were tastefully integrated, but also that clients were becoming more visually aware of their surroundings and the effects that could be created.

The dissemination of designs

As the demand for varied and sophisticated designs grew during the eighteenth century, it was clear that the craftsmen would need some additional sources of ideas apart from the customary models, and their own initiatives, which were often based on other examples they may have seen. Although architects were one medium for this dissemination, they tended only to operate within a particular sphere, so it was often to be the craftsmen themselves who developed these new sources for the wider market.

Whilst cabinet-makers or drawing masters wrote the works, it was book and print sellers who were the main medium for the physical distribution of them. Established in retail premises, they supplied printed catalogues of their stock for the trade and the client.[27]

The role of the printed designs were often two-fold. In one instance they would communicate ideas from the maker to customer, in another they would serve as ideas for the workman to interpret as he wished. In the first instance they could simply be a representation, but clearly the maker would often require scaled working drawings and templates rather than artfully drawn designs.

Despite the apparent profusion of pattern books, it is as well to remember that many designs became type forms, and for many examples of furniture the basic shape changed little over long periods.[28] The surface pattern, decoration, or even the choice of timber might alter the look, but often a shape remained. Nevertheless, the pattern books acted as inspiration for the artistic invention of numerous cabinet-makers. Indeed the ideas therein were intended to be exemplars only, and even if they were patented, this was not a bar to imaginative copying. Sheraton said as much when discussing library steps: 'this and the other design for library steps have obtained a patent, yet any part being materially altered will evade the Act, though the whole be nearly the same'.[29]

The pattern books

The publication of design books and the drawings within them were not meant to be manuals of craft instruction; it was usually assumed that the skilled working journeyman or master would be able to fill in the details from a conceptual or schematic offering from the pattern book.[30] In the case of engravings, which were often bizarre and fanciful, and rarely drawn by cabinet-makers themselves, there was often little chance of a direct copying by the cabinet-maker. In most cases it seems that the designs were guides that could be adapted by the maker to suit a particular taste, although there are of course many examples of objects directly relating to pattern designs.[31] In fact it becomes clear when inspecting the individual patterns that those intended for copying often have a plan section (sometimes with differing halves), details of parts and a measured scale, whilst those meant for inspiration are drawn in perspective and are often quite fanciful.[32]

The proliferation of pattern books justifies a brief discussion of some of the more important and influential ones here. One scholar has recently accounted for no less than seventy-six pattern books produced between 1744 and 1799.[33]

The first eighteenth-century design book to include furniture was apparently William Jones's *Gentleman or Builder's Companion* (1739), in which items of furniture were clearly an appendage to architecture.[34] This was closely followed by Batty and Thomas Langley's, *City and Country Builder's and Workman's Treasury of Designs* (1740), which included some furniture designs in the Kentian manner mixed in with French rococo designs lifted from Nicolas Pineau. Other editions of this work were published with additional plates in 1741, 1750 and 1756.[35] This publishing history is not unusual as many pattern books ran into a number of editions; what is revealing about it is the persistence of certain designs over a lengthy period. In both the above cases, the volumes were biased towards building but by 1741 William de la Cour began to publish plates of ordinary chairs which seems to have been the first to illustrate furniture designs alone.[36]

An example of the growing importance of printed sources and their specialist production was the work of Matthias Darly. He described himself as an engraver and drawing master, and would seem to have had an association with furniture-makers and designers as his premises faced Old Slaughters Coffee House in St Martin's Lane, close to the Academy and parts of the trade.[37] His work, *A New Book of Chinese Gothic and Modern Chairs* (1751), comprised eight plates of rather eccentric chairs. However, like other designs, they were resurrected, in this case by Manwaring in his *Chair-maker's Guide* as late as 1766.[38] In 1754 Darly and George Edwards published *A New Book of Chinese Designs* which was mainly of use to painters and japanners as it was full of landscapes and figures in a Chinese manner, but it did include some furniture designs in the Chinese taste. Darly continued to be productive, publishing design books in a variety of tastes. From 1765 to 1771 he showed designs for architecture and ornament at the Society of Artists, and in 1771 showed at the Free Society as a Professor and Teacher of ornament. His last work was *A New Book of Ornaments in the Present (Antique) Taste* published in 1772, which was among the first to show ornament in the neo-classical style. Darly is particularly fascinating in that his *œuvre* covers most of the main stylistic trends of the century.

Darly also worked as an engraver for other cabinet-makers who produced pattern books.[39] For example, he engraved 98 out of 147 plates in Chippendale's *Director*, as well as working for Ince and Mayhew on their *Universal System*. He was also commissioned for the engravings in the collection made by Sayer, under the title of 'The Society of Upholsterers' in 1760 (see below). Whilst Darly was, by trade, a drawing master and engraver, other authors of pattern books were themselves active in the furniture business.

Thomas Johnson was one such craftsman who published pattern books whilst working as a specialist carving sub-contractor to the trade. By 1763, he was described as a 'Carver, teacher of drawing and modelling' indicating the trend of his business towards designing and draughting.[40] His first book, entitled *Twelve Girandoles*, was published in 1755, whilst his second work, *A New Book of Ornaments*, followed soon after in 1758. This was dedicated to Lord Blakeney, grand President of the Anti-Gallican Association (founded in 1745 to encourage English trade and minimise French influence). Johnson was a member of the association, and in the dedication plate he particularly attacked the introduction of French papier mâché – not surprising as it was a less expensive imitative material that was likely to rival his wood carving business.[41]

Another carver who chose to publish his designs was Matthias Lock. His first published work, *Six Sconces* (1744), was quickly followed by *Six Tables* (1746), both of which demonstrate rococo motifs some time before they were generally popular. In 1752 he published *A New Book of Ornaments* in collaboration with H. Copland, and this was re-published in 1768. This long interval between issues of the same designs again gives some indication of the continuing demand these pattern books must have had in the trade.

In contrast to these trading designers was the work of Sir William Chambers. Chambers's importance was in providing first-hand knowledge of Chinese designs when most representations of the Orient were fanciful and frivolous. Chambers had visited China in the service of the Swedish East Company,[42] but his designs show an acquaintance with a wide range of other influences. His eclecticism was perhaps founded on his extensive education: having visited the Far East, he studied at the Ecole Des Arts, in Paris, and then took two trips to Rome for long periods (1750–1 and 1752–5). In 1757 he published his *Designs of Chinese Buildings, Furniture, Dresses, Machines and Utensils*, which he hoped 'might be of some use in putting a stop to the extravagancies that daily appear under the name of Chinese'.[43] His other achievements were mainly in the architectural field, but like Adam, he insisted on supervising the furnishing of any schemes he had a hand in planning. With the growth of the neo-classical style, Chambers played as important a role in spreading this style as he had done with the Chinese.

Around the middle of the century, one of the most well-known pattern books was published; indeed the importance of Thomas Chippendale's *The Gentleman and Cabinet-maker's Director* (1754) as one of the most influential pattern books of the period is not to be doubted.[44] Designed in the format of architectural treatises already issued, it included 'a short explanation of the five orders of architecture and rules of perspective: with proper directions for executing the most difficult pieces',[45] it was therefore aimed both at the sophisticated client and fellow craftsman.

Its success was also based on the dual satisfaction that the designs achieved: first, their acceptance by the gentry as high style, and by the provinces and colonies as a guide to good taste; and second, as a practical copy book for makers. Chippendale's press notice of the *Director* reveals something of his expected market:

As this work abounds with a great variety of elegant designs, every gentleman will have it in his power to make his own choice with respect to the furniture wanted: and will be able to point out such his choice to the workmen: who with a common capacity, may easily execute the same, the rules being plain and easy.[46]

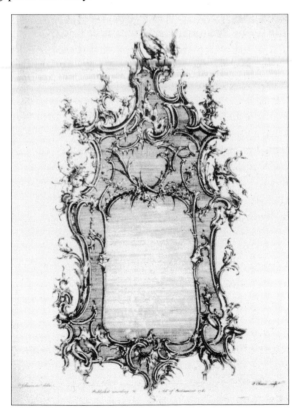

23 A printed design for an exuberant rococo style wall mirror-frame from a pattern book by Thomas Johnson, *c.* 1760.

It is clear from an analysis of the subscribers that approximately two-thirds of them were from the furniture trades, and this qualifies the second reason for its success.[47] Chippendale's own association with cabinet-making and his desire to make the designs as useful as possible is shown in the detailed advice that accompanies many of the plates. This advice includes particulars on setting out, planning details, construction, jointing and moulding descriptions.

This altruism was tempered by the fact that Chippendale clearly saw the work as an advertisement for his own firm and a direct source of orders as well. Gilbert (1978) has suggested that the appearance of the *Director* in 1754 coincided with Chippendale's decision to establish a business to deal with the public rather than simply supplying other members of the trade.[48] To do this would not only require a change in premises but also an initiative to attract a clientele. The *Director* was a useful tool in any attempt to establish his business in the face of the strong existing competition.

It was also important as it appears to be the first pattern book to include cabinet-work, as opposed to chair or carving patterns. This was, perhaps, a clever marketing ploy, or a reasoned response to the growing demand for fashionable, functional cabinet goods as well as the more decorative carved pieces.

Not surprisingly, it was not long before a competing cabinet-making business tried to produce a rival publication. In 1759 William Ince and John Mayhew began to bring out *The Universal System of Household Furniture*. This work was designed to be published in weekly numbers, each containing four plates, rather than to be subscribed to, as was the case with Chippendale's *Director*. In fact, the difficulties in production meant that the scheme was abandoned a little after the half-way stage and the engravings were published as a volume with other additions. The authors' intentions are clearly explained in the title page and owe quite a lot to the similar preface in the *Director*:

> The whole made convenient to the nobility and gentry, in their choice, and comprehensive to the workman, by directions for executing the several designs, with specimens of ornament for young practitioners in drawing.[49]

Clearly taking the same line as Chippendale, they tried to appeal to both customer and fellow tradesman. Chippendale's publication of a

24 A design for a 'toylet table' from Chippendale's *Director*, 1762. This rococo design demonstrates a combination of the cabinet-maker's and upholsterer's arts.

second edition of the *Director* was likely to have been a direct response to the Ince and Mayhew initiative.

It should be clear by now that one of the results of the production of pattern books was a common visual language defined by the trade and available to them and the public.

The dissemination of this language was also greatly assisted by parts of the publishing trade. Robert Sayer, a publisher and print-seller, was responsible for marketing the pattern books of Chippendale, Manwaring and Ince and Mayhew, and was instrumental in the publication of *Household Furniture in Genteel Taste* by A Society of Upholsterers, Cabinet-makers &c., which ran to four editions in the space of five years. The volume of sixty plates was reissued in 1762 with forty extra plates, and reprinted in 1763; a final edition from 1764 or 1765 contained an additional twenty plates.[50] The work, according to Ward-Jackson, was a compilation of 'rather plain and modest furniture . . . somewhat dull and lacking in originality'.[51] This comment unintentionally indicates the nature of the book and its market; it was aimed at the growing middle market for fashionable but safe furniture designs which could be interpreted by journeymen cabinet-makers. It is clear that this was not meant to be a rival to the established works, but rather a workaday trade volume. This is also suggested by the decision to use a fictitious society of authors which seems to be a marketing device.[52]

Competition between publishers was as strong as between makers. Henry Webley published Robert Manwaring's *The Cabinet and Chair-maker's Real Friend and Companion* in 1765, but in 1766 Robert Sayer brought out a rival volume called *The Chair-maker's Guide* by Robert Manwaring. Webley had to counter this by advertising the bona-fide volume with a comment that 'Many people, envious of the rapid Sale that the above book hath met with, hath published others something similar to this Title, be careful therefore to ask for the *Chair-maker's Friend* printed only for H. Webley'.[53]

The volume in question, *The Cabinet and Chair-maker's Real Friend and Companion*, was an interesting work which contained workaday schematic drawings. In the introduction, Manwaring considered that even though 'The art of chair-making as well as that of Cabinet-making hath of late years been brought to great perfection', it was still capable of improvement.[54] He went on to point out that although there had been a number of design books published before his, 'the practical workman has not been instructed in the execution of those designs'. Manwaring's avowed intent was to rectify this; though strangely, his volume only has one page of instructions for setting out chair rails and brackets. A generation later, Sheraton picked this point up and complained that the work was of limited assistance to the maker; the *Chair-maker's Guide* had only 'what a boy might be taught in seven hours'![55]

One example from many pattern books that brought fashionable designs within the reach of a wide furniture buying public was published in 1765. This was John Crunden's *The Joyner and Cabinet-maker's Darling or Pocket Director* which demonstrated the fret and lattice designs that were so popular, exemplifying the Gothic as well as the Oriental taste. Although an architect, Crunden recommended his designs as being applicable to 'bookcases, tea tables, tea stands, trays . . .'.[56]

The emphasis on drawing and perspective that was encouraged earlier on in the century was maintained by Thomas Malton. Although a cabinet-maker of some importance, Malton is best known for his work on perspective: his *Compleat Treatise on Perspective* was published in 1775.[57] Malton clearly understood the economic value of perspective drawing for cabinet-makers who were competent draughtsmen. In the eleventh section of the third book he says:

> Next to the architect, the cabinet-maker and upholder will find his account in a knowledge of perspective . . . There is nothing influences a gentleman more in favour of his workman, when he is pleased to want something whimsical and out of the way, than to take his Pencil and sketch out the idea the Gentleman had conceived . . . He who can do that, and at the same time display a little modern taste, in Ornament, being known, is certain of success, or of employ, at least.[58]

As in the beginning of the century, it was the architect who was able to bring together all the facets of an interior to achieve the completely integrated room or house. The work of Robert Adam was unsurpassed in this field. In particular, his classicising influence, which was based on Roman and Etruscan models, was to produce a new taste which was copied greatly in the 1770s and 1780s. His ideas of integration meant that he designed much furniture, and many examples were published in *The Works in Architecture of Robert and James Adam* (1778), which were avidly reproduced by others. The popularity of Adam's designs was perhaps based more on his touch of lightness and frivolity than any academic precedent; indeed it was often this gaiety that was criticised by contemporaries. Chambers called Adam's work 'filigraine toy work', whilst Horace Walpole considered it 'gingerbread and sippets of embroidery'.[59] Charles Heathcote Tatham was another detractor: 'The late Messrs Adam were the children of the Arabesque, yet I do not recollect one instance in which they successfully employed it'.[60] Success obviously bred a degree of resentment.

The influence of Adam on the artisanal level was found in the publication of Hepplewhite's *The Cabinet-maker and Upholsterer's Guide*, first published in 1788, reissued in 1789, with a third edition brought out in 1794.[61] Like others before him, Hepplewhite clearly

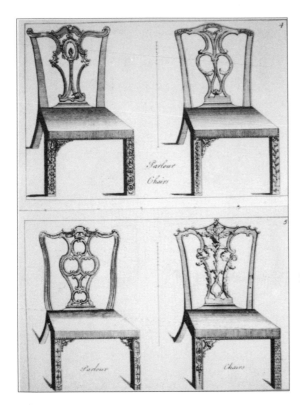

25 Designs for a variety of parlour or dining chairs by Robert Manwaring, 1765, which are intended for stylistic guidance only.

stated that his intention was to 'produce a work which shall be useful to the mechanic and serviceable to the gentleman'.[62] He clearly saw the role that pattern books could play in disseminating designs:

> Countrymen and Artisans, whose distance from the metropolis makes even an imperfect knowledge of its improvements acquired with much trouble and expense.[63]

It was perhaps the first important pattern book to be published since Chippendale's third edition of 1762, and was no doubt useful for other cabinet-makers, as it contained designs for much furniture that was practical and solid. Indeed, the author stated that his purpose was not intended to provide fashionable furnitures which were derided as the 'production of whim at the instance of caprice'; rather, it was to offer 'such articles only as are of general use and service'.[64] The representation of furniture that was not high-style, but was in fact quite

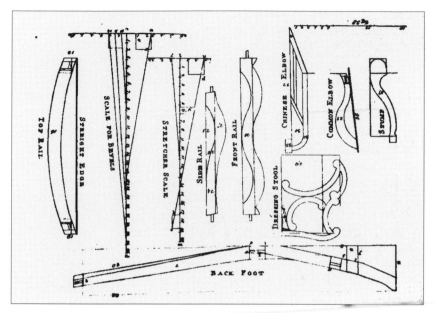

26 Crude scales and settling-out instructions for chair parts by Robert
Manwaring, 1765.

conservative, indicates a demand for modest not modish items. Indeed,
some items in his book are similar in design to ones published twenty
to thirty years previously. Hepplewhite's near contemporary, Thomas
Sheraton, commented that the designs in Hepplewhite's book 'had
caught the decline, and perhaps in a little time will suddenly die in
the disorder'.[65]

Towards the end of the century Thomas Sheraton published his *The
Cabinet-maker and Upholsterer's Drawing Book*. The first edition
appeared in fortnightly parts between 1791 and 1793, with a second
edition in 1794 and a third in 1802. The *Drawing Book* is divided into
three parts and these subdivisions give an indication of the author's
intentions. The first two parts, which were about geometry, drawing
and perspective, reinforce previous ideas that cabinet-makers should
be at least as well versed in drawing as they were in constructing
designs. Sheraton considered that although designs would change, the
fundamental skills of drawing remained. Indeed, his frontispiece illustration has the following motto: 'Time alters fashions and frequently

153

obliterates the works of art and ingenuity: but that which is founded on geometry and real science will remain unalterable.'[66] His comments on Chippendale's *Director* confirm this; he noted that although Chippendale's designs were now out-dated, the work had value for showing past styles and reinforcing the need for a knowledge of the rules of perspective.

The third section was 'intended to exhibit the present taste of furniture, and at the same time to give the workman some assistance in the manufacturing part of it'.[67] This was an important step as many of the previous pattern books had assumed a level of technical competency and only offered minimal practical advice. It may have been a response to the declining apprenticeship system, but it is clear that Sheraton considered that his market was only the trade. His definitions of the three types of persons who might be interested in his work is revealing as to the nature of the operation of parts of the trade.[68] The first were simply those who wanted new designs. There were others who wanted designs suitable for a broker's shop, 'to save them the

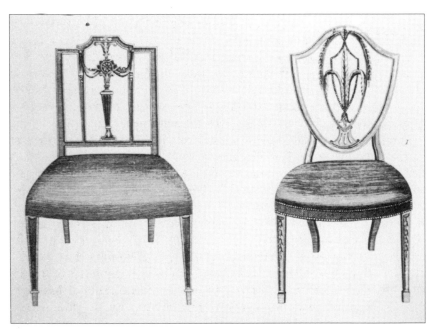

27 Two typical chair designs by Hepplewhite, from his *Guide* published in 1794.

trouble of borrowing a bason-stand to shew to a customer'. Others 'expected it to furnish a country ware-room to avoid the expense of making up a good bureau . . .' These last two remarks seem to suggest that the pattern book was being used by retail outlets as a sample book for customers to choose designs from, either to be made up on the premises or to be ordered from a workshop.[69]

Prints and visual literacy

It seems quite clear that as the century progressed, the impact of printed material grew apace. Visual sources were a great help to artisanal craftsmen who could interpret designs to their own skill level. For clients, the supply of visual matter was an enormous spur to the acquisition of notions of taste and decor, as well as being part of the planning process of interior schemes themselves. In addition, an attitude to learning and an appetite for historical and geographical knowledge was being made more and more accessible through periodicals, engravings and books.

The process had started some time before. Prints of furniture had been published for a long time prior to the eighteenth century, and a large number of continental prints were in circulation before the first British publications containing furniture in the 1730s. However, it seems that the main works of architectural design were responsible for promoting the particular styles which allowed people to see how they wanted to represent themselves through their interiors.

In the early part of the century, the Palladian revival was sponsored by the publication of William Kent's *Designs of Inigo Jones* (1727) and by Isaac Ware's edition of Palladio's treatise (1738). By the mid-century, Batty and Thomas Langley were promoting the Gothic. William Chambers's *Designs of Chinese Buildings* (1757) encouraged a scholarly interest in the East, whilst Robert Adam's *Ruins of the Palace of the Emperor Diocletian at Spalato* (1764) heralded the development of his own brand of neo-classicism followed by *The Works in Architecture of Robert and James Adam* (1778), which formally recognised their talents. The reaction to the exotic Adam style was invoked by Henry Holland who returned to a purer, more simple mode influenced by French design. This change in taste away from the Kentian massiveness of the early part of the century is confirmed by Archibald Alison:

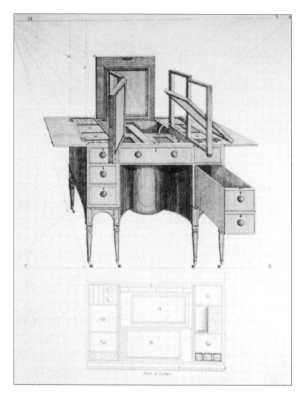

28 A design for a lady's dressing table by Sheraton, 1793. An example of a design incorporating space-saving features with ingenious mechanics.

All furniture . . . is beautiful in proportion to its quantity of matter, or the fineness or delicacy of it. Strong and massy furniture is everywhere vulgar and unpleasing.[70]

Continental design influences

Many designs were partly based on the assimilation of influences from the continent (especially France), which were then combined with national characteristics. This resulted in the application of foreign techniques and decorative motifs to essentially English (or other national) furniture types. The migration of practitioners and designers also played an important part in the process of changing styles during the century. The example of the Huguenot influence on the silver and silk industries indicates this. However, this is not to say that English influences were not received abroad; English craftsmen were often to be found in employment within Europe, whilst the colonisation of North America meant that English styles in that area were very strong.

Continental influences were brought about in three ways. First, by the impact of craftsmen moving from country to country, as well as from capital cities to provincial areas; for example, French, Italian and other artisans and artists who worked in London during the last quarter of the seventeenth and much of the eighteenth century clearly had an influence on fashion and taste.[71] Second the allure of actual objects being imported or exported created a desire for the 'exotic'. Thirdly, imported designs were being copied and ornamental print designs were being published in large quantities. The latter were often published in translation, for example, Daniel Marot's designs were published in Germany, Holland and England. In London, booksellers listed Le Pautre, Rossi, Boucher, Cuvilles and Babel amongst their stock of prints,[72] whilst conversely, various English pattern makers' designs were offered in French and German editions.

The disposition of English makers to foreign designs was ambivalent. Whilst Italian designs seem, on the whole, to have been acceptable, there was considerable difficulty with attitudes towards French design. Some thought that English manufacturers were too reliant on French émigré designers to supply new designs; others complained that there were fewer facilities for training in England than there were in France, so English designers were disadvantaged. Therefore an institution equivalent to the Academy in France was considered essential for the promotion of English design.[73]

Concerns over the French influence on English life were brought together under the banner of the Anti-Gallican Association. The association was founded in 1745 to encourage English trade and 'to oppose the insidious arts of the French Nation'.[74] It was intended that

> from the endeavours of its members to promote British manufactures to extend the commerce of England and discourage the introduction of French models and oppose the importation of French commodities.[75]

The anti-French attitude was long-lived, and was revealed in a variety of ways. Daniel Defoe suggested that the French were eminent at producing a fine show on the outside, whilst lacking the necessities on the inside.[76] In 1757 Boitard published a print entitled 'The imports of England from France', which was clearly anti-Gallican in intent. In the same year a novel entitled *The Anti-Gallican* was written by

E. Long.[77] The reaction continued, no doubt fuelled by xenophobic attitudes derived from the Napoleonic Wars. In 1802 the pretentious 'frenchifying' of the cabinet-makers' vocabulary was criticised in the *Gentleman's Magazine*:

> words entirely foreign have been gently pressed into our service, not by philologists and lexicographers, but by cabinet-makers and auctioneers, to give dignity to table and chairs, to exalt cupboards and brackets.[78]

Despite this Francophobe attitude, many of the more enterprising furniture suppliers knew that fashion knows no boundaries in either direction. The taste for French furniture and furnishings meant that French cabinet-makers were likely to meet with success if they established themselves in London.[79] It also meant that English cabinet-makers would import furniture and become involved in dubious customs-dodging practices (see below) as well as visiting France on purchasing expeditions.[80] In some cases English firms would employ French immigrant labour as company policy.[81]

The taste for French designs did not subside at the end of the century and contemporaries still commented upon the problem. Sheraton complained that all the time London fashion tried to ape Paris, the former's reputation would sink as Paris became the leading supplier:

> This we must bring upon ourselves, by foolishly staring after French fashions, instead of exerting ourselves to improve our own, by granting suitable encouragement to designers and artists for that purpose.

He continued by blaming the retailer:

> Instead of this, when our tradesmen are desirous to draw the best customers to their ware-rooms they hasten over to Paris, or otherwise pretend to go there, plainly indicating either our own defects in cabinet making or extreme ignorance.[82]

As already noted, the trade was not all one way. English work was considered interesting on the Continent, and it is revealing that Webley's architectural and pattern book sellers offered 'large allowances . . . to those who export them [pattern books] abroad'.[83] For example, in 1762 a French edition of Chippendale's *Director* was published as *Le Guide du Tapissier, de l'Ebeniste et de tous ceux qui travailent en meubles*; Ince and Mayhew's *Universal System* and Adam's *Works in Architecture* both had editions published in French or supplied with sub-titles. A German edition of Sheraton's *Drawing Book* was published in Leipzig in 1794. As if in confirmation of these developments, Hepplewhite was able to say that 'English taste and workmanship have of late years been much sought for by surrounding nations'.[84]

The comparison of quality between French and English craftsmanship was also commented upon by Sheraton: 'Were it not for the excellence of French brass mounts by which they set off cabinet work, it would not bear comparison with ours, neither in design nor neatness of execution.'[85] Interestingly, he suggested that further improvements might follow from the establishment of a national brass foundry 'sponsored by noblemen'. He also suggested a national public timber yard, alleging that improvements to trade and the national credit would result.

To put design into another framework, Margaretta Lovell's (1991) 'diffusion model' is useful. She has posited an argument to explain the spread of an aesthetic idea or development.[86] She suggests the image of a pebble thrown into a pond to show how design dissipation takes place and is watered down as it reaches the extremities. This, for example, helps to relate the success of Chippendale's *Director*, first as high style, both in England and America, and second with a diffused impact in provincial and vernacular furniture. It also helps to explain France's exertions to remain at the epicentre of fashion and taste. Powerful commercial interests, well aware of their position of superiority in design and production, ensured that France remained a leader of European taste and trade for much of the century.

All the discussions above have tended to relate to high style merchandise, indicating the difficulties in establishing the roles of design in lower status goods. Whilst Lovell's model is useful as a general position, more work needs to be done to discover any further links between pattern books, designers and the making of 'common' furniture.

Notes

1 D. Diderot, *Dictionnaire raisonne des sciences, des arts et des metiers*, 1751–72 (1793), 'Dessin en architecture', Forman's translation in *American Seating Furniture, 1630–1730* (New York, Norton, 1988), p. 6.
2 See C. Saumarez-Smith, *Eighteenth-Century Decoration* (London, Weidenfeld and Nicolson, 1993), pp. 135–42.

3 R. Dossie, *Handmaid to the Arts* (1758), Preface.
4 *Ibid.*
5 Quoted in Saumarez-Smith, *Eighteenth-Century Decoration*, p. 135.
6 W. Sleater, *An Essay on Perfecting the Fine Arts in Great Britain and Ireland* (Dublin, 1767), p. 39, quoted by Saumarez-Smith, *Eighteenth-Century Decoration*, pp. 135–40.
7 Quoted by P. Thornton, *Authentic Decor. The Domestic Interior 1620–1920* (London, Weidenfeld and Nicolson, 1984), p. 140.
8 D. Pye, *The Nature and Art of Workmanship* (Cambridge, Cambridge University Press, 1968).
9 This section is indebted to J. C. Jones, *Design Methods* (London, John Wiley, 1981).
10 See N. Cross 'The changing design process' in R. Roy and D. Wied, *Product Design and Technological Innovation* (Open University Press, 1985).
11 R. Campbell, *The London Tradesmen*, [1747] (Newton Abbot, David and Charles, 1969), p. 171.
12 Thomas Sheraton advertised his teaching of drawing on his trade card. See A. Heal, *The London Furniture-makers, from the Restoration to the Victorian Era, 1660–1840* (London, Batsford, 1953).
13 A. Paulson, *Hogarth, his Life, Art and Times* (New Haven and London, Yale University Press, 1971), pp. 369–75.
14 John Pye, *Patronage Of British Art* (1845), quoted by D. Fitzgerald, 'Gravelot and his influence on English furniture', *Apollo*, xc (August 1969), p. 142.
15 D. Fitzgerald, 'Chippendale's place in the English rococo', *Furniture History*, iv (1968).
16 P. Kirkham, *The London Furniture Trade, 1770–1870* (Furniture History Society, 1988), p. 97.
17 S. Jervis, *Dictionary of Design and Designers* (Harmondsworth, Penguin, 1984).
18 C. Gilbert, 'The early furniture designs of Matthias Darly', *Furniture History*, xi (1975).
19 *Gentleman's Magazine* (February 1756), pp. 61–2; quoted in Saumarez-Smith, *Eighteenth-Century Decoration*, p. 138.
20 'An account of the Life of Mr Edwards', *Anecdotes of Painters* (London, 1808), quoted in Kirkham, *London Furniture Trade*, pp. 99–100.
21 M. Heckscher, 'Gideon Saint: an eighteenth-century carver and his scrap-book,' *The Metropolitan Museum of Art Bulletin*, xxvii (1969), pp. 299–311.
22 P. Thornton, *Seventeenth-Century Interior Decoration in England, France and Holland* (Yale University Press, 1978), p. 52.

23 For more on the architects and their designs see, J. Lever, *Architects' Designs for Furniture* (London, Trefoil, 1982); S. Jervis, *Dictionary of Design and Designers* (Harmondsworth, Penguin, 1984); P. Ward-Jackson, *English Furniture Designs of the Eighteenth Century* (London, Victoria and Albert Museum, 1984).

24 C. Gilbert, *The Life and Work of Thomas Chippendale* (London, MacMillan, 1978), p. 27.

25 Melbourne House papers, quoted by Gilbert, *Chippendale*, p. 96.

26 The most accessible pictorial sources for these are Thornton, *Authentic Decor*, and Saumarez-Smith, *Eighteenth-Century Decoration*.

27 T. Friedman, 'Two eighteenth-century catalogues of ornamental pattern books, *Furniture History*, XI (1975).

28 See L. Wood, *The Lady Lever Art Gallery Catalogue of Commodes* (London, HMSO, 1994), for a detailed discussion of the commode furniture type.

29 Sheraton, *Drawing Book*, Appendix, p. 42.

30 Although in varying degrees the working cabinet-makers who designed pattern books included some information; see Sheraton especially.

31 Although see Y. Hackenbrock, 'Pattern books and eighteenth-century design', *Antiques*, LXXIV (September 1958), pp. 225–32.

32 Compare, for example, Chippendale's *Director* and Matthew Darly's *A New Book of Chinese Gothic and Modern Chairs*. Many of the designs in pattern books were intended to be adapted to suit the amount of decoration required.

33 Information from Michael Snodin, Victoria and Albert Museum, 16 April 1994.

34 Pattern books and engraved designs had of course been available prior to the eighteenth century. See for examples, S. Jervis *Printed Furniture Designs before 1650* (Furniture History Society, 1974).

35 Ward-Jackson, *English Furniture Designs*, p. 35.

36 Snodin points out in his revision of Ward-Jackson's *English Furniture Designs* that De La Cour published eight books of ornament. The fifth book has the subtitle *Useful for all manner of furniture and other things*.

37 For this and other aspects of the art and design world see M. Girouard, 'English art and the rococo', *Country Life* (1966), part 1, 13 Jan., pp. 58–61, part 2, 27 Jan., pp. 188–90, part 3, 3 Feb., pp. 224–7.

38 C. Gilbert, 'The early furniture designs of Matthias Darly', *Furniture History*. Darly's connection with the furniture trade continued in respect of his own pattern book, Manwaring's reprint of it, the engraving of most of the plates in Chippendale's *Director*, followed by further engraving work for Mayhew and Sayer.

39 Ward-Jackson, *English Furniture Designs*.

40 Mortimer, *The Universal Directory* (1763).
41 Jervis, *Dictionary of Design*. Also see H. Hayward, *Thomas Johnson and the English Rococo* (London, Tiranti, 1964).
42 For Chambers, see J. and E. Harris, *Sir William Chambers* (London, Zwemmer, 1970).
43 Quoted in Ward-Jackson, *English Furniture Designs*, p. 17.
44 C. Gilbert, 'The subscribers to Chippendale's *Director*, a preliminary analysis', *Furniture History*, x (1974), and Heckscher, 'Philadelphia Chippendale: the influence of the *Director* in America', *Furniture History*, xxi (1985). For a detailed study of the history of the publication see Gilbert, *Chippendale*, pp. 65–92.
45 Extracted from the title page of Chippendale's *The Gentleman and Cabinet-maker's Director* (1754).
46 *York Courant* (20 April 1762), quoted in Gilbert *Chippendale* p. 92, n. 58. See also the preface to the *Director* in which Chippendale refers to the 'Gentlemen and Cabinet-makers' referred to in the title; 'the work [is] calculated to assist the one in the choice and the other in the execution of the designs'.
47 Gilbert, 'Subscribers to Chippendale's *Director*'.
48 Gilbert, *Chippendale*, p. 65.
49 W. Ince and J. Mayhew, *The Universal System of Household Furniture* (1759–62).
50 Information from Gilbert, *Chippendale*, p. 89.
51 Ward-Jackson, *English Furniture Designs*, p. 52.
52 This is the interpretation of C. Gilbert (1982).
53 See C. Gilbert, 'Smith, Manwaring, Sayer and a newly discovered set of designs', *Furniture History*, xxix (1993).
54 *Ibid.*
55 Sheraton, *Drawing Book*, p. 9.
56 J. Crunden, *The Joyner and Cabinet-maker's Darling or Pocket Director* (1765). The full title includes this passage.
57 For Malton, see S. Redburn, 'The furniture designs of Thomas Malton 1775–9', *Furniture History*, xi (1975).
58 Redburn, 'Furniture Designs of Thomas Malton'.
59 Quoted in E. Harris, *The Furniture of Robert Adam* (London, Tiranti, 1963).
60 C. H. Tatham to Henry Holland jun, 4 April 1796, Soane Ms. Quoted in Harris, *Furniture of Robert Adam*, p. 43.
61 It is now considered that these works were published posthumously by Alice Hepplewhite, his widow, who carried on this business after his death. See G. B. Peck, 'Alice and George Hepplewhite's Cabinet-maker and Upholsterer's Guide', *Woman's Art Journal*, 8 (Fall 1987/Winter

1988); Ian Caldwell, 'Working women in the eighteenth century', *The Antique Collector* (October 1985), pp. 78–81.

62 A. and C. Hepplewhite, *The Cabinet-maker and Upholsterer's Guide* (1794) Preface to the third edition.

63 Hepplewhite, *Guide*.

64 Hepplewhite, *Guide*, Preface to the third edition, 1794.

65 Sheraton, *Drawing Book*, p. 10.

66 Sheraton, *ibid.*, Frontispiece illustration inscription.

67 Sheraton, *ibid.*, p. 352.

68 Sheraton, *ibid.*, p. 354.

69 It seems as if pattern books were not the only method of offering samples. It has been suggested that painted boards with full size designs for chair backs were used for sampling.

70 A. Alison, *Essays on the Nature and Principles of Taste* (1790 sixth edition 1825), cited in E. Joy, *The Connoisseur's Complete Period Guides* (London, Connoisseur, 1968), p. 822.

71 For example, Daniel Marot, Gaetano Brunetti, Hubert Gravelot.

72 Friedman, 'Two eighteenth-century catalogues of ornamental pattern books', *Furniture History* XI (1975).

73 See above and Saumarez-Smith, *Eighteenth-Century Decoration*, pp. 19–22, 138–9. Sheraton also makes a similar suggestion, see below.

74 A. Coleridge, *Chippendale Furniture* (London, Faber, 1968), p. 64. For the Anti-Gallican Association see C. Alister, 'The Anti-Gallicans', *Transactions of the Greenwich and Lewisham Antiquarian Society*, VII (1970), pp. 211–17 and E. Mew, 'Battersea enamels and the Anti-Gallican Society', *Apollo*, VII (1928), pp. 216–22. Information from S. Pryke, 'The extraordinary billhead of Francis Brodie', *Regional Furniture*, IV (1990), pp. 98–9.

75 G. Wills, *English Furniture, 1760–1900* (London, Guinness Superlatives, 1969), p. 37

76 D. Defoe, *The Complete English Tradesman*, [1727] (New York, Kelley, 1969), vol. 1, p. 263.

77 See also M. Snodin (ed.), *Rococo Art and Design in Hogarth's England*, V & A exhibition catalogue (London, May–Sept. 1984) p. 16.

78 G. de Bellagiue, 'English marquetry's debt to France', *Country Life* (13 June 1968), pp. 1594–8, quoting the *Gentleman's Magazine* (September 1802).

79 For example, the cabinet-maker Langlois.

80 Chippendale visited France in 1768, and Mayhew went at least prior to 1786.

81 See Wood, Catalogue of *Commodes*, pp. 199, 200, 202, for possible Ince and Mayhew employment of French-trained labour.

82 T. Sheraton, *The Cabinet Dictionary* (London, 1803) vol. 1, p. 116.
83 Friedman, 'Two eighteenth-century catalogues'.
84 Hepplewhite, *Guide*, Preface to the third edition, 1794.
85 Sheraton, *Dictionary*.
86 M. Lovell, '"Such furniture as will be profitable". The business of cabinet-making in eighteenth-century Newport', *Winterthur Portfolio*, xxvi (1991).

5   Consumption

Consumption is not simply the final part of the model I have chosen
to use: its importance lies in its demonstration of the cross-disciplinary
nature of furniture studies. Economically, consumption is the outlet
for production; socially, it represents a wide range of attitudes
(e.g. emulation, status, morality and fashion), and for design studies,
it can often help in an explanation of changing room use, ideas of
comfort, utility and ingenuity.[1]

There are five particular aspects of eighteenth-century consumption
that help to throw light upon attitudes to design generally and furniture
in particular. These are ideas about emulation, morality, fashion, comfort and convenience and room use.

Emulation

The growth of eighteenth-century consumption has sometimes been
overwhelmingly explained by theories of emulation. Thorstein Veblen
and his *Theory of the Leisure Class*,[2] have often been invoked to
support the idea of emulation of one's superiors as the fuel that fed
the will to consume. It is not necessary to simply rely on Veblen.
Indeed 150 years prior to Veblen, it was the observant Daniel Defoe
who pointed out that 'the poorest citizens strive to live like the rich,
the rich like the gentry, the gentry like the nobility and the nobility
striving to outshine one another, no wonder that all the sumptuary
trades encrease'.[3] Another contemporary writer was also aware of the
change in demand brought about by emulation:

> In England the several ranks of men slide into each other almost imper-
> ceptibly, and a spirit of equality runs through every part of their con-
> stitution. Hence arises a strong emulation in all the several stations and
> conditions to vie with each other . . . In such a state as this, fashion
> must have uncontrolled sway. And a fashionable luxury must spread
> through it like a contagion.[4]

Lady Kildare demonstrated the point well in a letter to her husband in 1757, when she said: 'I shall wish to have our house look sprucish. Every mortal's house here [in London] is so pretty and smart, and well furnished, that I do long to have ours so too a little'.[5]

In spite of these contemporary comments, our analyses of the reasons for consumption are now a lot less clear-cut than either Defoe's or Veblen's. Consumption processes might in fact indicate a number of differing messages. These could include the desire to establish a status difference, the desire to establish a particular community distinction, or the desire to establish an individual identity.[6] The latter was particularly true in towns, were spending on furnishings was part of the process of establishing one's family, particularly if others in the town had little knowledge of one's ancestry. Contrary to this, the well-established rural family often had little need to demonstrate their position in a hierarchy. As status already existed and was acknowledged, conspicuous consumption of fashions and furnishings may well have been tempered by this awareness.[7]

Colin Campbell (1993) has suggested that the theory of emulation, which simply uses purchasing power to attain an equal status, should be questioned. The trickle-down phenomenon does not necessarily indicate motives of emulation, that is, the facility to copy does not mean this is the reason; perhaps there is an actual desire for goods for their own sake.[8] This desire is referred to below. Clearly then, there can co-exist examples of imitation or copying, emulation which is trying to equal or even excel, as well as examples of personal or group distinction.

What were the conscious motives or intentions of the consumer? When consequences are recognised as objects, the analysis of intention can be useful. In other words, we can use furniture objects (amongst others) to assist in interpreting eighteenth-century consumer ambitions. Campbell suggests that the key to this understanding is a recognition of personal characteristics; the individual's desire to express ideals in themselves.[9] The particular tastes of the eighteenth century, which included the rococo, the Gothic, and the neo-classical, all expressed differing ideals and attitudes. In the case of furniture and interiors, the selection of particular merchandise directly relates to the expression of individuals' ideas of themselves. Not only do interiors and their furnishings tell others about the occupants, but they also remind the owners of themselves and their position.[10] Whilst this remains the case, the home will inevitably be bound up with individual self-concepts. Overlaying these ideas is the hegemony of taste, and social hierarchy which were discussed in the introduction.

The accepted symbolic meanings of objects as 'codes' were intended to establish both differentiation and integration. The former was aimed at separating the owner and emphasising his/her individuality, whilst in the latter, the object symbolically expressed the integration of the owner into a context which was both narrow (the building) and broad (the social stratum).[11]

Therefore, one of the most valuable symbolic functions of goods, and especially of furnishings, was 'making visible and stable the categories of culture'.[12] This process was not lost on contemporaries. Sheraton clearly demonstrated this when giving advice to upholsterers upon their role:

> When any gentleman is so vain and ambitious as to order the furnishings of his house in a style superior to his fortune and rank, it will be prudent in an upholsterer, by some gentle hints to direct his choice to a more moderate plan.[13]

In addition, Sheraton noted that even 'in furnishing a good house for a person of rank, it requires some taste and judgement, that each apartment may have such pieces as is most agreeable to the appropriate use of the room'.[14] So not only did the retailer have to make sure that the standard of furnishing was appropriate to a social level, but also that the particular schemes were suitable for particular room types.

The distinctions between categories of culture can also be seen in the differences between 'old' and 'new' wealth. In the case of old wealth (gentry and nobility), McCracken (1988) has posited the idea of 'patina' as a representation of status prior to, and after, the eighteenth century. He goes on to suggest that during the eighteenth century the fashion system took over and status was to be found in new things rather than old.[15] This in turn encouraged regular changes in styles enabling distinctions to be continually made. The differences between inherited and self-made wealth were unwittingly commented upon by the contemporary author, G. Lichtenberg, whilst on a visit to the papier mâché maker, Baskerville: 'The rooms are furnished in the fine taste of those people who, instead of inheriting their wealth, have earned it on their own'.[16] This can of course, be interpreted in two ways: either literally, or as satire.

As Sheraton was well aware (see above), this bourgeois preoccupation with good taste meant that the newly wealthy often had to employ upholsterers to assist with the choice of tasteful furnishings:

> [The upholsterer] tells one immediately what colours go together, how much each article costs, what one must choose in order to guard against the style becoming old-fashioned after some years, what changes must be made in a house . . . and so on and so on.[17]

This is not surprising as many people had little or no experience of purchasing stylish house furnishings on a regular basis. It was also the basis for the upholsterer, later the retail furnisher, to be considered as an arbiter of taste during the centuries that followed.

The shifts in ownership and spending patterns of eighteenth-century consumers can be developed using Lorna Weatherill's (1988) conclusions. The ownership patterns she has recognised include the idea that often the minor gentry were less likely to own particular goods than commercial and professional classes, despite the former's higher social standing.[18] She cites the example of window curtains which, from the data used, shows the following ownership range: 28 per cent of dealing trades, 26 cent of gentry, 13 per cent of craft trades, 5 per cent of yeomen. Other spending pattern examples illustrate the distinction between the urban and rural distribution of goods. The possession of looking glasses in London was 77 per cent, in major towns, 58 per cent, in other towns 50 per cent, and in rural or village areas 21 per cent, thus confirming the preponderance of these status objects in cities.

The differences between the urban and the rural, as well as between status groups, were also reflected in the total interior effect. *The Book of Trades* (1804) commented on the distinctions:

> What a difference is there between the necessary articles of furniture to be found in a cottage and the elegantly furnished house of a merchant or peer. In the former there is nothing but what is plain, useful, and almost essential to the convenience of life: in the latter, immense sums are sacrificed to magnificence and show.[19]

The choices of the wealthy had implications in the growth of cosmopolitanism, a society life and the development of specialist suppliers.

One fed upon the other and created a self-fulfilling urban economy. Whilst this urban economy satisfied the demand for luxuries, decencies and necessities, the rural economy fluctuated in its responses. The diffusion of ideas, tastes and product styles is therefore inevitably affected by the nature of the receiver.

Demand for particular goods was also derived from other needs. One such demand was due to the development in social habits, for example, tea drinking, social entertaining, reading and writing, which meant that practical, functional furniture was required, and this will be discussed further below. Another demand came from people who desired objects for their own intrinsic worth: the polished surfaces, dramatically grained and figured veneers, coloured timbers, and contrasting inlays of wood and metals all excited the visual appetite, as well as satisfying other egotistical demands.

The visual results also reflected status. Whether it was a pine dresser with simple ceramic objects on view, or a mahogany sideboard with a full display of a silver service, the instinct was the same: an exhibition of prestige. The display was attractive for the owner as a reminder of his or her position, but more importantly it was a sign for guests or visitors. These markers therefore clearly extended beyond a simple parading of objects.

The development of polite society had ramifications for furniture as much as other decorative arts. This meant that markers that placed one in society were often more than signifiers of position. For example, the proper provision of comfort and pleasure for visitors and guests was clearly important. Sophie von la Roche indicated as much when she wrote of a visit to Lord Harcourt. She describes the reception room and its contents:

> Chests in the finest workmanship, holding the necessaries for all kinds of games, and lined on top with books of all varieties and languages; a piano, music, violin, . . . numerous sofas and all kinds of arm and easy chairs; ladies work tables besides, so as all the guests may do exactly as they please.[20]

Clearly Harcourt was a considerate and thoughtful host. Sophie's comments also serve to remind us that as new fads and tastes entered society so new pieces of furniture had to be devised or adapted. Whatever the reasons for them, many of these motives for consumption gave rise to questions about the morality of the process.

Morality

Although many contemporary writers extolled the benefits of consumption,[21] there were some voices raised against it. Consumption as a 'vice' was denounced by particular commentators. Defoe wrote a chapter discussing tradesmen who 'by the necessary consequences of their business are obliged to be accessories to the propagation of vice, and the encrease of wickedness of the times'.[22] The sort of merchants that Defoe complained about were the tailors and mercers whom he saw as tempters and manipulators of vanity. According to Defoe, the same problems occurred in furnishings:

> The Upholder does the like in furniture, till he draws the gay ladies to such excesses of folly that they must have their houses new furnished every year; everything that has been longer than a year in use must be called old, and to have their fine lodgings seen by persons of any figure above twice over, looks ordinary and mean.[23]

To overcome this trend and to stop 'all excesses in cloathing, furniture and the like'[24] would have required sumptuary laws and this idea was unwelcome in the political climate of the eighteenth century.

Conversely, the idea of sensibility was seen as important. Sensibility represented a feeling of goodness, emotion and a response to beauty, of which any lapses were considered to breed bad taste. Therefore 'taste' became an important part of an individual's moral character. This clearly gave support to the supposed 'vice' of being 'in the fashion'. Indeed, a lack of virtue could be expressed by failing to show the correct judgement in matters of taste, therefore objects that demonstrated good taste also indicated respectability. Not to be in fashion was perhaps seen to imply a dubious moral standing, therefore fashion consciousness was not necessarily seen as the seeking of status but more as a protector of one's own good name.[25]

In the case of furniture, Ince and Mayhew, in the preface to their *Universal System*, point out that even if large amounts of money are spent on furnishings, this should be balanced with decorum and grace to obtain a tasteful effect:

> In furnishing all should be with Propriety-Elegance should always be joined with a peculiar neatness through the whole house, or otherwise an immense expense may be thrown away to no purpose either in use or appearance.[26]

The dichotomy between the vice of supplying attractive and fashionable goods and the morality of clients who were trying to show a degree of taste, was no doubt of little consequence in the actual market place.

Fashion

Although the fashion system was particularly influential in matters of personal dress and adornment, furniture was also affected by the changes fashion demanded. Defoe, the astute observer of his times, noted that 'the fashions alter now in the more durable kind of things, such as Furniture of houses, Equipages, Coaches, nay even of Houses themselves'. This meant that

> this must needs give a new turn to the trade, and that of course gives new methods and new measures to the Manufacturers, obliges them to a continual study of novelty, and to rack their inventions for new fashions, introduces new customs, and even gives a turn to Trade it self.[27]

One hundred years later, in its advice to new entrants to the furniture trade, a guide published in 1829 had the following to say:

> In a business where change and caprice rule with unbounded sway – in which the fashion of today may become obsolete tomorrow – an inventive genius and discriminating judgement are certainly essential qualifications.[28]

Plus ça change! Novelty and new innovations were clearly one key to a successful furnishing business.

This need to change, to be seen to be fashionable, and to reject the taste of the previous generation was to become noticeable even in rural districts. The transitions were commented upon by a joiner, James Spershott of Chichester, Sussex. His memoirs included this passage which referred to his youth in the early eighteenth century:

> I observ'd in those days the household furniture . . . was almost all of English oak . . . but with younger people it was now in fashion to have deal dressers with shelves over for pewter, etc. Their tables and chests of drawers of Norway oak called wainscot. With the higher sort, walnut tree veneering was most in vogue and esteem'd for its beauty above anything else . . . The best chairs were turn'd ash, dyed or stuffed, with Turkey or other rich covers.[29]

Even if rural areas were being affected by fashions, it was the urban middling classes who were disproportionately responsible for the surge in demand for fashionable goods. Writing in a similar vein to Spershott, but this time referring to urban homes in Bath, John Wood saw that

> Walnut tree chairs, some with leather and some with damask or worked bottoms supplied the place of such as were seated with cane or rushes; the oak tables and chests of drawers were exchanged; the former for such as were made of mahogany, the latter for such as were made either of the same wood or with walnut tree; handsome glasses were added to the dressing tables[30]

This is a fine example of 'trading up' in terms of household goods. In contrast, an inventory of a cottage in New Brentford, Middlesex from 1768, shows the range of household effects that an artisan-labourer possessed. Although not so elegant as the Bath example, it shows an interesting mix of the old and new, combined with some idea of comfort.

The bedroom furniture included a four-poster bedstead and a half tester turn-up bedstead, both with textile furnishings. The home boasted five tables, two of which were described as wainscot dining tables. There were four cane and five rush-bottomed chairs as well as a leather-covered elbow chair. For storage they had a deal clothes chest, a wainscot chest with drawers veneered in front and a mahogany tea chest. Other items included eight prints and two small looking glasses.[31]

The fact that the home comforts had improved for a wide swathe of the population impressed Josiah Tucker. He wrote in the last quarter of the eighteenth century that

> Were an inventory to be taken of household goods and furniture of a peasant, or mechanic in France, and of a peasant or mechanic in England the latter would be found on average to exceed the former in value by at least three to one'.[32]

He went on to say that the English had more in the way of furniture, carpets and curtains than were to be found anywhere else in Europe. Even allowing for a degree of patriotic exaggeration, there had clearly been great strides in the material well-being of large groups of English peoples.

However, reaction was never far away. By 1825, William Cobbett raised complaints against the new furniture and fashions that had displaced the old. He wrote of a Wealden farmhouse which was 'formerly the scene of plain manners and plentiful living'.[33] It was once all furnished with oak pieces, some of which had the advantage of being many hundreds of years old, but were all now in a state of decay and disuse. Amongst many complaints, the worst introduction for Cobbett was 'the mahogany table, and the fine chairs, and the fine glass, and all as bare-faced [an] upstart as any stock-jobber in the kingdom can boast of'.[34]

These comments reflect some of the shifts that occurred in common English furnishing habits over the century. These changes were no doubt welcomed by the consumers even if they were criticised by some commentators of the time.

Another comparative example will demonstrate the nature of improvements. The furniture in the living room of one farmer in 1676 simply comprised 'one longe table, 6 joyned stooles, one cuppbord, 3 chairs and one little table'. Things had improved considerably by the 1750s. A typical farmhouse in the Yorkshire Dales was furnished with a dresser, a table, a clock, chairs and a long settle in the fore house. In the parlour and closets were beds and bedding, chests of drawers, a little table, chairs and a corner cupboard. In the bedrooms were two chaff beds, a chest, two tables, four chairs and accessories.[35] By comparison, the craftsman-potter was even better off in the 1740s:

In the Hall a clock and case, a looking glass, a writing desk and table and stand, a dozen Sedge [matted] chairs. In the parlour a corner cupboard and china and a tea table, an oval table, a tea table, a card table a dressing table and hand board, twelve cane chairs.[36]

These contrasting examples help to confirm Tucker's observations about the home comforts of the English. With finance the key to stylish decoration, it was clear that some people were able to buy the latest in luxury furnishings, whilst many others were still 'making do'. Parson Woodforde of Weston, Norfolk, wrote that in November 1789 he had purchased two second-hand mahogany tables, a second-hand mahogany dressing table and one new mahogany washstand.[37]

Those who were not living in their own homes had even less in the way of furnishing comforts. This description of a rented room from 1767 illustrates the point:

a half-tester bedstead with brown linsey-woolsey furniture, a bed and a
bolster . . ., a small wainscot table, two old chairs with cane bottoms,
a small looking glass six inches by four in a deal frame painted red and
black, a red linsey-woolsey curtain.[38]

As has already been intimated, a desire for attractive and fashionable home furnishings was an important and continuing feature of
eighteenth-century life. One specific aspect of a desire for comfort
was combined with an interest in ingenuity and science.

Comfort and convenience

A *delight in ingenuity*

In addition to the practicalities that ingenious furniture items brought,
there was also a delight in ingenuity for its own sake. What might be
called playful furniture was evident at times throughout the century.
In the 1740s, the example of Potter and his mechanical furniture, which
included harlequin rising tables, gaming tables and rise and fall breakfast tables, is a valuable demonstration of this interest.[39] But the appeal
was also practical. In Potter's breakfast table, for example, by releasing
catches the tray-top would descend and two flaps could then cover
the void to make a clear top.

Interest continued into the 1750s and a fine example of craftiness
of workmanship can be found in the Murray cabinet with its seventeen
secret compartments opened by pins, as well as such niceties as spring
loaded keyhole covers.[40]

By the end of the century, there was a great demand for this sort
of furniture. Sheraton's designs included ladies' writing tables which
had spring-loaded pen and ink drawers; a spring-weighted screen
operated by lead weights and pulleys;[41] a lady's dressing table with
rising back mirror and side mirrors;[42] and the harlequin table, so called
because it used complicated mechanisms that were similarly employed
in *commedia dell'arte*.

An example of an ingenious device which also indicated a more
relaxed attitude to parts of the interior was Benjamin Crosby's patent
'machine or stand for books'[43] which was a system for making a
bookcase in any convenient shape based on a central column. Clearly
devised for use in a variety of rooms, it was part of a range of
moveable bookcases which were designed so that 'a lady can move

to any sitting room'.[44] This taste for mechanical and moveable furniture was also related to a wider interest in machines, tools and 'mechanicks' generally.[45]

The example of Merlin and his mechanical furniture will be encountered below in the case of medical furniture. He was also at the forefront of metamorphic or combined-function furniture. The sorts of objects that could be found in Merlin's premises included:

> neat little writing- reading- or working-tables, combined with charming soft toned pianos . . . Others with pianos concealed, and clever desks with lights attached for quartettes set up in less than three minutes, which if not required for music might be converted into a nice piece of furniture for playing chess.[46]

Amongst other pieces of furniture that the 'ingenious mechanick' Merlin designed was the Quartetto music cabinet which 'contains flutes, violins and music books; and by touching a spring key, it will rise to a proper height and form music desks for four performers'.[47] Perhaps the most incredible example of Merlin's attempts to amuse and interest the public's demand for furniture was the 'curious new invented tea table by which any lady can fill twelve cups of tea and shift them round by the pressure of the foot, without the assistance of her hands'.[48] The success of this rather unlikely piece is not recorded!

An interesting insight into trade practice is also revealed in Merlin's catalogue. Merlin clearly encouraged furniture-makers to use his designs and he made the following offer:

> any ingenious cabinet-makers or mechanics who are desirous of making and copying any of Mr Merlin's curious and useful pieces of mechanism, Mr Merlin will recommend to the Nobility and gentry by favouring him with their address.[49]

Why were some furniture types extremely successful while other ideas were not? The popularity of particular models is now difficult to judge, but there were clearly many reasons for success or failure in the marketplace. As far as innovative furniture types are concerned, it may be that common attitudes to innovation, type forms and image were widespread. The fickle nature of public taste seems arbitrary, but is very real. To be successful, a newly introduced item must fall within the bounds of consumer taste, expectation and experience. Most of the examples mentioned in this section would perhaps have been developed from an existing type that was already familiar.

As far as dual-purpose furniture is concerned, it could be argued that this furniture type reflected an interest in mechanisation which was widespread amongst sections of the purchasing public.[50] In a number of cases, these special-purpose items were patented, and even if they were not officially patented, they would often be promoted as such thus giving them the correct cachet.

Metamorphic furniture

As has been shown, convenience as well as ingenuity for its own sake was a growing part of attitudes in eighteenth-century interiors and their furnishing. To achieve this, many new furniture types were introduced, and a whole range of objects were produced which integrated different functions into one item. This sort of furniture design is perhaps indicative of how furniture-makers responded to the

29 A Merlin quartetto music cabinet which contained 'flutes, violins, and music books: and by touching a spring key, it will rise to a proper height, and form music desks for four partners'.

problem of a very varied range of demands. Some authors have suggested that the trend reflects a space-saving requirement that arose from a population increase and a demand for furniture convenient for use in crowded town dwellings.[51] This, however, is only one side of the story. There was clearly a delight in metamorphic and dual-purpose furniture that was enjoyed by those with both large and small houses.

Nevertheless, items that had modes of combining functions within one piece of furniture were often space-saving as well. For the customer, this no doubt added to the convenience as well as to the amusement value of a piece. For the trade they were also potentially very profitable.

A flurry of patent activity in the last quarter of the eighteenth century indicates the increasing potential of metamorphic furniture at this time. The first patent with a particular space-saving intention was Eckhardt's portable table and portable chair of 1771, which was 'so contrived as to answer all the purposes of the common tables and chairs, and at the same time to lay in the compass of a small box'.[52]

Space-saving dining tables were also the subject of a number of other patent applications, the first being Sweetnam and Higgs's 'improvements in the construction of tables'.[53] The principle of this patent was that a double flap top would be able to flip over, swivel round and extend the table to twice its original size. The table also had a hollow-frame top which was designed to hold shaving, dressing or writing requisites.

These two patent tables indicate something of the different reasons for their demand. Eckhardt's would be useful in simplifying the export or transport of tables etc., whilst Sweetman and Higgs's would be a practical matter of introducing a table that could accommodate a variety of persons at different times.

As dining became more of a social custom, adjustable-size dining tables continued to gain the attention of patent designers, and in 1800 Richard Gillow designed an extending dining table which used wood or metal sliders to pull apart the two tops, ready for the insertion of extra flaps.[54] Between 1802 and 1807, four more patents were taken out which related to altering the size of tables. Brown's patent extension table was based on the 'lazy-tongs' principle with a cross rail and legs between each pair of tongs;[55] this was successfully marketed by Wilkinson & Co. of Ludgate Hill. A further improvement on the extension of dining tables was invented by George Remington in 1807.

This device consisted of a lazy-tongs action which expanded tables in a concertina motion similar to Brown's patent, two years previous, but this patent relied on a pair of legs being attached to each set of tongs.[56] Further examples included tables which operated by the use of pulleys, endless chains and developments of the lazy-tongs and screw motions. All this activity certainly reflects a particular consumer interest in this form of table.

Not all inventions that related to space saving involved dining tables. The requirement was further advanced by the patent of John Elwick in 1800 which was for a new and improved method of framing 'together chairs and sofas of every kind and sort whatsoever and which invention is intended to be applied to every description of household furniture'.[57] This patent, designed to help the needs of exporters, was made by the son of Edward Elwick of the firm of Wright and Elwick. The idea was based on the 'knock-down' principle. By having screw-tapped holes and stretchers with screws inserted into them, an item could be assembled at its destination. This was clearly a pragmatic solution to the space problem for exporters and no doubt helped save considerable freight costs.

In addition to the physical need for space-saving furniture, there was also a demand for dual-purpose items and this was often, though by no means always, related to the size of the family. The example of press beds is instructive. The idea of beds in cupboards had, for a long time, been in use in vernacular homes, but in polite society, sensibility and social pressure suggested that a bed in a dining or living room was not *de rigeur*. This idea may also have been related to concerns about health. As early as 1691, Thomas Tryon was complaining that press bedsteads did not allow proper air circulation,[58] and over 100 years later Loudon warned that press bedsteads were 'objectionable, as harbouring vermin and being apt soon to get out of order when in daily use'.[59]

Regardless of these warnings, press beds were to remain popular throughout the century. Ideal for garret bedrooms and servants, they were also made for grander clients. Imposing examples might well have followed the 1772 patent of Thomas Gale, who invented a mechanism for a wardrobe/bedstead that raised the false doors to make a tester for the bed which then unfolded from the inside. When closed, the whole object resembled a bookcase or wardrobe.[60] The models made for David Garrick and Sir Edward Knatchbull are of a high quality, whilst the records of the Gillow firm show they produced a range of models for most tastes.[61]

The press bedstead was an interesting example of a basic product type that was available in a number of varieties, each of which indicated a different status. At the top of the range was the library press bed which incorporated shelving for books on either side of a middle section covered by double doors. According to Richard Gillow these were intended 'to stand in a Dining Room as a handsome piece of furniture to make an additional bedroom occasionally'.[62] A little less imposing was the wardrobe press bed. This was a wardrobe shape that combined a pull-out bed hidden behind wood or mirror doors. At the bottom of the selection were bureaux and table press beds, where the beds unfolded from behind or underneath.[63] Oliver Goldsmith referred to this dual image in his *Deserted Village*:

> The chest contrived a double debt to pay
> A bed at night, a chest of drawers by day.[64]

As mentioned above, a particular notion of decorum, in which the alternative use of a piece of furniture is hidden, was part of a wider feeling that the specialised use of space, rational systems of storage and the careful planning of limited resources was both practical and morally superior. The example of a product from the Seddon workshop which was commented upon favourably by Sophie von la Roche is revealing of this trend. The item, a sideboard, had a spring in the place where the drawers were indicated, which opened up into a lead-lined compartment, fitted out to keep wine bottles cool. In addition:

There were two foot stools of the same wood, and made to match . . .
In these foot-stools are two tiny cupboards, one lined with sheet iron and neat grillers, on which plates can be heated by the red hot iron beneath them; the other is meant to keep salt cellars and other table utensils.[65]

Certainly rational and well-planned, it must have impressed the diarist as much for its ingenuity in design as its fine workmanship.

Other ideas for the use of space were more bizarre. Sheraton designed a sideboard with a secret pot-cupboard door 'which has not a turning buckle but a thumb spring which operates a rod that springs the door open'. This was planned to meet the need of assembled male company as it was not socially acceptable to leave the room to visit the lavatory.[66] This local custom, and the furniture specially designed to accommodate it, was commented upon by a French visitor, Louis Simond:

> Drinking much and long leads to unavoidable consequences. Will it be credited that in a corner of the very dining room, there is a certain convenient piece of furniture, to be used by anybody who wants it.[67]

In fact it was not only sideboards that accommodated this contrivance. Ideas of decorum encouraged the 'deception table' which was designed to appear like a common Pembroke table, but it actually assumed the purpose of a pot-cupboard.[68] In other cases it might be simply designed to fit under a sideboard but with the same purpose.

The need for portability in furniture, like other innovations, also seems to have stemmed from someone perceiving a demand and then planning to meet it. The needs of an army and navy that were more often abroad than at home obviously demanded furniture that could be taken around on tours of duty. Some families liked to take some furniture with them as they moved from town to country and back again, or if they

30 An example of a metamorphic cabinet press bed that resembles a chest of drawers when closed.

31 The bureau bed when open revealing a folding bed frame.

emigrated to other parts of the world they would require furniture both for the journey and for the new home. The concept of flat-packing chairs and table together was no doubt appreciated on board ships where space was at a premium, whilst many other ideas based on customer demand were the epitome of convenience.

Whatever sort of furniture was actually chosen, its relation to room use was always considered to be significant.

Room use

Halls, ante-rooms and vestibules

The role of the hall as an introductory statement of what might be found in the rest of the house, often meant that the decoration and furnishings would want to act either as a foil to the main interior or sometimes to be a dramatic statement in their own right. In 1768 Isaac Ware pointed out a distinction between the purpose of halls in town and country dwellings. In the town, halls did not need to be elegant as the area was a place for servants, whereas in the country it ought to be large and noble as it could serve a variety of functions.[69]

Whatever the case, for much of the century the main items to be found in the hall were chairs or benches specifically designed for that situation. These could represent another self-positioning possibility:

> [the chairs] are such as are placed in halls, for the use of servants or strangers waiting on business – they are generally made of all mahogany with turned seats and the crest or arms of the family painted on the centre of the back.[70]

Hall chairs were devised solely for one location and tended to follow a particular pattern. Both Chippendale and Ince and Mayhew illustrate the form in their pattern books, and interestingly, both suggest a painted finish if mahogany should prove too expensive. Hall benches followed a similar style to the hall chairs. In either case, the rather fanciful idea that these were made with hard seats and backs to remind users of their place in society is less likely than the more practical idea that with continual use, as well as contact with wet or dirty clothing, plain wooden chairs would be easier to maintain.

Although by no means exclusive to the hall and ante rooms, console and pier tables may be discussed here. The pier table, often designed to be part of a comprehensive decorative scheme, was usually supported by two front legs, the back being fixed to the wall. In elaborate schemes the support may have taken the form of a lion or fish, while in many cases pier tables were intended to complement looking glasses that were mounted between the architraves of windows. Clearly both these table types have no special use over and above being part of the scheme; indeed this non-functional aspect was often part of the message that was being portrayed to visitors.

Dining rooms

The eighteenth century saw an uncertain attitude to the role of the dining room, although the range and variety of tables associated with eating give clues to this important event. An assortment of arrangements therefore result. In the seventeenth century it had been *de rigeur* to have a dining table (round, oval or rectangular) set up in the dining room, with cupboards and side tables around the walls. Chairs were also arranged against the walls.[71] During the eighteenth century, the range of possibilities grew.

A number of small tables in the same room were often used, whilst it was not unusual for meals to be taken in a variety of rooms dependant upon one's whim at the time. Chairs were still generally arranged around the room when not in use.

From around 1780 a set of dining tables (or in fact one large table) was the mode. This big table often comprised three or more sections. The Reverend James Woodforde explained in his diary that his 'new tables are three in number, all of the very best mahogany and new, the middle one is a very large one and very wide, the other two are half rounds, to add to the middle table'.[72] Other sorts of extending tables included the horseshoe table made from segments that were brought together to form a semicircle.

The sideboard table was used 'for a dining equipage, on which the silver plate is placed',[73] whilst the sideboard was introduced in the last quarter of the eighteenth century, designed to hold all the necessaries for serving and dining.

As with the sideboard, other furniture items associated with dining were often based on the demand for convenience. Breakfast tables, for example, were designed on a small scale and were often fitted with two small flaps to extend the top for convenience. They also had an enclosed shelf fitted below the top to accommodate used crockery. Tea tables were often planned with a fretted gallery, presumably designed to avoid knocking cups off the top, whilst other tea tables were made with multi-dished tops apparently designed for securing cups and saucers whilst serving tea.[74]

The style and function of the dining room was reflected in its furnishings. Adam proclaimed that '[dining rooms] are considered as the apartments of conversation, in which we [males] are to pass a great part of our time'.[75] In another vein, Sheraton uses adjectives such as 'handsome', 'large' and 'substantial', to evoke an idea of the required furniture style for a dining room, thus giving a hint of the sort of impression that was to be projected.[76] Impressions were also important in the furnishing of a library.

Libraries and book rooms

Even quite modest homes would not have been complete without a library of some sort. Depending on the scale of the room and the collection of books, prints and drawings, there would be a whole range

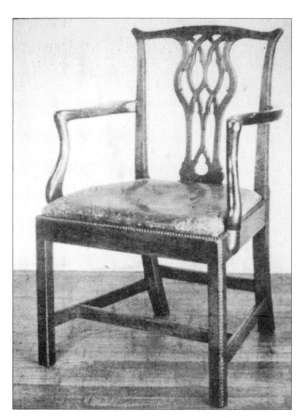

32 Solidly elegant Georgian taste. A mahogany armchair with a Gothic influenced splat, *c.* 1755.

of furniture accessories deemed necessary. Solely for reading, there could be specially-designed reading and writing chairs, which remained popular throughout the century. Although made in a variety of fashionable styles, they were all contrived so that they could be sat upon astride with the book set upon an adjustable shelf on the back rail.[77] This moved around the whole armpiece so that the appropriate angle could be selected.

Reading tables and stands were also introduced to support books at various slants. These were either freestanding upon a pedestal, or designed to sit on a table. They feature in Ince and Mayhew's *Universal System of Household Furniture* and also in the 1797 edition of *The Prices of Cabinet Work*.[78] More sophisticated were the combined writing and reading tables variously known as artists, architects, or Cobb tables. These combined rising tops with drawer space and

33 An elegant extending two-pedestal dining table with reeded pillars, which can be enlarged by the addition of extra leaves.

accessories. The reason they were called Cobb tables was explained in Smith's (1828) description of them. He said that John Cobb 'was the person who brought that very convenient table into fashion that draws out in front, with upper and inwards rising desks, so healthy for those who stand to write, read or draw.[79] The use of the word 'convenient' clearly relates to the design of a whole range of furniture that was planned to make the use of the library as efficient and as pleasant as possible.

An essential item in larger libraries was the double kneehole table. This was made up from pedestals with drawers or cupboards which supported a top, itself fitted with drawers. Often large enough to accommodate two people, and frequently being of fine quality in design and finish, they could take pride of place within the library setting.

In most libraries, furniture items intended to assist access would also have been indispensable, as books were often shelved to the cornice. These items took a wide variety of forms, usually as steps or ladders, including telescopic poles, miniature staircases, as well as convertible tables or chairs that had built-in steps. Sometimes they were architectural in conception and resembled a flight of stairs, whilst in other cases they were hidden away until required. These

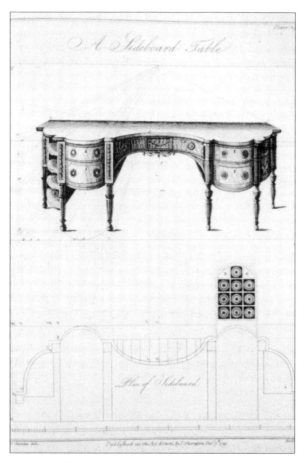

34 A sideboard table design by Thomas Sheraton, showing the plan complete with drawer details.

metamorphic models were often based upon the 1774 patent of Robert Campbell.[80] In a similar vein was the metamorphic library chair which could be deftly turned from an elbow chair into a set of steps.[81]

Inevitably, the most important items of the library, especially if the architect had not supplied built-in storage, were the bookcases. Although the well-known example of the Pepys's bookcases (considered to be the first, and now in Magdalene College, Oxford) dates from 1666, bookcases were only to grow in popularity during the eighteenth century. The free-standing press or library case, often based on architectural forms, was the mainstay of library rooms, and this continued to be the case into the nineteenth century. In smaller or more private rooms, book storage was often integrated to form a composite piece called a bureau bookcase.[82]

It has been suggested that the library lost much of its 'all-male' connotations towards the end of the century.[83] The influence of the female and the change of role for the library from a studious space to a more family-orientated room meant that a wider range of activities were included which called for more specialised furniture. Examples might include writing tables for both men and women, screen tables designed to shield one from the heat of a fire[84], and specially designed chairs for convenient and comfortable sitting at these table types.[85]

Bedrooms, closets and dressing rooms

The ascending order of importance of a suite of rooms as described by Isaac Ware in 1756 indicates a changing role for particular apartments.[86] The progression from the saloon, via antechamber, drawing room, bed chamber and finally to the dressing room represents a move towards making the closet and dressing room have a greater importance than the reception rooms. The opportunity for personal display in dressing rooms was therefore too good to miss, thus explaining why much dressing furniture is often of fine quality and taste. Mrs Boscawen, writing in 1748, recorded proudly that 'This afternoon I saw company in my dressing room for the first time since it being finished'.[87]

For women's dressing rooms, a range of special tables, boxes and stools, mirrors and chests of drawers were developed, whilst for men, shaving stands, dressing glasses and storage items were introduced. Dressing tables were known and used in the seventeenth century, but during the eighteenth century they became much more elaborate. They incorporated a wide variety of toilet requisites and could be very complex and costly objects. An interesting example of an extreme design is the Rudd or reflecting dressing table. This was a four-legged table with pull-out drawers, some being fitted with mirrors that lifted up at various angles. First illustrated in Hepplewhite's *Guide* (1788), it was also shown in a simplified form in the *Cabinet-maker's London Book of Prices*. The model was again published in 1797, but by 1803 Sheraton could claim that it was 'not much in present use'.[88] Perhaps this indicates the relatively short span of popularity of a novel item.

35 A convertible table with a set of library steps within, using Campbell's 1774 patented principle.

It would appear that the terms 'dressing' and 'toilet' table were interchangeable during the century. Chippendale refers to a 'toylet' table in the *Director*, and Ince and Mayhew show a 'toiletta', derived from Chippendale's example.[89] Both are fancifully draped and fitted with an adjustable mirror glass.

Dressing tables were not exclusively for women. Sheraton designed one to 'accommodate a gentleman or lady with conveniences for dressing',[90] although men tended to use dressing units, variously known as dressing stands, commodes or chests. There were differences between these items, the chest usually being a chest of drawers with the top drawer fitted out for convenience. The dressing commode seems hardly different except that the chest might have been fitted with a hinged top having a mirror on the underside, whereas the commode would frequently have had a free-standing toilet mirror stood upon it.[91] The dressing chest fulfilled the taste for multi-purpose furniture as

36 A satinwood
ladies' worktable
after a Sheraton
design, complete
with basket,
writing slope and
fire screen built-in.

it was compact and was fitted with a variety of drawers: one for a night stool, one for a square bidet, one for a basin and two cups and one for a water bottle. In addition, a glass frame was usually hinged under the top.[92]

Apart from these, other special-use items included shaving tables and stands, the distinction generally being that the stands did not have basins. Night tables, introduced in the mid-century, are illustrated in Ince and Mayhew's *Universal System*, with one example conveniently offering a rising top for reading. Night tables, bidets, etc. were often disguised to look like another furniture type or were hidden within another unit. (See dressing rooms above.)

The necessaries of ablutions were completed by the close stool or chair. Close stools, also known as 'conveniences', were common during the century.[93] They were often disguised, as in the close-stool chair, which was made with a hinged seat with an extended apron to

37 An example of the delight in ingenuity in furniture during the latter part of the eighteenth century. The Rudd or Reflecting dressing table, designed so that the sitter could see themselves from most angles.

conceal its true purpose. Whereas the chair simply had a deeper apron than normal, the 'chest' version was quite a contraption in the metamorphic furniture tradition. Sheraton describes it as having

> the appearance of a small commode, standing upon legs: when it is used the seat part presses down to a proper height by hand, and afterwards it rises by means of lead weights hung to the seat by lines passing over pullies at each end, all of which are inclosed in a case.[94]

Eighteenth-century bedroom and dressing furniture was clearly intended to provide the maximum in convenience and personal comfort. This requirement was also found in the saloons and drawing rooms.

Drawing rooms

The quest for comfort is one of the key issues in eighteenth-century furniture and upholstery. Discussion of this trend is related to two other important developments during the period. These were the growing distinction between the public and private apartments of a large house, and the gradual separation of work from the home, both of which brought about an increase in private furniture designed for relaxation.

Towards the end of the century, the drawing room or saloon was arguably the most important room in the house.[95] It was the main reception room and like other rooms, was to be furnished in accordance with the demands of social politeness, manner and appropriate taste. This meant using the 'correct' furnishings. Sheraton gave an example of this when he warned against introducing books, pictures and globes into the drawing room as these would interfere with conversation. On the other hand, 'The grandeur then introduced into the drawing room is not to be considered as the ostentatious parade of its proprietor, but the respect he pays to the rank of his visitants'.[96] This respect might manifest itself in furniture designed with comfort and luxury in mind.

The aspirations of home-makers towards this ideal were noted by William Cowper:

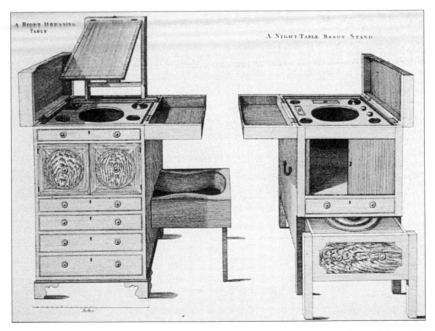

38 Designs by Sheraton for bedroom furniture. A bidet dressing table and a night table offer a range of useful facilities.

Thus first Necessity invented stools
Convenience next suggested elbow chairs
and Luxury the accomplished sofa last.[97]

The parallels between Cowper's comments, and those of Joshua Reynolds and Daniel Defoe quoted above are remarkable for their consistency in describing the ladder of desire, in particular, the desire for a more relaxed approach to interiors, their furnishing and their use, which becomes more noticeable as the century progresses. In the early 1770s, Lady Louisa Conolly described the use of the gallery in Castletown which reflects this trend towards cosiness: 'In the gallery where we live 'tis the most comfortable room you ever saw, and quite warm; supper at one end, the company at the other, and I am writing in one of the piers at a distance from it all.'[98]

Towards the end of the century much of the architectural formality had been watered down to a framework for the casual arrangement of furniture, as a result of the demand for comfortable surroundings. Comfort in this case would mean ease and convenience as well as support. A contemporary commentator gives a flavour of this idea of comfort: 'The furniture of houses generally speaking consists of large chairs, the seats of which are in part stuffed up very full and covered with Morocco leather, and partly of mahogany tables.'[99]

It seems reasonable to suggest that there was a change in the manner of polite sitting during the latter part of the eighteenth century. People began to sit in a different way as the revival of couches, day-beds and reclining chairs gives ample evidence of a more casual and 'lolling' type of relaxation.

Indeed, an enquiry was being made into the relationship between posture and postural defects by Nicholas Andry, who published *L'Orthopédie ou l'art de prévenir et de corriger dans les enfants les déformités du corps* in Paris during 1741.[100] Although this would appear to be a specific medical enquiry, it is perhaps emblematic of an interest in posture and sitting.

In France a compromise was reached between comfort and style by using two sorts of chairs. The *sièges meublants* were designed to complement the architectural shell and remain in one position, whereas he *sièges courants* were lighter in weight and style, and were intended to be moved about at will within the less formal rooms. Sheraton commented upon this French distinction saying, 'where their drawing rooms are fitted up in the most splendid manner, they use a sett of small and plainer chairs, reserving the others merely for ornament.'[101]

Comfort, of course, meant more than upholstery and easy chairs. It meant leisure and convenience as well. In these matters, the eighteenth century was developing fast. The practical demands created by two related issues furthered the cause of comfort in the widest sense. The combined effects of improvements in health, hygiene and comfort often went together and nowhere so much as in the treatment of invalids. These demands were important stimuli to inventors, so in many cases the products were the subject of patents.

One of the first concerns of patentees in this field was to produce furniture that would relieve the suffering of patients who were bed-ridden or incapable of self-propulsion. Indeed, the very first furniture patent listed in July 1620 relates to a back frame designed to relieve sick persons who were permanently prostrate. By the eighteenth-century, retailers were offering furniture that provided relief from gout and insomnia as well supplying methods of propulsion for the infirm. Between 1727 and 1744 Hodson of Frith Street, London, operated a 'Looking glass and cabinet warehouse' which had amongst the stock advertised 'many well contrived machines for weak or sickly people'.[102]

One of the most successful of the eighteenth-century designers of adaptable chairs and furniture was John Joseph Merlin. Merlin specialised in mechanical furniture, which has already been discussed, but he also introduced a number of varieties of invalid and exercising chairs.

These chairs often reflected a current health fad. The portable Hygeian chair for example, was designed to allow people to swing themselves in exercise.[103] The idea that swinging might be a remedy for 'pulmonary consumption and hectic fever' was promoted by James Carmichael Smyth in a pamphlet published in 1787.[104] The chair was noted by Mrs Powys in her diary of 1788, in which she recorded that the physicians said these chairs were without doubt conducive to good health; she commented that 'their motion I found easy and pleasing'.[105] Even if the medical evidence sounds of dubious value, in was no doubt a pleasant experience. Another of Merlin's chairs was positively odd. This was the Valetudinarian chair, designed to show increases in weight by eating and drinking, and subsequent decreases by perspiration![106] The more well-known 'gouty chair', which in its simplest form was a self-propelled chair on wheels, often with a footrest, had a precedent in the *Receuil d'Ouvrages Curieux de Mathématique et de Méchanique*, published in Paris in 1751 by Grollier de Servière.[107]

Merlin's exhibition of mechanical objects also included the Morpheus chair which was 'made to fall back and form a bed for the repose of the infirm. It has curtains and a calash over the head with a cradle for the legs, and also wheels about at pleasure'.[108] Priced at 40 guineas it must have been a more splendid object than the simple mechanical easy chair or gouty chair that Merlin also advertised at 14 to 20 guineas.[109]

It seems that there was a degree of success in addressing comfort in a physical sense, but it was to be a demand for convenience and amusement that spawned a wonderful variety of furniture in the latter part of the century that has been put under the title of metamorphic furniture.

This discussion about furniture use has been intentionally wide-ranging without losing sight of the actual objects that are part of the material culture of the eighteenth century. Consumption is of course not to be viewed in isolation, and is an integral part of the process that this book has tried to investigate. Indeed, it can also be seen to be a new starting point, since consumption is inevitably the motivation for demand, necessitating further design and production.

Notes

1 The disciplines that impinge on consumption could, of course, be widened to include other branches of historical studies as well as politics, geography etc.

2 T. Veblen, *Theory of the Leisure Class* (1899, Unwin reprint, 1970).

3 D. Defoe, *The Complete English Tradesman* [1727] Vol II, part 2, p. 167.

4 N. Forster, *An Enquiry into the Present High Price of Provisions* (1767), quoted in N. McKendrick *et al.*, *The Birth of Consumer Society* (Bloomington, Indiana University Press, 1982), p. 11.

5 The Correspondence of Emily, Duchess of Leinster, vol. 1, p. 59, quoted in J. Fowler and J. Cornforth, *English Decoration in the Eighteenth Century* (London, Barrie and Jenkins, 1974).

6 For work in this area see P. Bourdieu, *Distinction: A Social Critique of the Judgement of Taste* (London, Routledge, 1984); M. Douglas and B. Isherwood, *The World of Goods: Towards an Anthropology of Consumption* (Harmondsworth, Penguin, 1980), D. Miller, *Material Culture and Mass Production* (Oxford, Oxford University Press, 1987).

7 See J. Sleep, 'Consumer behaviour across an urban hierarchy, 1650–1725', *Regional Furniture Newsletter*, XXI (1994), pp. 12–13.

8 C. Campbell 'Understanding traditional and modern patterns of consumption in eighteenth-century England: a character action approach', in J. Brewer and R. Porter (eds), *Consumption and the World of Goods* (London, Routledge, 1993), pp. 40–57.

9 *Ibid.*

10 This particular role for the interior reached it peak in the mid-nineteenth century.

11 M. Csikszentmihalyi and E. Rochberg Halton, *The Meaning of Things: Domestic Symbols and the Self* (Cambridge, Cambridge University Press, 1981), pp. 38–9.

12 Douglas and Isherwood, *The World of Goods*, p. 59.

13 T. Sheraton, *The Cabinet Dictionary* (London, 1803), p. 215.

14 *Ibid.*

15 G. McCracken, *Culture and Consumption* (Bloomington, Indiana University Press, 1988).

16 Quoted in H. Huth, *Lacquer of the West. The History of a Craft and Industry, 1550–1950* (Chicago, 1971), p. 117.

17 *London und Paris*, VI, 1800, pp. 184–7, quoted in P. Kirkham, *The London Furniture Trade, 1700–1870* (Furniture History Society, 1988), p. 67.

18 L. Weatherill, *Consumer Behaviour and Material Culture in Britain, 1660–1760* (London, Routledge, 1988), p. 191, Table 8.2.

19 *The Book of Trades or Library of Useful Arts* (London, 1804), part III, pp. 123–5.

20 C. Williams (trans.), *Sophie in London* [1786] (London, Cape, 1933), p. 275.

21 See 'The consumer revolution in eighteenth-century England', in McKendrick *et al.*, *Birth of a Consumer Society*, pp. 9–34, especially the references to Mandeville's *Fable of the Bees*.

22 D. Defoe, *The Complete English Tradesman* [1727] (New York, Kelley, 1969), vol. II, part 2, p. 149.

23 *Ibid.*

24 Jonathan Swift quoted in McKendrick *et al.*, *Birth of a Consumer Society*, p. 19.

25 See P. Tristram, *Living Space in Fact and Fiction* (London, Routledge, 1989), for details of similar approaches in eighteenth- and nineteenth-century literature, p. 162. Also Joyce Appleby, 'Consumption in early modern social thought', in Brewer and Porter, *Consumption and the World of Goods*.

26 W. Ince and J. Mayhew, *Universal System of Household Furniture* (London, 1762), Preface.

27 Defoe, *Complete English Tradesman* [1727], part 2, p. 6.

28 J. Stokes, *The Complete Cabinet-maker and Upholsterer's Guide* (London, 1829), p. 4.

29 Quoted in D. Knell, *English Country Furniture* (London, Barrie and Jenkins, 1992), p. 76.

30 J. Wood, *An Essay towards a Description of Bath*, 1749, in B. Denvir, *The Eighteenth Century: Art Design and Society* (Harlow, Longman, 1983).

31 Middlesex Sessions Books 1229, 1768. (Middlesex Guildhall), quoted in E. Joy, *The Connoisseur's Complete Period Guides* (London, Connoisseur, 1968), p. 592. The preparation of inventories during the eighteenth century declined dramatically after the first quarter of the century. There are some useful examples in M. Spufford, *The Great Reclothing of Rural England* (London, Hambledon Press, 1984). For the later part of the century auction records may prove useful in determining the range of furnishings owned in a household.

32 Josiah Tucker, *A Selection from his Economic and Political Writings*, ed. R. L. Schuyler (1931). Quoted in McKendrick *et al.*, *The Birth of a Consumer Society*, p. 25.

33 W. Cobbett, *Rural Rides* (1830) (Harmondsworth, Penguin, 1967), p. 226, entry for 20 October 1825; also see C. Gilbert, *English Vernacular Furniture, 1750–1900* (New Haven and London, Yale University Press, 1991), p. 43.

34 Cobbett, *Rural Rides*, p. 226.

35 Gilbert, *English Vernacular Furniture*, p. 32. The inventory of Mathew Heslop of Langton-upon-Swale 1751. The total value of his furniture and furnishings was £21. Compare this with the value of his livestock and crops at £88. See also Jan de Vries 'Between purchasing power and the world of goods, understanding the household economy in early modern Europe', in Brewer and Porter (eds), *Consumption and the World of Goods*, pp. 100, 104, where he argues that growing numbers of possessions did not increase the value of estates, rather their relative value fell.

36 Weatherill, *Consumer Behaviour*, pp. 33–4.

37 Joy, *Connoisseur's Complete Period Guides*, p. 834.

38 'Consideration on the Expediency of Raising . . . the Wages of servants that are not domestic, particularly Clerks in Public Offices' (B.M.T. 152/4, 1767), quoted in Joy, *Connoisseur's Complete Period Guides*, p. 834.

39 C. Gilbert and T. Murdoch, *John Channon and Brass-inlaid Furniture*,

1730–1760 (New Haven and London, Yale University Press, 1993), p. 18.

40 Temple Newsam, Leeds. See also Gilbert and Murdoch, *John Channon*.

41 T. Sheraton, *The Cabinet-maker and Upholsterer's Drawing Book* (1793), p. 388.

42 *Ibid.*, p. 397.

43 B. Crosby, Patent No. 3153, 25 July 1808.

44 Sheraton, *Cabinet Dictionary*.

45 The nobility amusing themselves with turning machines is one example. See K. Maurice, *Sovereigns as Turners* (Zurich, Verlag Ineichen, 1985).

46 Williams (trans.) *Sophie in London*, p. 140.

47 Michael Wright, *John Joseph Merlin, the Ingenious Mechanick*, Exhibition catalogue (London, Kenwood, 1985), p. 76.

48 *Ibid.*, item IX. Noted by Sophie von la Roche, *Sophie in London*, p. 140.

49 *Morning and Evening Amusement at Merlin's Mechanical Museum*, 1803, Catalogue, Wellcome Museum reprinted in Wright, *John Joseph Merlin*, Exhibition catalogue.

50 M. J. Ettema, 'History, nostalgia and American furniture', *Winterthur Portfolio*, XVII (1982), p. 140.

51 Edward Joy, *English Furniture, 1800–1851* (London, Sotheby, 1974).

52 A. G. Eckhardt, Patent No. 995, 29 July 1771.

53 R. Sweetman and J. Higgs, Patent No. 2007, 13 August 1794.

54 R. Gillow, Patent No. 2396, 1 May 1800.

55 R. Brown, Patent No. 2898, 26 November 1805. The lazy tongs were simply based on a concertina movement.

56 G. Remington, Patent No. 3090, 16 December 1807.

57 J. Elwick, Patent No. 2420, 1 July 1800.

58 T. Tryon, *The Way to Health, Long Life and Happiness* (London, 1691), p. 440.

59 J. C. Loudon, *An Encyclopaedia of Cottage, Farm and Villa Architecture and Furniture*, revised edition (London, 1839), pp. 331–2.

60 T. Gale, Patent No. 1002, 1 February 1772.

61 Garrick's press bed/wardrobe is in the Victoria and Albert Museum. For the Knatchbull commission see C. Gilbert, *The Life and Work of Thomas Chippendale* (London, 1978), p. 231. A number of examples are shown in the Gillow ES (estimate sketch books) held at Westminster Central Library, London.

62 Richard Gillow, letter to Matthew Wilson, November 1778. See Gillow's Letter Book, 1778–81, 344/169. Gillow Archive.

63 For press beds see C. Edwards, 'Press Beds', *Furniture History*, XXVI (1990).

64 Cited in J. Gloag, *Dictionary of Furniture*, revised edition (London, Unwin Hyman, 1990), p. 537.

65 Williams (trans.), *Sophie in London*, p. 174.

66 The reason for this seems to be that if one left the room it was seen as an opportunity to avoid further drinking by not returning.

67 Louis Simond, 'The reason the English keep a commode close by' (1815), quoted in P. Greenhalgh, *Quotations and Sources on Design and Decorative Arts* (Manchester, Manchester University Press, 1993).

68 Sheraton, *Cabinet Dictionary*, p. 192.

69 Fowler and Cornforth, *English Decoration*, p. 66.

70 Sheraton, *Cabinet Dictionary*, p. 250.

71 For a full description see R. Holme, *The Academy of Armoury* [1688] (London, Roxburgh Club edn, 1905), vol. 2, pp. 15–16.

72 Quoted in Gloag, *Dictionary of Furniture*, entry for compass table.

73 Sheraton, *Cabinet Dictionary*, p. 304.

74 See Gilbert and Murdoch, *John Channon*, pp. 113–20.

75 Cited in P. Thornton, *Authentic Decor. The Domestic Interior, 1620–1920* (London, Weidenfeld and Nicolson, 1984), p. 147.

76 Sheraton, *Cabinet Dictionary*, p. 218.

77 *Ibid.*, p. 17 and plate 5.

78 *The Prices of Cabinet Work* (1797) Plates 26 and 11 respectively.

79 J. T. Smith, *Nollekens and his Times* (London, 1828), vol. II, pp. 243–4.

80 Robert Campbell, Patent No. 1086, 11 November 1774. This patent referred to making library steps in writing, library, dining, card, breakfast, dressing or other tables. The continuing success of the design may be gauged by the fact that Morgan and Sanders were making library steps based on Campbell's principle in the early nineteenth century; see B. Austen, 'Morgan and Sanders and the patent furniture-makers of Catherine Street', *Connoisseur* (November 1974), pp. 130–91. They are illustrated in Sheraton, *Drawing Book*, Plates 5 and 22. Although Campbell patented the design in 1774, Sheraton writing in *c*. 1793 pointed out that if makers did not want to bother with altering the model to avoid the patent, the steps were available from Robert Campbell and Son, Marylebone Street, London, 'with a sufficient allowance for selling them again'. (Appendix, p. 43.)

81 For library steps, see further, E. H. Pinto, 'Georgian library steps', *Antiques*, LXXXIII (January 1963), pp. 102–4.

82 This term was not contemporary. It was coined in the nineteenth century. At the time the piece was known as a desk and bookcase.

83 Thornton, *Authentic Decor*, p. 150.

84 For example see *The Price of Cabinet Work*, plate 6.

85 Sheraton, *Drawing Book*, Appendix, plate 10.

86 Sir Isaac Ware, *A Complete Body of Architecture* (London 1756), book III, p. 328, quoted in Tristram, *Living Space*.
87 Fowler and Cornforth, *English Decoration*, p. 81.
88 Sheraton, *Cabinet Dictionary*.
89 Gloag, *Dictionary of Furniture*.
90 Sheraton, *Cabinet Dictionary*, p. 202. See also plate no. 214 in Thornton, *Authentic Decor*.
91 Even with this distinction there appear to be examples of both versions.
92 *The Prices of Cabinet Work*.
93 See A. Heal, *The London Furniture-makers, from the Restoration to the Victorian Era, 1660–1840* (London, Batsford, 1953), p. 181.
94 Sheraton, *Cabinet Dictionary*, pp. 274–5. The nineteenth-century term 'commode', for this furniture type, might have derived from this description.
95 In larger houses the saloon would have been the main reception room, whilst the drawing room was a more relaxed family room.
96 Sheraton, *Cabinet Dictionary*, p. 218.
97 W. Cowper, 'The Task', quoted in E. S. Cooke (ed.), *Upholstery in America and Europe from the Seventeenth Century to World War I* (New York, Norton, 1987), p. 11.
98 Fowler and Cornforth, *English Decoration*, p. 75.
99 M. Grosley, *A Tour of London or New Observations on England* (1772), vol. 1, pp. 72–3.
100 Quoted in J. Rykwert, *The Necessity of Artifice* (London, Academy Editions, 1982).
101 Sheraton, *Drawing Book*.
102 Heal, *London Furniture-makers*, p. 80.
103 Item VI in Catalogue of Merlin's Mechanical Exhibition, 1787–9, Princeton University Library, quoted in Wright, *John Joseph Merlin*, Exhibition Catalogue, p. 138.
104 J. C. Smyth, *An Account of the Effects of Swinging Employed as a Remedy in the Pulmonary Consumption and Hectic Fever*, London 1787, quoted in Wright, *John Joseph Merlin*, Exhibition Catalogue.
105 *Passages from the Diaries of Mrs. Philip Lybbe Powys* Emily Climenson (ed.), 1899, p. 232, quoted in G. Wills, *English Furniture 1760–1900* (London, Guinness Superlatives, 1969), p. 159.
106 Item xx in Catalogue of Merlin's Mechanical Exhibition, 1787–9, Princeton University Library reprinted in Wright, *John Joseph Merlin*, Exhibition Catalogue.
107 Rykwert, *Necessity of Artifice*. See also P. Thornton, *Seventeenth-Century Interior Decoration in England, France and Holland* (Yale

University Press, 1978), pp. 196–8, for a discussion of the precedents for gouty chairs found in invalid chairs for royal usage.

108 Item VII in Catalogue of Merlin's Mechanical Exhibition, 1787–9, Princeton University Library reprinted in Wright, *John Joseph Merlin*, Exhibition Catalogue, p. 138.

109 Item XII in Catalogue of Merlin's Mechanical Exhibition, 1787–9, reprinted in Wright, *John Joseph Merlin*, Exhibition Catalogue, p. 139.

Bibliography

Adams, R., *Ruins of the Palace of the Emperor Diocletian at Spalato*, 1764.

Adams, R., *The Works in Architecture of Robert and James Adam*, 1778.

Aitken, W., 'Papier mâché manufacture' in S. Timmins (ed.), *Birmingham Resources and Industrial History*, 1866.

Alexander, D. G., *Retailing in England during the Industrial Revolution*, London, Athlone, 1970.

Alison A., *Essays on the Nature and Principles of Taste*, 1790.

Alister, C., 'The Anti-Gallicans', *Transactions of the Greenwich and Lewisham Antiquarian Society*, VII, 1970, pp. 211–17.

Ames, K., and Ward, G.,(eds), *Decorative Arts and Household Furnishings in America, 1650–1920*, 1989.

Austen, B., 'Morgan and Sanders and the patent furniture-makers of Catherine Street', *Connoisseur*, November 1974, pp. 180–91.

Austen, B., *Tunbridge Ware and Related European Decorative Woodware*, London, W. Foulsham and Co., 1989.

Baarsen, R., 'Japanese lacquer and Dutch furniture in the seventeenth and eighteenth centuries', *Antiques*, CXLI, April 1992, pp. 632–41.

Bacon, B., 'Timber and the design of furniture', *Connoisseur*, April 1980, pp. 294–5.

Bacon, B., 'Exotic timber trade', *Connoisseur*, March 1980, pp. 184–7.

Bailey, W., *The Advancement of Arts, Manufactures, and Commerce, or a Description of the Useful Machines and Models Contained in the Repository of the Society for the Encouragement of Arts, Manufactures and Commerce*, London, 2 vols, 1772.

Bamford, F., 'A Shetlander in St Martin's Lane 1775', *Furniture History*, XI, 1975.

Barnett, H. G., *Innovation: the Basis of Cultural Change*, New York, 1953.

Barrow, J., *Dictionarium Polygraphicum*, 2 vols, London, 1751.

Barton, N., 'Rise of a royal furniture-maker I and II', *Country Life*, 10, February 1966, pp. 293–5, 360–2.

Beard, G., 'Thomas Chippendale's fire insurance', *Furniture History*, II, 1966.

Beard, G., 'William Kent and the cabinet-makers', *The Burlington Magazine*, CXVII, December 1975, pp. 867–84.

Beard, G., 'Vile and Cobb: eighteenth-century London furniture-makers', *Antiques*, CXXXVII, June 1990, pp. 1394–405.

Bibliography

Beard, G., 'Three eighteenth-century cabinet-makers, Moore, Goodison and Vile', *The Burlington Magazine*, CXIX, July 1977, pp. 479–86.

Beard, G. and Gilbert, C. (eds), *Dictionary of English Furniture-makers*, Leeds, Furniture History Society, 1986.

Bellagiue, G. de, 'Engravings and the French eighteenth-century marqueteurs', *The Burlington Magazine*, CVII, May 1965, pp. 240–50, and July 1965, pp. 357–62.

Bellagiue, G. de, 'English marquetry's debt to France', *Country Life*, 13 June 1968, pp. 1594–8.

Benhamou, R., 'Imitation in the decorative arts of the eighteenth century', *Journal of Design History*, IV, 1991, pp. 1–14.

Berg, M., *Manufacture in Town and Country before the Factory*, Cambridge, Cambridge University Press, 1983.

Berg, M., *The Age of Manufactures, 1700–1820*, London, Fontana, 1985.

Bergeron, H., *L'Art du Tourneur*, Paris, 1816.

Bigelow, D., *Gilded Wood Conservation and History*, Madison, Connecticut, Sound View Press, 1991.

Bimont, *Principes de l'Art du Tapissier*, 1770.

Bjerkoe, E., *The Cabinet-makers of America*, New York, 1957.

Bodley, H., *Nail-making*, Aylesbury, Shire Albums, 1983.

The Book of Trades or Library of Useful Arts, London, 1804.

Borsay, P., 'The English urban renaissance' *Social History*, V, 1977.

Bourdieu, P., *Distinction: a Social Critique of the Judgement of Taste*, London, Routledge, 1984.

Bowett, A., 'The commercial introduction of mahogany and the Naval Stores Act of 1721', *Furniture History*, XXX, 1994.

Boynton, L., 'The bed bug and the Age of Elegance', *Furniture History*, I, 1965.

Boynton, L., 'William and Richard Gomm', *The Burlington Magazine*, CXXII, June 1980, pp. 395–400.

Boynton, L., 'The Moravian Brotherhood and the migration of furniture-makers in the eighteenth century', *Furniture History*, XXIX, 1993.

Bradley-Smith, H. R., *Chronological Development of Nails: Blacksmith's and Farrier's tools at Shelburne Museum*, no. 7, n.d.

Brewer, J. and Porter, R. (eds), *Consumption and the World of Goods*, London, Routledge, 1993.

Brooks, R. C., 'Origins, usage and production of screws: an historical perspective', *History and Technology*, VIII, 1990, pp. 51–76.

Caldwell, I., 'Working women in the eighteenth century', *Antique Collector*, October 1985, pp. 78–81.

Campbell, R., *The London Tradesmen* [1747], Newton Abbot, David and Charles, 1969.

Carson, M., 'Thomas Affleck, a London cabinet-maker in colonial Philadelphia', *Connoisseur*, March 1968, pp. 187–91.

Chambers, W., *Cyclopaedia or Universal Dictionary of Arts and Sciences*, 2 vols, London, 1728.

Chambers, W., *Designs of Chinese Buildings, Furniture, Dresses, Machines and Utensils*, 1757.

Champness, R., *The Worshipful Company of Turners of London*, London, Lindley-Jones and Brother Ltd, 1966.

Chippendale, T., *The Gentleman and Cabinet-maker's Director*, London, 1754.

Clabburn, P., *The National Trust Book of Furnishing Textiles*, London, Viking, 1988.

Clarke, E,. *A Tour Through the South of England, Wales and Parts of Ireland Made During the Summer of 1791*, London, 1793.

Clunas, C., 'Design and cultural frontiers, English and Chinese furniture workshops', *Apollo*, CXXVI, October 1987, pp. 256–63.

Clunie, M. B., 'Joseph True and the piecework system in Salem', *Antiques*, XI, May 1977, pp. 1006–13.

Cobbett, W., *Rural Rides* (1830), Harmondsworth, Penguin, 1967.

Cole, W. A., 'Trends in eighteenth-century smuggling', *Economic History Review*, 2nd Series, X, 1958, pp. 395–409.

Coleridge A., *Chippendale Furniture*, London, Faber, 1968.

Collyer, J., *The Parent's and Guardian's Directory and the Youth's Guide in the Choice of a Profession or Trade*, London, 1761.

Cooke, E. S., 'Craftsman client relations in the Houstanic valley 1720–1800', *Antiques*, CXXV, January 1984, pp. 272–80.

Cooke, E. S. (ed.), *Upholstery in America and Europe from the Seventeenth Century to World War I*, New York, Norton, 1987.

Cornforth, J., 'Princely Pietre Dure', *Country Life*, 1 December, 1988, pp. 160–5.

Cotton, G., '"Common" chairs from the Norwich chair-makers Price Book of 1801', *Regional Furniture*, II, 1988, pp. 68–92.

Cotton, W., *The English Regional Chair*, Woodbridge, Antique Collectors Club, 1990 .

Cotton, W., 'The north country chair-making tradition: design, context and the Mark Chippindale deposition', *Furniture History*, XVII, 1981.

Crafts, N. F. R., 'British Economic growth, 1700–1831', *Economic History Review*, 2nd series, XXXVI, 1983, pp. 177–99.

Cross, J., 'The changing role of the timber merchant in early eighteenth-century London', *Furniture History*, XXX, 1994.

Cross, N., 'The changing design process' in R. Roy and D. Wied, *Product Design and Innovation*, Open University Press, 1986.

Bibliography

Crunden, J., *The Joyner and Cabinet-maker's Darling or Pocket Director*, 1765.

Csikszentmihalyi, M. and Rochberg Halton, E., *The Meaning of Things: Domestic Symbols and the Self*, Cambridge, Cambridge University Press, 1981.

Darly, M., *A New Book of Chinese Gothic and Modern Chairs*, 1751.

Darly, M. and Edwards, G., *A New Book of Chinese Designs*, 1754.

Darly, M., *A New Book of Ornaments in the Present (Antique) Taste*, 1772.

Darrow, F. L., *The Story of an Ancient Art: From the Earliest Adhesives to Vegetable Glue*, Lansdale, Pennsylvania, Perkins Glue Co., 1930.

Davis, D., *A History of Shopping*, London, Routledge, 1966.

Defoe, D., *The Complete English Tradesman*, [1727], New York, Kelley, 1969.

Denvir, B., *The Eighteenth Century: Art Design and Society, 1689–1789*, Harlow, Longman, 1983.

Deville, J., *Dictionaire du Tapissier de l'Ameublement Francais*, Paris, 1878–80.

DeVoe, S., *English Papier Mâché of the Georgian and Victorian Periods*, London, Barrie and Jenkins, 1971.

Dickinson, G., *English Papier Mâché, its Origin, Development and Decline*, n.d., *c*. 1926.

Dickinson, H., *James Watt, Craftsman and Engineer*, Cambridge, Cambridge University Press, 1936.

Dickinson, H., 'Joseph Bramah and his inventions.' *Transactions of the Newcomen Society*, XXII, 1941–2, pp. 169–86.

Dickinson, H., 'Origin and manufacture of wood screws', *Transactions of the Newcomen Society*, XXII, 1941, pp. 79–90.

Diderot, D., *Dictionnaire raisonne des sciences des arts et des metiers*, 1751–72, 1793.

Doley, A., 'Le meuble en verre', *Oeil*, CCCIX, April 1981, pp. 46–53.

Dossie, R., *The Handmaid to the Arts*, 1758, 1764.

Douglas, M. and Isherwood, B., *The World of Goods: Towards an Anthropology of Consumption*, Harmondsworth, Penguin, 1980.

Edwards, C., 'Press Beds', *Furniture History*, XXVI, 1990.

Edwards, C., *Victorian Furniture*, Manchester, Manchester University Press, 1993.

Edwards, R., 'A great Georgian cabinet-maker. New light on the firm of Seddon', *Country Life*, 21 October 1933, pp. 415–18.

Edwards, R. and Jourdain, M., *Georgian Cabinet-Makers c. 1700–1800*, London, Country Life, 1955.

Edwards, R., *The Shorter Dictionary of English Furniture*, London, Country Life, 1964.

Edwards, R., 'Patrons of taste and sensibility: English furniture of the eighteenth century', *Apollo*, LXXXII, December 1965, pp. 449–61.

Eland, G. (ed.), *Purefoy Letters*, 2 vols., 1931.

Ettema, M. J., 'Technological innovation and design economics in furniture manufacture', *Winterthur Portfolio*, XVI, 1981.

Ettema, M. J., 'History, nostalgia and American furniture' *Winterthur Portfolio*, XVII, 1982.

Evans, N., 'A history and background of English Windsor furniture', *Furniture History*, XV, 1979.

Evelyn, J., *Account of Architects*, 1664.

Evelyn, J., *Sylva, a Discourse of Forest Trees*, 1664, 1670, 1776.

Fairbanks, J. C. and Bates, E. B., *American Furniture 1620 to the Present*, London, Orbis, 1981.

Fales, D., *American Painted Furniture, 1660–1880*, New York, Dutton, 1972.

Fastnedge, R., Preface and descriptive notes in *Shearer Furniture Designs from the Cabinet-maker's London Book of Prices*, [1788], London, Tiranti, 1962.

Fastnedge, R., *Sheraton Furniture*, London, Faber, 1962.

Fastnedge, R., 'A manual for Georgian cabinet-makers', *Country Life*, 10 June 1965, pp. 144–5.

Fisher, F. J., 'The development of London as a centre of conspicuous consumption in the sixteenth and seventeenth centuries', *Transactions of the Royal Historical Society*, XXX, 1948, pp. 37–50.

Fitzgerald, D., 'Chippendale's place in the English rococo', *Furniture History*, IV, 1968.

Fitzgerald, D., 'Gravelot and his influence on English furniture', *Apollo*, XC, 1969, pp. 140–7.

Ford, B., (ed.), *Eighteenth-Century Britain*, Cambridge, Cambridge University Press, 1991.

Forman, B., 'Mill-sawing in seventeenth-century Massachusetts', *Old Time New England*, LX, Spring 1970, pp. 110–30.

Forman, B., *American Seating Furniture, 1630–1730*, New York, Norton, 1988.

Fowler, J., and Cornforth, J., *English Decoration in the Eighteenth Century*, London, Barrie and Jenkins, 1974.

Friedman, T., 'Two eighteenth-century catalogues of ornamental pattern books, *Furniture History*, XI, 1975.

Gaynor, J. M. A., and Hagedorn, N. L., *Tools Working Wood in Eighteenth-Century America*, Colonial Williamsburg, 1993.

A General Description of All Trades, London, 1747.

Giedion, S., *Mechanisation Takes Command*, New York, Oxford University Press, 1948, reprinted 1969.

Bibliography

Gilbert, C., 'Furniture by Giles Grendey for the Spanish trade', *Antiques*, XCIX, April 1971, pp. 544–50.

Gilbert, C., 'The subscribers to Chippendale's *Director*, a preliminary analysis', *Furniture History*, X, 1974.

Gilbert C., 'The early furniture designs of Matthias Darly', *Furniture History*, XI, 1975.

Gilbert, C., 'Wright and Elwick of Wakefield, 1748–1824. A Study of Provincial Patronage', *Furniture History*, XII, 1976.

Gilbert, C., *The Life and Work of Thomas Chippendale*, London, MacMillan, 1978.

Gilbert, C., 'London and provincial books of prices, comment and bibliography', *Furniture History*, XVIII, 1982.

Gilbert, C., 'An early cabinet and chair work price list from York', *Furniture History*, XXI, 1985.

Gilbert, C., *English Vernacular Furniture, 1750–1900*, New Haven and London, Yale University Press, 1991.

Gilbert, C., 'Smith, Manwaring, Sayer and a newly discovered set of designs', *Furniture History*, XXIX, 1993.

Gilbert, C. and Murdoch T., *John Channon and Brass-inlaid Furniture, 1730–1760*, New Haven and London, Yale University Press, 1993.

Gillow Chairs and Fashion, Travelling Exhibition Catalogue, North-west Museums Service, Lancaster, 1991.

Girouard, M., 'English art and the Rococo', *Country Life*, part 1, 13 Jan., 1966, pp. 58–61, part 2, 27 Jan., pp. 188–90, part 3, 3 Feb., pp. 224–7.

Giusti, A. M., *Pietre Duri-Hardstones in Furniture*, Philip Wilson, 1992.

Gloag, J., *A Social History of Furniture Design*, London, Cassell, 1966

Gloag, J., *Dictionary of Furniture*, revised edition, London, Unwin Hyman, 1990.

Goodison, N., *Ormolu, the Work of Matthew Boulton*, London, Phaidon, 1974.

Goodison, N., 'The V & A metalwork pattern books', *Furniture History*, XI, 1975.

Goodman, W. L., *The History of Woodworking Tools*, London, Bell, 1964.

Goodman, W. L., 'Christopher Gabriel, his book', *Furniture History*, XVII, 1981.

Goodman, W. L., *British Plane-makers from 1700*, 3rd edn, 1993, Needham Market, Roy Arnold, 1993.

Greenhalgh, P., *Quotations and Sources on Design and Decorative Arts*, Manchester, Manchester University Press, 1993.

Grosley, M., *A Tour of London or New Observations on England*, 1772.

Gusler, W. B., 'Variations in eighteenth-century casework', *Fine Woodworking*, XXIII, July/August 1980, pp. 50–3.

Hackenbrock, Y., 'Pattern books and eighteenth-century design', *Antiques*, LXXIV, September 1958, pp. 225–32.

Hall, I., 'Patterns of elegance: Gillows furniture designs', *Country Life*, 8/15 June 1978, pp. 1612–15, 1740–2.

Harris, E., *The Furniture of Robert Adam*, London, Tiranti, 1963.

Harris, J., *Sir William Chambers*, London, Zwemmer, 1970.

Harris, E., 'Batty Langley, a tutor to Freemasons 1696–1751', *The Burlington Magazine*, CXIX, May 1977, pp. 327–35.

Havard, H., *Dictionnaire de l'Ameublement et de la Decoration*, Paris, 1890–94.

Hayward, H., *Thomas Johnson and the English Rococo*, London, Tiranti, 1964.

Hayward, H. and Kirkham, P., *William and John Linnell: Eighteenth-Century London Furniture-makers*, London, Studio Vista, 1980.

Hayward, J., 'English brass-inlaid furniture', *Victoria and Albert Museum Bulletin*, vol. 1, part I, January 1965, pp. 11–25; vol. 2, part II, April 1966, pp. 65–70 .

Hayward, J., 'A further note on Christopher Fuhrlohg, *The Burlington Magazine*, CXIX, July 1977, pp. 486–93.

Heal, A., *The London Furniture-makers, from the Restoration to the Victorian era, 1660–1840*, London, Batsford, 1953.

Heckscher, M., 'Gideon Saint: an eighteenth-century carver and his scrapbook', *The Metropolitan Museum of Art Bulletin*, XXVII, 1969, pp. 299–311.

Heckscher, M., 'Philadelphia Chippendale: the influence of the *Director* in America', *Furniture History*, XXI, 1985.

Hecksher, M. and Frances Gruber Safford, 'Boston japanned furniture in the Metropolitan Museum of Art', *The Magazine Antiques*, CXXIX, May 1986, pp. 1047–59.

Hepplewhite, A. and Co., *The Cabinet-maker and Upholsterer's Guide*, 1788.

Hewitt, B., Kane P., Ward G., *The Work of Many Hands, Card Tables in Federal America, 1790–1820*, New Haven, Yale University Press, 1982.

Hill, J. H., 'History and technique of japanning and the restoration of the Pimm highboy', *American Art Journal*, 8, November 1976, pp. 59–84.

Himmelheber, G., 'The craftsmanship of David Roentgen', *Connoisseur*, September 1976, pp. 17–21.

Hinckley, F. L., *Directory of Historic Cabinet Woods*, New York, Crown, 1960.

Hogarth, W., *The Analysis of Beauty*, 1753.

Holden, E W., 'Note on sawpits', *Archeological Journal*, CXXXII, pp. 231, 1975.

Holley, D., 'Upholstery springs', *Furniture History*, XVII, 1981.

Holme, R., *The Academy of Armoury*, [1649, 1688] 1905.

Bibliography

Honor, H., 'Pietre Dure and the Grand Tourist', *Connoisseur*, June 1958, pp. 212–15.

Hope, T., *Household Furniture*, London, 1807.

Hoppus E., *The Gentleman's And Builder's Repository*, 1737, 1748, 1760.

Houston, J. F., *Featherbedds and Flock Bedds, Notes on the History of the Worshipful Company of Upholders of the City of London*, Three Tents Press, Sandy, 1993.

Howard, G. S., *The New Royal Encyclopedia*, London, 1788,

Hughes, G. B., 'George Seddon of London House', *Apollo*, LXV, May 1957, pp. 177–81.

Hughes, G. B., 'Windsor chairs in palace and cottage,' *Country Life*, May 1962, pp. 1242–3.

Hughes, G. B., 'Costly elegance of gilded chairs', *Country Life*, 28 November 1963, pp. 1398–9.

Hughes, G. B., 'Furnishers of Georgian Mayfair', *Country Life*, 19 November 1964, pp. 1328–9.

Hughes, G. B., 'Georgian fretwork' *Country Life*, 9 December 1971, p. 1664.

Humell, C. F., 'Samuel Rowland Fisher's Catalogue of English Hardware', *Winterthur Portfolio*, I, 1964.

Hummel, C. F., *With Hammer in Hand. The Dominy Craftsmen of East Hampton, New York*, published for the Henry Francis du Pont Winterthur Museum by the University Press of Virginia, Charlottesville, 1968.

Hunter-Steibel, P., 'Exalted hardware the bronze mounts of French furniture', *Antiques*, CXXVII, January 1985, pp. 236–45.

Hutchinson, C., 'The Leeds cabinet and chair-makers Book of Prices', *Furniture History*, X, 1974.

Hutchinson, C., 'George Reynoldson, upholsterer of York 1716–1764, *Furniture History*, XII.

Huth, H., *Lacquer of the West. The History of a Craft and Industry, 1550–1950*, Chicago, 1971.

Huth, H., *Roentgen Furniture*, London, Sotheby, 1974.

Ince, W. and Mayhew, J., *The Universal System of Household Furniture*, 1759–62.

Jervis, S., 'Giles Grendey, 1693–1780', *Country Life*, 6 June 1974, pp. 1418–19.

Jervis, S., *Printed Furniture Designs before 1650*, Furniture History Society, 1974.

Jervis, S., *Dictionary of Design and Designers*, Harmondsworth, Penguin, 1984.

Jobe, B., 'Boston Furniture Industry 1720–45', in W. Whitehill (ed.), *Boston Furniture of the Eighteenth Century*, Virginia, 1974.

Johnson, T., *Twelve Girandoles*, 1755.

Johnson, T., *A New Book of Ornaments*, 1758.

Jones, E. C., 'The fashion manipulators: consumer tastes and British industries 1660–1800', in Cain L., and Uselding, P. (eds), *Business Enterprise and Economic Change. Essays in honour of H. F. Williamson*, Kent State, Kent State University Press, 1973.

Jones, J. C., *Design Methods*, London, John Wiley, 1981.

Jones, P. D'A, and Simons, E. N., *The Story of the Saw*, Newman Neame for Spear and Jackson, 1961.

Jones, W., *Gentleman or Builder's Companion*, 1739.

Journals of the House of Commons.

Joy, E., 'Chippendale in trouble at the customs', *Country Life*, 24 August 1951, p. 569

Joy, E., 'Eighteenth-century London furniture industry', *Apollo*, LXXVI, May 1962, pp. 185–8.

Joy, E., 'The overseas trade in furniture in the eighteenth century', *Furniture History*, I, 1965.

Joy, E., *The Connoisseur's Complete Period Guides*, London, Connoisseur, 1968.

Joy, E., *English Furniture 1800–1851*, London, Sotheby, 1974.

Kane, P., *300 years of American seating furniture. Chairs and Beds from the Mabel Brady Garvan and other collections*, Yale University, New York Graphic Society, 1976.

Kane, P., 'Samuel Gragg: his bentwood fancy chairs', *Yale University Art Gallery Bulletin*, XXXIII, No. 2, Autumn 1971, pp. 26–37.

Kearsley, G., *Table of Trades*, 1786.

Kebabian, P. and W. Lipke, *Tools and Technologies: America's Wooden Age*, Vermont, University Press, 1979.

Kellett, J. R., 'The breakdown of gild and corporation control over the handicraft and retail trade in London', *Economic History Review*, X, 1958, pp. 381–94:

Kent, W., *The Designs of Inigo Jones*, 1727.

Kinmonth, C., *Irish Vernacular Furniture 1700–1950*, New Haven and London, Yale University Press, 1993.

Kirk, J. T., *American Furniture and the British Tradition to 1830*, New York, 1982.

Kirkham, P., 'The careers of William and John Linnell', *Furniture History*, III, 1967.

Kirkham, P., 'Samuel Norman, a study of an eighteenth-century craftsman', *The Burlington Magazine*, III, August 1969, pp. 500–511.

Kirkham, P., 'The partnership of William Ince and John Mayhew 1759–1804', *Furniture History*, X, 1974.

Bibliography

Kirkham, P., 'Inlay, marquetry and buhl Workers in England *c.* 1660–1850', *The Burlington Magazine*, CXXII, June 1980, pp. 415–19.

Kirkham, P., *The London Furniture Trade, 1700–1850*, Furniture History Society, 1988.

Knell, D., *English Country Furniture*, London, Barrie and Jenkins, 1992.

Lacquer: an International History and Collecting Guide, London, Bracken Books, 1989.

The Ladies Amusement or the Whole Art of Japanning Made Easy, London, n.d. *c.* 1760.

Langley, B. and T., *City and Country Builder's and Workman's Treasury of Designs*, 1740.

Latham, B., *Timber. A Historical Survey of its Development and Distribution*, London, Harrap, 1957.

Learmont, D., 'The Trinity house chairs, Aberdeen', *Furniture History*, XIV, 1978.

Learoy, S., *English Furniture Construction and Decoration 1500–1910*, London, 1981.

Legg, P., 'The Bastards of Blandford', *Furniture History* XXX, 1994.

Lever, J., *Architects' Designs for Furniture*, London, Trefoil, 1982.

Lindsey, G., 'Papier mâché', in Bevan (ed.), *British Manufacturing Industries*, 1876.

Linnard, W., 'Sweat and sawdust, pit-sawing in Wales', *Folk Life*, XX, 1981–2, pp. 41–55.

Lock, M., *Six Sconces*, 1744.

Lock, M., *Six Tables*, 1746.

Lock, M., *A Book of Tables, c.* 1768.

Lock, M. and Copland, H., *A New Book of Ornaments*, 1752.

Loudon, J. C., *Arboretum and Fruticetum Britannicum*, vol. 2, London, Longman, 1844.

Loudon, J. C., *Encyclopaedia of Cottage, Farm And Villa Architecture and Furniture* (revised edition), London, 1839.

Lovell, M., '"Such Furniture as will be profitable." The business of cabinet-making in eighteenth-century Newport,' *Winterthur Portfolio*, XXVI, 1991.

Luff, R. W., 'The craftsmanship of English walnut furniture', *Antique Collector*, June/July 1972, pp. 151–7.

Luff, R. W., 'The top made to rise: architects' or artists' tables made for the country house library', *Antique Collector*, June 1961, pp. 138–41.

Macquer, Phillipe de, *Dictionaire Raisonne Universal des Arts et Metiers*, 5 vols, Paris, 1773.

Mantoux, P., *The Industrial Revolution in the Eighteenth Century* (revised edn) 1961.

Manwaring, R., *The Cabinet and Chair-maker's Real Friend and Companion*, 1765.

Manwaring, R., *The Chair-maker's Guide*, 1766.

Margon, L., *Construction of American Furniture Treasures*, New York, 1975.

Martin, T., *The New Circle of the Mechanical Arts containing Practical Treatises on the Various Manual Arts, Industries and Manufactures*, London, 1819.

Mathias, P., *The Transformation of England, Skills and Diffusion of Innovations in the Eighteenth Century*, London, Methuen, 1979.

Maurice, K., *Sovereigns as Turners*, Zurich, Verlag Ineichen, 1985.

Mayes, L. J., *The History of Chair-making in High Wycombe*, London, Routledge, 1960.

McCracken, G., *Culture and Consumption*, Bloomington, Indiana University Press, 1988.

McKendrick, N., Brewer, J. and Plumb, J. H., *The Birth of Consumer Society*, Bloomington, Indiana University Press, 1982.

McNeill, I., *Joseph Bramah, a Century of Invention, 1749–1851*, Newton Abbot, David and Charles, 1968.

McQuoid, P., *The Age of Mahogany*, (1906), reprinted, Woodbridge, Antique Collectors Club, 1987.

McQuoid, P., and Edwards, R., *Dictionary of English Furniture*, revised edition, London, Country Life, 1954.

The Method of Learning to Draw in Perspective . . . Likewise a New and Curious Method of Japanning, London, 1732.

Mew, E., 'Battersea enamels and the Anti-Gallican Society', *Apollo*, VII, May 1928, pp. 216–22.

Miller, D., *Material Culture and Mass Production*, Oxford, Oxford University Press, 1987.

Milne, E. C., *History of the Development of Furniture Webbing*, 1983 (private print), Leeds.

Montgomery, C., *American Furniture. The Federal Period*, New York, 1966.

Montgomery, F., *Textiles in America, 1650–1870*, New York, Norton, 1984.

Morris, C. (ed.), *Journal of Celia Fiennes*, London, 1947.

Mortimer, T., *The Universal Directory*, 1763.

Mortimer, T., *A New and Complete Dictionary of Trade and Commerce*, London, 1766.

Moxon, J., *Mechaniks Exercises or the Doctrine of Handy Works etc.*, 1677, Praeger reprint, 1970.

Mui, H. C. and L. H., *Shops and Shopping in Eighteenth-Century England*, London, Routledge, 1989.

Mukerji, C., *From Graven Images, Patterns of Modern Materialism*, New York, Columbia University Press, 1983.

211

Bibliography

Murdoch, T. (ed.), *The Quiet Conquest: the Huguenots 1685–1985*, London, Museum of London, 1985.

Mussey, R. D., 'Old finishes and early varnishes', Fine Woodworking Techniques 6, *Fine Woodworking*, March/April 1982, pp. 71–5.

New, S., 'The use of stains by furniture-makers, 1660–1850', *Furniture History*, XVII, 1981.

Neve, R., *The City and Country Purchaser's and Builder's Dictionary*, 1726, Reprint, Newton Abbot, David and Charles, 1969.

Nicholson, P. and M., *Practical Cabinet-maker and Upholsterer*, London, 1826.

Oliver, J. L., *The Development and Structure of the Furniture Industry*, Oxford, Pergamon, 1966.

Ostergard, D., *Bentwood and Metal Furniture, 1850–1946*, University of Washington Press, 1987.

Pair, W., *The Carpenters and Joiners Repository*, 1778, 1792.

Paulson, A., *Hogarth, his Life, Art and Times*, New Haven and London, Yale University Press, 1971.

Peck, G. B., 'Alice and George Hepplewhite's cabinet-maker and upholsterer's guide,' *Woman's Art Journal*, 8, Fall 1987/Winter 1988.

Peyer, R. de., *A Bibliography of Eighteenth-Century Furniture Studies Using the Blaise line*, Regional Furniture Society. n.d.

Pinto. E., 'The Georgian chamber horse', *Country Life*, 20 October 1955, pp. 846–7.

Pinto, E., 'Georgian library steps', *Antiques*, LXXXIII, January 1963, pp. 102–5.

Plas, S., *Les Meubles a Transformation et a Secret*, Paris, 1975.

Porter, R., *English Society in the Eighteenth Century*, London, Allen Lane, 1982.

Postelthwayt, M., *The Universal Dictionary of Trade And Commerce*, 2 vols, 1751–5.

Pradere, A., *French Furniture-makers*, London, Sotheby's, 1989.

Pryke, S., 'A study of the Edinburgh furnishing trade taken from contemporary press notices 1708–1790', *Regional Furniture*, III, 1989, pp. 52–67

Pryke, S., 'The extraordinary billhead of Francis Brodie', *Regional Furniture*, IV, 1990, pp. 81–99.

Pryke, S., 'Pattern furniture and estate wrights in eighteenth-century Scotland', *Furniture History*, XXX, 1994.

Pye, D., *The Nature and Art of Workmanship*, Cambridge, Cambridge University Press, 1968.

Quimby, I. (ed.), *The Craftsman in Early America,* New York, 1984.

Ramond, P., *La Marqueterie*, Dourdan, 1981.

Randall, R. H., 'Templates for Boulle singerie', *The Burlington Magazine*, CXI, September 1969, pp. 206–9.

Redburn S., 'The furniture designs of Thomas Malton 1775' *Furniture History*, XI, 1975.

Reynolds, J., *Seven Discourses*, 1778.

Rieder, W., 'Furniture smuggling for a Duke', *Apollo*, XCII, September 1970, pp. 206–9.

Roche, S., Courage, G., Devinoy, P., *Mirrors*, Paris, 1956, London, 1985.

Rolt, R., *A New Dictionary of Trade and Commerce*, 1756.

Roth, R., Nineteenth-century American patent furniture in *Innovative Furniture in America*, New York, 1981.

Roubo, A. C., *L'Art de Menuisier*, Paris, 1772.

Rykwert, J., *The Necessity of Artifice*, London, Academy Editions, 1982.

Salaman, R., *Dictionary of Tools Used in the Woodworking and Allied Trades 1700–1970*, London, Unwin Hyman, 1975.

Salmon, W., *Polygraphics*, 1672, 1675, 1678, 1685.

Salverte, F. de, *Les Ebenistes du XVIIIe siecle*, 1927.

Samuel, R., 'Workshop of the world, steam power and hand technology in mid-Victorian Britain', *History Workshop*, III, 1977.

Saumarez-Smith, C., *Eighteenth-Century Decoration*, London, Weidenfeld and Nicolson, 1993.

Sayer, R., *The Ladies Amusement or the Whole Art of Japanning Made Easy*, 1762.

Schlereth, T. J., *Material Culture Studies in America*, Nashville, AASLH, 1982.

Schweig, B., *Mirrors*, London, Pelham Books, 1973.

Shammas, C., 'The domestic environment in early modern England and America', *Journal of Social History*, XIV, 1980, pp. 1–24

Shammas, C., *The Pre-industrial Consumer in England and America*, Oxford, Oxford University Press, 1990.

Shearer, T., *The Cabinet-makers' London Book of Prices etc.*, 1788.

Sheraton, T., *The Cabinet-maker and Upholsterer's Drawing Book*, 1793.

Sheraton, T., *The Cabinet Dictionary*, London, 1803.

Siddons, G., *The Cabinet-maker's Guide* (5th edn), London, 1830.

Sims, W., *200 years of History and Evolution of Woodworking Machinery*, Burton Lazars, Walders Press, 1985.

Sleater, W., *An Essay on Perfecting the Fine Arts in Great Britain and Ireland*, Dublin, 1767.

Sleep, J., 'Consumer behaviour across an urban hierarchy 1650–1725', *Regional Furniture Newsletter*, XXI, Winter 1994, pp. 12–13.

Smith, A., *Wealth of Nations*, London, Methuen, 1961.

Smith, G., *The Laboratory or School of Arts*, 1756.

Smith, H. T., 'Marquetry and parquetry in France in the eighteenth century', *Apollo*, LXXII, December 1960, pp. 169–72.

Bibliography

Smith, J. T., *Nollekens and his Times*, 2 vols., London 1828.

Smith, N. A., *Old Furniture; Understanding the Craftsman's Art*, New York, Dover, 1991.

Snodin, M. (ed.) *Rococo Art and Design in Hogarth's England*, V & A exhibition catalogue, London, May–Sept. 1984.

Society of Upholsterers, *Household Furniture in the Genteel Taste for the year 1760*, 1760.

Spufford, M., *The Great Reclothing of Rural England*, London, Hambeldon Press, 1984.

Stabler, J., 'English newspaper advertisements as a source of furniture history', *Regional Furniture*, V, 1991, pp. 93–102.

Stalker, J., and Parker, G., *A Treatise of Japanning And Varnishing*, 1688.

Steer, F. W. (ed.), *Farm and Cottage Inventories of Mid-Essex, 1635–1749*, 1950.

Stokes, J., *The Complete Cabinet-maker and Upholsterer's Guide*, 1829.

Stratmann, R., 'Design and mechanisms in the furniture of Jean-François Oeben', *Furniture History*, IX, 1973.

Streeter, C., 'Marquetry tables from Cobb's workshop', *Furniture History*, X, 1974.

Stuart, S., *Gillow Chairs and Fashion*, Exhibition Catalogue, North-west Museums Service, 1991–92.

Stuart, S., 'Prices for workmen in Lancaster – the earliest surviving cabinet-makers' price list', *Regional Furniture*, II, 1988, pp. 19–23.

Sturmer, M., 'Bois des Indes and the economics of luxury furniture in the time of David Roentgen', *The Burlington Magazine*, CMIX, December 1978, pp. 799–805.

Sturmer, M., 'An economy of delight', court artisans of the eighteenth century', *Business History Review*, Winter 1979, pp. 497–528.

Summerson, Sir John, *Georgian London*, Harmondsworth, Penguin, 1962.

Sweeney, K. M., 'Furniture and furniture making in mid-eighteenth-century Wethersfield Connecticut', *Antiques*, CXXV, May 1984, pp. 1156–63.

Symonds, R. W., 'Eighteenth-century brassfounder's catalogue', *Antiques*, XIX, February 1931, pp. 102–5.

Symonds, R. W., 'Furniture trade in the eighteenth century', *Connoisseur*, February 1933, pp. 89–97.

Symonds, R. W., 'English furniture-making in the eighteenth century', *Connoisseur*, November 1936, pp. 253–61.

Symonds, R. W., 'English looking glass plates and their manufacture', *Connoisseur*, May 1936, pp. 243–9 and July 1936, pp. 9–15.

Symonds, R. W., 'English cane chairs: the rise and decline of an industry between 1664–1747', *Antique Collector*, Sept.–Oct. 1937, pp. 102–6.

Symonds, R. W., 'The chairmaker', *Connoisseur*, November 1938, pp. 234–40.

Symonds, R. W., 'Craft of the English turner,' *Apollo*, XXIX, May 1939, pp. 223–6.

Symonds, R. W., 'Craft of the cabinet-maker', *Connoisseur*, May 1940, pp. 200–7.

Symonds, R. W., 'Export trade of furniture to colonial America', *The Burlington Magazine*, MCLXXVII, November 1940, pp. 152–60.

Symonds, R. W., 'English eighteenth-century furniture exports to Spain and Portugal', *The Burlington Magazine*, LXXVIII, February 1941, pp. 57–64.

Symonds, R. W., 'English gesso furniture', *Connoisseur*, June 1942, pp. 105–11.

Symonds, R. W., 'Craft of furniture-making in the eighteenth century', *Antique Collector*, March–April 1946, pp. 54–9.

Symonds, R. W., 'Craft of the carver and gilder', *Antiques Review*, December 1950, pp. 13–20.

Symonds, R. W., *Furniture-making in Seventeenth- and Eighteenth-Century England*, London, Connoisseur, 1955.

Symonds, R. W., 'The craft of the eighteenth-century upholsterer', *Antique Collector*, June 1956, pp. 103–8.

Talbot, A., 'Factors influencing the introduction and development of tools in the seventeenth and eighteenth centuries', *Working Wood*, Winter 1980, pp. 16–19.

Taylor, V. J., *Construction of Period Country Furniture*, 1978.

Thornton, P., *Seventeenth-Century Interior Decoration in England, France and Holland*, New Haven, Yale University Press, 1978.

Thornton, P., *Authentic Decor. The Domestic Interior 1620- 1920*, London, Weidenfeld & Nicolson, 1984.

Tinniswood, A., *A History of Country House Visiting: Five Centuries of Tourism and Taste*, Oxford, Oxford University Press, 1989.

Toller, J., *Papier Mâché in Great Britain and America*, London, 1972.

Tristram, P., *Living Space in Fact and Fiction*, London, Routledge 1989.

Tryon, T., *The Way to Health, Long Life and Happiness,* London, 1691.

Valuable Secrets Concerning Arts and Trades, London, 1775.

Veblen, T., *Theory of the Leisure Class*, 1899, Unwin reprint, London, 1970.

Verlet, P., *Les Meubles Francais du XVIIIe Siecle*, 2 vols, 1956.

Voss Elder, W. and Stokes J. E., *American Furniture, 1680–1880*, Baltimore, Baltimore Museum of Art, 1987.

Walton, K.-M., *The Golden Age of English Furniture Upholstery 1660–1840*, Temple Newsam, 1973.

Walton, K.-M., 'The worshipful company of upholsterers of the City of London', *Furniture History*, IX, 1973.

Bibliography

Walton, K-M., 'Eighteenth-century cabinet-making in Bristol', *Furniture History*, XII, 1976.

Ward, G. (ed.), *Perspectives on American Furniture*, New York, 1988.

Ward, J., 'The work of Coxed and Woster in Mulberry wood and Burr Elm', *Apollo*, LV, November 1941, pp. 104–6.

Ward-Jackson, P., *English Furniture Designs of the Eighteenth Century*, 1959, Victoria and Albert Museum, 1984.

Watson, F. J., 'Furniture guilds of eighteenth-century Paris', *Antiques*, LXXIII, May 1958, pp. 465–9.

Watson, F. J. B., 'Tradition and change in furniture-making in nineteenth-century Paris,' *Apollo*, LXXXIII, May 1966, pp. 343–50.

Watson, F. J. B., 'The craftsmanship of the Ancien Régime,' *Apollo*, XC, September 1969, pp. 180–9.

Weatherill, L., *Consumer Behaviour and Material Culture in Britain, 1660–1760*, London, Routledge, 1988.

Weil, M., 'A cabinet-maker's price book', Ian Quimby (ed.), *American Furniture and its Makers, Winterthur Portfolio*, XIII, 1979.

Welsh, P., *Woodworking Tools 1600–1900*, Contributions from the Museum of History and Technology, *United States National Museum Bulletin*, No. 241, Smithsonian Institution, 1966.

Werner, A., 'Eighteenth-century japanning Garret', *Tools and Trades Journal*, III, 1985, pp. 84–96.

White, J., *Arts Treasury of Rarities and Curious Inventions*, London, 1770.

White, L., 'Furnishing your house and garden in the 1760s', *Antique Collecting*, CCCXXI, 4 September 1986, pp. 51–4.

Whitehead, J., *The French Interior in the Eighteenth Century*, London, Laurence King, 1992.

Whiteley, W. T., *Artists and their Friends in England, 1700–1799*, 1928.

Williams, C. (trans.) *Sophie in London*, [1786], London, Cape, 1933.

Wills, G., *English Looking Glasses, a Study of Glasses, Frames and Makers, 1672–1820*, Country Life, 1965.

Wills, G., 'Furniture smuggling in eighteenth-century London', *Apollo*, LXXXII, August 1965, pp. 112–17.

Wills, G., *English Furniture 1760–1900*, London, Guinness Superlatives, 1969.

Wilson, G., 'Boulle', *Furniture History*, VIII, 1972.

Wood, L., *The Lady Lever Art Gallery Catalogue of Commodes*, London, HMSO, 1994.

Wragg, R. B., 'The history of Scagliola' *Country Life*, 10 October 1957, pp. 718–21.

Wright, M., *John Joseph Merlin, the Ingenious Mechanick*, Exhibition catalogue, London, Kenwood, 1985.

Wrigley, E. A., 'A simple model of London's importance in changing English society and economy 1650–1750', *Past and Present*, xxxvii, July 1967, pp. 44–70.

Zimmerman, P., 'A Methodological Study in the Identification of some important Philadelphia Chippendale Furniture', *Winterthur Portfolio*, xiii, 1979.

Zimmerman, P., 'Workmanship as evidence, a model for object study', *Winterthur Portfolio*, xvi, 1981.

Unpublished sources

Joy, E., *Some Aspects of the London Industry in the Eighteenth Century* (unpublished MA thesis, London, 1955).

Nichols, S., *Gillows and Company of Lancaster England, An Eighteenth-Century Business History* (University of Delaware, MA thesis, 1982).

Walton, K.-M., *Eighteenth-Century Upholstery in England with Particular Reference to the Period 1754–1803: the Work and Status of the Upholsterer* (Unpublished M Phil, Leeds, 1980).

Index

Index